14 DAYS

14 DAYS

Making the Conservative Movement in Canada

BRUCE CARSON

McGill-Queen's University Press
Montreal & Kingston • London • Ithaca

ISBN 978-0-7735-4351-5 (cloth)
ISBN 978-0-7735-9196-7 (ePDF)
ISBN 978-0-7735-9197-4 (ePUB)

Legal deposit second quarter 2014
Bibliothèque nationale du Québec

Printed in Canada on acid-free paper that is 100% ancient forest free
(100% post-consumer recycled), processed chlorine free.

McGill-Queen's University Press acknowledges the support of the
Canada Council for the Arts for our publishing program. We also
acknowledge the financial support of the Government of Canada
through the Canada Book Fund for our publishing activities.

Library and Archives Canada Cataloguing in Publication

Carson, Bruce, author
    14 days : making the Conservative movement in Canada / Bruce
Carson.

Includes bibliographical references and index.
Issued in print and electronic formats.
ISBN 978-0-7735-4351-5 (bound). – ISBN 978-0-7735-9196-7 (ePDF). –
ISBN 978-0-7735-9197-4 (ePUB)

    1. Conservatism – Canada. 2. Conservative Party of Canada.
3. Canada – Politics and government – 1993–2006. 4. Canada – Politics
and government – 2006–. I. Title. II. Title: Fourteen days.

JC573.2.C3C37 2014   320.520971   C2014-900770-1
                                                 C2014-900771-X

This book was typeset by True to Type in 10.5/13 Sabon

To my late mother and father,
Margaret and Robert Carson

Contents

Prologue

As I put the finishing touches on this book in the late fall of 2013, the prime minister has been playing both offence and defence. He completed a major shuffle of his Cabinet in July and, in mid-October, delivered a Speech from the Throne and announced the signing of the Canada–European Union Free Trade Agreement. He hopes all this will allow his Conservative government to rebound in the polls and attain a second majority mandate in the next election. For the first time since forming the government in 2006, the prime minister is dogged by problems that have hurt his popularity, as well as that of his government. While he still retains credit for Canada's economic performance through the depression/recession, there is discontent with his governing style, the ever-simmering Senate expense scandal, which has resulted in the suspension of three former Conservative senators, and a lack of policy direction. The two main opposition parties, the NDP and the Liberals, have settled on new leaders who will take them into the 2015 election. (Although an election could be called before 2015, there must be one in 2015 at the latest, so I've chosen to use that year throughout when referring to the next election.) The concluding chapter of this book attempts to set out these issues and describe new directions for the government as it tries to gain back the initiative held almost without a break since 2006. However, this work is not about the destination, but rather the journey of the federal conservative movement represented by the Progressive Conservative Party, the Reform and Alliance parties, and finally the Conservative Party of Canada over the past twenty years from opposition to government, and then the exercise of the levers of government.

As the saying goes, "a week is a long time in politics." Here, I am suggesting we examine what amounts to two weeks – fourteen remarkable political "days," or periods, starting in 1993 and ending in 2013. This book chronicles the major events in the history of the conservative movement during this period, anchoring them to fourteen significant dates. There could, and should, be endless discussion about whether these are the right times or days to peg in the inexorable march from 1993 back to majority government in 2011. There were many days, both good and bad, that led a disparate group of people, all claiming some relationship to conservative philosophy in Canada, to move from the split evidenced by the 1993 election results, which left the PC Party with two seats and the Reform Party with fifty-four seats, to a minority government in January 2006 and then to a majority government in 2011.

The days that form the main events of the following chapters were chosen because, in my opinion, they were pivotal. Important events leading up to the particular day, the day itself with whatever occurred, and then the denouement are discussed from my perspective. I was involved with the PC Party throughout most of this period, and then with the Conservative Party either in a staff function or other related position.

But this is more than a diary of events. It is an opportunity to look at the personalities who were critical to those days and the surrounding period, or were affected by them: leaders and would-be leaders, Cabinet ministers, and staff who played and still play such an important role in the service of Canadians. I believe only by working with elected officials, their political staff, and the public service that supports them, does one really come to appreciate the time and dedication behind the phrase "public service," and the resultant service to the public that is Canada and all Canadians.

So this is a story about events and the people who were there and shaped them as conservatism proceeded from opposition to government. Events are analyzed based on their historic importance as seen through the eyes of someone who was also there and worked with or for most of the participants, especially from the PC Party side of the conservative movement. The mind-numbing 1993 election results for the PC Party and the maturing of the Reform Party as a real political force; both parties' attempts to grow in the period between the 25 October 1993 election and the disappointing-yet-reassuring PC results in the 1997 election; Official Opposition status for Reform, even with no real breakthrough in representation east of Manitoba: all are chronicled.

Leadership changes. Another election in 2000. How many elections must occur before one party is killed off or surrenders? The inevitable result of the infighting was another Liberal majority. The leadership issues surrounding, first, Stockwell Day and then Joe Clark are detailed, as each searched for the magic formula that would end the Liberal hegemony and bring some form of conservative party back to government. First the PC and Democratic Reform Caucus (DRC) combined, and then came the leadership battle for the newly formed Alliance Party. Clark and the PCs put all their money – which wasn't much – on a Day win over Harper. A gross miscalculation! With a Harper victory, the PC–DRC alliance was no more, a new leader would be sought for the PC Party, and Joe Clark's dream of returning to 24 Sussex evaporated.

A new PC leader, Peter MacKay, was chosen, but his victory was immediately clouded by a deal with David Orchard, the man Joe Clark called "a tourist" in the PC Party during the 1998 leadership campaign. In Peter MacKay, the PCs had found a leader whose roots went way back in the Party, whose whole family history was about being in politics to be the government and not languish as the perpetual opposition. These were the familial traits that Peter would bring to his new job.

While there may be many differences between Harper and MacKay, they possessed one vitally important similarity: they both wanted to put an end to the Liberal Party domination of the Canadian federal political landscape. What prompted both leaders to see merger as the only option? For Harper, it was the Perth–Middlesex by-election loss; for MacKay, it was his political instincts and the urging of those closest to him, including former prime minister Brian Mulroney, shortly after his leadership win in Toronto.

While the negotiation of something like a remarriage with a pre- and post- and yet another pre-nuptial agreement is never easy or smooth, deliberations moved surprisingly quickly, and with little real disagreement, other than the method of choosing the leader, which was eventually resolved. The discussions about the founding principles were anything but acrimonious because there was an end game: forming a government. That could only be done with founding principles that appealed to a broad cross-section of Canadians. And that end justified sacrifice and compromise.

As merger progressed, Paul Martin and the Liberal Party steam-rolled into action – but riding in the sidecar was the beginning of the sponsorship scandal. While Martin did win in 2004, he was held to a minority, which NDP leader Jack Layton enjoyed running. When the Martin Liberal government was brought down in November 2005, Justice Gomery was riding in the sidecar and the steamroller had start-ed to run out of steam. Halfway through the 2005–06 extraordinary election campaign, Justice Gomery's report on the Liberal Party and the sponsorship fund was joined by an RCMP letter stating the start of an investigation into the Liberal's income trust issues. That pretty much ended the Martin juggernaut. The RCMP announcement, com-bined with a methodical, policy-based Conservative campaign, secured a Conservative minority government.

On 6 February 2006, the first Conservative government since Brian Mulroney's in 1988 was sworn in. Some pretty green timber went into forming the Cabinet, but even given the lack of experience and the sit-uation it faced, it was a Cabinet that performed remarkably well.

Cabinet making, the issues, and dealing with the known and the unknown became a way of life for a group that decided collectively that hard work could compensate for lack of experience. Prime Min-ister Harper chose to force the 2008 election. Anticipating an eco-nomic downturn, he did not want to face the anemic Stéphane Dion giving the government economic advice in daily question period without a fresh mandate from Canadians. As Harper searched for an issue on which to base an election call, Dion gave the prime minister a clear-cut one to take to the people. Dion's Greenshift was a policy tailor-made for the prime minister to attack. A carbon tax may have been at its root, but it was a massive restructuring of the Canadian tax system and redistribution of income at a most inopportune time. It was clear that a worldwide recession similar to that of the 1930s was going to be, if it wasn't already, upon us. What better issue to fight a general election on for a prime minister with a master's degree in economics?

Unfortunately for the prime minister, a majority was not in the cards; but neither was there a win for Dion, who said he would stand down as Liberal leader when a new leader was elected sometime in spring 2009. Rumblings for Harper's resignation, which he expected, did not occur, and with the Liberals in apparent disarray, the fall economic update was delivered. The resultant constitutional issues around coalition and prorogation formed a whole new chapter in

Canadian constitutional history. In the end, Liberal leadership changed once again and the prime minister settled into governing during a global financial crisis. A stimulus budget was prepared, passed in February 2009, implemented – and it worked! The Clerk of the Privy Council, Kevin Lynch, after discussions he and I had in late December 2008 and early January 2009, put his mind to ensuring that the stimulus money got out the bureaucratic door. We agreed that it didn't matter how good the budget was; if the money flowed at its usual bureaucratic snail's pace (as it did with the Obama stimulus budget package in the United States), Canada would not get through the recession unscathed. The term "shovel ready" was the funding mantra, and under Minister of Transport John Baird's supervision, with the prime minister's support, the money flowed and an economic disaster was averted. The rest of 2009 and 2010 were spent governing through serious economic conditions based on the stimulus budget, and ensuring that Canada fared as well or better than most countries in the world.

The lead-up to the 2011 election was pivotal as the opposition leaders positioned themselves for the inevitable spring election, likely they thought over the budget. The Liberals decided that alleged corruption and contempt of Parliament meant that Canada was no longer a democracy under Harper and his Conservatives, and that issue could be configured into a winning ballot question for them. While the NDP supported that view, it went its own way on an economic tack: jobs and policies designed to appeal to middle- and low-income Canadians, especially with emphasis on enriching the Canada Pension Plan. The Bloc repeated its old message and did not do its homework. It was becoming irrelevant and didn't know it! The prime minister had only one message: the need for a strong, stable, national majority government to deal with the economy. No one believed or understood the Liberal campaign. The Bloc just trotted out its usual formula, a little rusty and outdated. And Jack Layton, while not entirely well, put on a stellar campaign.

The unexpected result for the NDP was Official Opposition status, with the Grits in third place and the Bloc virtually wiped out. But the PM finally had his majority! .

What to do now and when to do it? What wonderful questions to face with a majority government, with a seasoned Cabinet. Focus then turned to the reshaping of Canadian federalism and Canadian foreign policy under what I have termed the Harper Doctrine.

Finally, after looking back, it is time to look ahead at the challenges and opportunities both for the left as well as for the prime minister as he enters the last years of this majority mandate. As the left in Canadian politics heads toward the next federal election in 2015, are there lessons to be learned from the right and what occurred between 1993 and 2006? Certainly, leadership and an enormous capacity for hard work have been the hallmarks of the Harper years. Could the left benefit from concentrating more on certain policy areas? How could the left better deal with areas in which it may be perceived as weak? Merger, or measures of co-operation short of merger, which looked to be a possibility in the early post-Layton and Ignatieff days, are just not on – at least not before the next election.

Should the Conservatives win the 2015 election, it would mean that Stephen Harper could be prime minister longer than any other Conservative leader except for our first prime minister, Sir John A. Macdonald. If successful, history may record how Harper has reshaped this country and prepared it for the second quarter of the twenty-first century. Even to contemplate such a thing is exciting for conservatives, because in the history of Canada, conservatives don't often assume the role of government and effect, on a continuing basis, real change to the future path of this great country.

However, storm clouds are gathering for the prime minister and his party. Has Harper's method of governing caught up with him? Scandals have reached into the Senate and the Prime Minister's Office, while Canadians seem to be looking for more than economic reassurance from the federal government. How all of these matters are dealt with, including new policy development, will result in either the end of the Harper era or its continuation beyond 2015. Will this majority mandate be squandered, or will the government be able to right itself and be that government for all Canadians that the prime minister professed it to be in his 2008 election acceptance speech?

14 DAYS

The Resignation. With Kim Campbell's resignation, it was back to the drawing board for the PC Party. (Courtesy of Kenneth Ginn/Prime Minister's Office, 1992. Reprinted by permission)

Nowhere but Up:
Post–Election Day 1993

In order to have a comeback, there must be something to come back from. For the Progressive Conservative Party of Canada, going from 158 to 2 Members of Parliament in one election was the something, and 25 October 1993 was the day it happened. No ordinary feat, it was a long time in the making. The same can be said of the Reform Party: going from 1 seat to 52 seats in one election took a lot of planning and hard work. Rising from virtual obscurity to substantial third-party status, with a robust group of members – some with consider-able provincial experience – was an accomplishment that Preston Manning and his colleagues had every right to be proud of.

How did this happen? Where did the PC Party go wrong and where did Reform go right – or at least right enough to emerge as an electoral force that, as the future would demonstrate, would not disappear?

There has always been conjecture that if the PC Party had replaced former prime minister Brian Mulroney with Jean Charest instead of Kim Campbell just months prior to what would be the next federal election, the two-seat debacle would not have occurred. Or, as the thinking goes, there might have been a defeat, but at least Official Opposition status would have been preserved. I am not so sure.

When Chief Electoral Officer Jean-Pierre Kingsley stated that if the election date was post–25 October, a new enumeration would have to be carried out – at a cost of approximately $25 million to taxpayers (since the enumeration for the referendum on the Charlottetown Ac-cord was no longer considered valid) – opposition parties were given the biggest gift they could receive: they knew the election date. It was a period of economic restraint, the deficit was at a record high, so

Campbell, the newly minted prime minister, who supposedly cared about taxpayer dollars, would go with a pre–26 October date, which she did.

Knowing when E day was going to be, the Liberals, NDP, and Reform as well as the Bloc in Quebec went to work developing platforms. The Liberal Red Book and its election scripting are the best examples of their kind for the period. The PC Party had just run a leadership race, had been the governing party since 1984, and believed it could run on its record, which was considerable. It could also run *away* from its record by putting new policies in the window – such as those espoused by Prime Minister Campbell during the leadership campaign. The problem was that only Charest, under the guidance of the Honourable Robert de Cotret, had put new policies in the window during that campaign.

Working with the late Bob de Cotret on Charest's campaign team was, at that time in my life, a great experience, one that I have always been grateful for and that I remember fondly. We got to do it again in 1998 for the Right Honourable Joe Clark, when he contested and won the PC leadership after Charest went to Quebec City. (So working together in leadership contests, Bob and I were 1–1.) I first met Bob in his West Block office after he had left Cabinet and was waiting for his appointment to the World Bank to be finalized. During this interregnum, he took on the task of being Charest's director of policy, speechwriting, and whatever else Charest needed.

It was a small but enthusiastic group supporting Charest. Our task was to develop, put flesh on the bones of, the policy theories that Jean and Bob had put together. These included dealing with the deficit and debt, job creation, health care, and the future of Canada under his leadership. Charest first articulated these parts of his platform in spring 1993 to the Canadian Home Builders Association. These themes were further developed, and Charest referred to them continuously in speeches and in the leadership debates, of which he only lost one.

If PM Campbell was going to run away from the record of Brian Mulroney, this was what she was going to have to run on.

But the problem was deeper than lack of a coherent platform. It was the one matter that will always lead to defeat: underestimating your opponent. No one in the PC camp or war room believed that Canadians would vote en masse to elect a Liberal government that would see Jean Chrétien become prime minister. Many times it was said that Canadians would not want to be represented on the world stage by this man. He was characterized as second-rate, barely articulate in either official language, and, in the words used later in that decade to describe Ontario Liberal leader Dalton McGuinty, "not up to the job." So, if you don't believe your opponent is worthy, why bother getting ready or training for the fight? Thus, the PCs did neither.

The Reform Party was put in the same box as the Liberals, treated with equal disdain. It had one seat. Would it actually get to the twelve seats needed to achieve official party status in the House of Commons?

Intellectually, the PC brain trust knew that the PC party was not regarded fondly in western Canada, even though most of the Cabinet heft came from out west – Joe Clark, Don Mazankowski, Bill Mc-Knight, and Harvie Andre, to name just a few. Matters such as the movement of the Air Canada repair depot from Winnipeg to Montreal on top of two failed attempts by Prime Minister Mulroney to strike a constitutional deal that would see Quebec sign on to the Constitution Act, 1982, which contained the Canadian Charter of Rights and Freedoms, were enough to shake loose PC support in the West. The West was tired of electing government members they believed, who would then go to Ottawa and come back to tell westerners what they should be doing and thinking. Preston Manning's Reform Party appealed to this sense of isolation and exclusion, and the perception of not being heard.

The only opponent not underestimated was Bloc leader Lucien Bouchard – he was a known quantity, tough and forceful. But even though he was taken seriously, he was not running a national campaign. He was only after 75 seats in Quebec – considerable in any election – but taking him seriously just meant that some of those 75 seats might be in play for the Bloc to grab.

Both the Liberals under Chrétien and Reform under Manning were gearing up for the electoral fight of their lives, knowing with some degree of accuracy when election day would be. They had put in place – Reform thanks to Stephen Harper and the Grits thanks to Paul Martin and Chaviva Hošek – platforms that set out their approach to governing and the proposals they would implement.

Predictably, Reform addressed economic issues with fervour. For example, a timetable for eliminating the deficit was presented. The Grits, in a first for Canadian federal politics, advanced its platform in what Chrétien referred to as the "Red Book." It was a detailed list of what the Liberals would do when elected. As he said many times during the campaign, voters could come to him two or three years down the road, point to a paragraph in the Red Book and ask him what he had done about that particular promise. It was more than a gimmick; it fueled an electorate's desire to hold politicians accountable, and now the electorate had a tool.

Reform promised a balanced budget in three years, or it would call an election. It also promised to review federal spending, either reducing or eliminating certain expenditures to provide a lower level of taxation; to lower the cost of doing business; and to lower the cost of living for all Canadians. The Liberal Red Book, "Creating Opportunity: The Liberal Plan for Canada," was 112 pages in length, and for the first time, actually costed the promises made. It didn't matter if it was a pipe dream or if some of the promises were not actually doable; it was out there for all to see as a credible prop for Jean Chrétien.

All of this caught the PC campaign team off guard. Those in charge had no idea they would face this level of organization among opposition parties. The PC Party put together a "Blue Book" to counter the Red Book, but it was playing catch up; it was too late. And the prime minister had already made her infamous statement about elections not being the time to discuss public policy.

Much has been written about the campaign (or lack thereof), the debates, and the PC advertisements featuring Jean Chrétien's face. Suffice to say that those running the PC campaign thought they were still fighting yesterday's battles with Prime Minister Mulroney at the helm. Like him or not – and I do, very much – if need be, he was and still could be a helluva campaigner. Not to get biblical, but at any time, day or night, where two or three would gather in his name or that of the PC Party, he would be there, with a smile, a reassuring word, and policies to fit the occasion. Campbell did not approach campaigning with that necessary level of enthusiasm, preparedness, and zeal, and the party suffered a disastrous defeat.

But the defeat was due to considerably more than just a poor campaigner as leader. There was also lack of hard work, lack of preparation, and supreme overconfidence combined with gross underestimation regarding the Reform Party and the Grits. Underestimating the task at hand will get a government defeated every time, and it sorely was on 25 October 1993.

So that is where the road began, the road leading back to being the Government of Canada, for all of those who identified with the conservative movement in our country, be they Red Tories, Blue Tories, soft Quebec nationalists with conservative views, or dyed-in-the-wool Reformers.

Post–October 1993, the PC and Reform parties went to work to see where they would end up three or four years hence, at the next general election.

The PC Party was in disarray. Staffers were let go, and it was really up to Senator Gerry St Germain, as party president, to save what was left of the furniture. Defeat might not have been a surprise, but its enormity caught most off guard. Questions had to be answered: personnel questions, logistical questions, but most importantly, leadership questions. Prime Minister Campbell did not retain her seat in the House of Commons, which, to all intents, was a great blessing. Jean Charest had retained his seat in Sherbrooke, and Elsie Wayne, the popular former mayor of St John, New Brunswick, had won the only other PC seat.

The first order of business was to secure Campbell's resignation. The second was to convince Charest, rejected only a couple of months before, and still smarting, to ascend to the precarious and vacant PC Party throne. There was no plan B. The only alternative – and it really wasn't one at this juncture – was to have the Party led from within the Senate. But what would that say about electoral chances next time?

André Pratte, in his book on Charest, says that Charest accepted the leadership task willingly.[1] That is not what I recall as senators met with Charest to convince him to take over. He was still getting over his loss to Campbell, which had caused quite a rift and a long process of reflection for him after the leadership vote. Now he was being asked to take over a tattered, torn, and really down-and-out party, whose only saving grace at the time was its majority in the Senate.

Charest did accept the task, took over and went to work addressing the issues that had lead to the virtual obliteration of the Party. He recognized that the Party needed restructuring, funding, and policies – he characterized the task before him as the three Rs: Restructure the Party, Renew the Policy, and Return to Power.

There were two silver linings to this dark storm cloud. First, despite only having two seats, the Party had the support of voters in every part

of the country. So, at least there was something upon which to
build. Second, there was the Senate, ably led by Senator John Lynch-
Staunton, who had held leadership roles in the Senate in the Mulroney government. But Lynch-Staunton's pivotal role might never
have been, since the vote for a new leader in the Senate was close.
While all ballots were subsequently destroyed, rumour persists that
Lynch-Staunton won by only one vote over Senator Bill Doody from
Newfoundland. His victory in this crucial vote, in which only senators
participated, meant that PC leadership in both chambers was solid.

John Lynch-Staunton, with whom I worked closely for many years,
was fluently bilingual, and intellectually and politically smart; possessed a wonderful sense of humour, as well as a vicious temper; and
had an incredible penchant for hard work. He read the Senate debates
and, until his death in September 2012, always enjoyed catching the
Liberals unawares, whether the Conservatives were in government or
opposition. While he was a partisan, he brought common sense to that
partisanship. On very few occasions – most notably over the Pearson
International Airport contracts – did he believe the Conservative senators should vote together to defeat the Liberal government's legislation or policy agenda. He was ideal for the job because he loved and
respected the Senate and also wanted to do all he could to help bring
the Party back to government. For the most part, he got along with and
was supportive of Charest's leadership. Through agreement with Lynch-
Staunton, all the research needed by the Party was run out of a small
but talented research group, funded by senators pooling money from
their research budgets.

The PC Party began to rebuild on two tracks: one was the three *R*s
being pursued by Charest in the House of Commons and internally
within the Party itself; the other was the legislative, or parliamentary,
track, which focused somewhat on the House of Commons, but in
reality, the heavy lifting was to be done by the Senate.

The Reform side of the equation, under Preston Manning went to
work, readying itself for government, which surely would come after
the next election. The best example of the influence over public policy exercised by Reform was creating an appetite within the country
and in the Chrétien government for fiscal responsibility in the form
of a balanced budget as soon as possible. Manning's "zero in three"
plank in the 1993 Reform platform was, in the main, implemented by
the Liberals. This demonstrated that Reform's economic policies were
not as draconian as they had been portrayed in the 1993 election.

While doing well on economic policy, Manning was never able to successfully convince Canadians east of the Manitoba–Ontario border of the efficacy of Reform's social policies, and the need for economic reform to be followed by action on social policy.

While Charest was working tirelessly on the party-rebuilding project, which would go to a Party congress in Hull, Quebec, in 1995, senators began to look for things to do to occupy their time usefully and also allow them to contribute positively to the Conservative public policy process. Chrétien gave them two early opportunities when the government established two special joint committees, one on defence policy and the other on foreign affairs. Both committees were to sketch out for the government where Canada should go and how it should get there in both of these areas. While there could have been one committee on both subjects – to ensure advice from one didn't contradict the other – two joint committees kept members of all parties and senators busy, doing useful and needed work. How much better could it get?[2]

Well, much better, if you are willing to take the gamble that Lynch-Staunton and Eric Berntson, his deputy leader, were ready to undertake.

The contracts that were let during the latter part of the Mulroney administration for the redevelopment and refurbishment of Pearson International Airport in Toronto had been a source of constant conflict between the new Liberal government on one side and PC senators and those who held the contracts for the work on the airport on the other. In this matter, PC senators were supported by the Reform Party.

There were two issues that Chrétien capitalized on in the election. The previous Mulroney government had committed Canada to an expensive helicopter purchase program to replace the aging Sea Kings. There were also contracts signed by the Mulroney government to refurbish the Pearson Airport in Toronto. In both instances, Chrétien promised to cancel the contracts when he became prime minister. So as well as writing "zero helicopters"[3] on 4 November 1993 shortly after he became prime minister, Chrétien took the same pen to the Pearson Airport redevelopment contracts and cancelled them. Not only did he cancel them, but Allan Rock, then minister of justice, brought in a bill that, if passed, would eliminate the contractor's right to sue for damages for breach of contract. Lynch-Staunton and Berntson, and many others, had had enough. As the PCs still had a majority in the Senate, which meant a majority on special investigative committees, it was high time a Senate special committee looked into and pronounced on this whole Pearson Airport contract affair.

An arrangement was reached with the Senate leadership on the government side and the Special Senate Committee on the Pearson Airport Agreements was struck.[4] Senator Finlay MacDonald volunteered to chair the committee; along with him on the PC side were Marjory LeBreton, David Tkachuk, and Duncan Jessiman. From time to time, Lynch-Staunton and Berntson exercised their right as ex officio members to sit in on the proceedings. This was a tremendous help, especially at the beginning, when it was obvious we were not prepared for what amounted to a full-frontal assault by the government, its senators and staff, and public service officials.

As much as the PC opposition senators believed there were valid points to be made and that everything to secure the Pearson Airport contracts was completely legal and above reproach, the new Chrétien Liberal government had its position and story to tell. The government placed Senator Michael Kirby as deputy chair of the Pearson Airport committee. The government believed it could take advantage of the hearings to solidify its position that the contracts were signed at the eleventh-and-a-half hour, when the PC government knew it was going to be defeated, and had no right either in law or convention to formalize or sign the contracts. And it was alleged that the contracts were awarded to friends and cronies of the PC Party who had little or no experience with this type of massive development. The Liberal government had already cancelled the contracts and was ready to use the committee hearings to justify its actions, taking the position that no damages were owed since the contracts were not legally authorized in the first place. The previous PC government had no authority to enter into the contracts when it did.

The PC senate caucus was absolutely convinced that it held all the cards in the matter, and believed the hearings and the concluding report would demonstrate how right they were. Quite frankly, if it occurred this way, it would be a morale booster for Jean and Elsie, PC senators, and all those who were still PC supporters. If it was done right, this might become part of the silver bullet that all were looking for, that would point the remnants of the PC Party back toward the path to respectability and then government. That was the plan.

In the first week or so, it did not look like the plan would come close to being executed. I do not believe that anyone on the PC side, and maybe even on the government side, realized what they were getting into. The special committee, because of the importance of the subject matter and the fact that there were numerous breach of contract lawsuits claiming damages, took on the demeanour of a quasi-judicial hearing. Gary O'Brien, a senior clerk at the time and now clerk of the senate, was assigned full time to the committee; he was invaluable in keeping the procedural issues straight and advising on process as well as procedure. Senior Ottawa legal counsel, John Nelligan, Q.C., was retained as counsel to the committee. The proceedings and the questioning of witnesses were based on departmental documents, memorandums, and letters that the Department of Transport produced for the committee on a regular basis. The accounting firm of Lindquist Avey was retained to catalogue the documents, keep track of them, and ensure the integrity of that part of the process.

The situation resulted in the government's Liberal senators having a distinct advantage: they had officials who were ready to brief them, and in some cases – not all – these officials had not been supportive of the process that led to the signing of the contracts. While both sides jointly agreed to the witness list, the government side had the benefit of advice from officials who were fully knowledgeable about the contracting process and, hence, the most effective order for witnesses to appear so as to support the government's contentions.

I believe Liberal senators received full briefings from departmental officials on the contracts, as well as the nature and scope of the documents. I also believe, but only have one instance to support it, that the government side was privy to more documents than the PC senators, which gave them a more thorough appreciation of the contracting process. My suspicions were aroused because of the nature of the Liberal questions. They seemed to have before them a clearer picture of what had transpired than did PC senators. Their questions also seemed to be alleging facts and searching for answers that were not apparent from reading and reviewing the available documents. The one incident that proved my suspicions correct occurred on a Thursday afternoon, when the committee and staff were looking forward to a week break in the hearings. This was near the beginning of the process, and Senator Michael Kirby drew a witness's attention to a particular part of a document. The paragraph being quoted was unfamiliar, and Senator Tkachuk raised an objection, specifically asking the chair, clerk, John Nelligan, and Senator Kirby which document he was referring to and how it came to be in his possession, when no one on the PC side had ever seen it. Senator Kirby simply explained that it was in his package and he had no idea how he came to have a document that the opposition senator did not have.

I discussed the matter at length with committee counsel John Nelligan. He told me – and it would not be the last time I heard him utter the phrase – "Bruce, you have to accept the word of the honourable senators."

My point here is to show what an enormous task this small group of PC senators, with limited resources, had in front of them as they tried to take on the entire weight of the federal government and its attendant bureaucracy.

The first week had not started well, and by mid-week, the PC Senate leadership was wondering how this good idea of striking a committee and holding hearings to justify the former government's action could go so far off track. Mid-week, Lynch-Staunton and Berntson visited the daily morning preparatory meeting, held in Senator Tkachuk's office in the Victoria Building, where the hearings were taking place. They weren't there to give everyone a pat on the back or commiserate about the enormity of the task ahead. They arrived loaded for bear, extremely critical of our side's performance.

As time went on, however, a rhythm developed for the hearings and for preparation on the PC side. The committee was fortunate – and PC senators, very fortunate – to have Jack Stillborn, Ph.D., seconded to it by the Parliamentary Research Branch of the Library of Parliament. It was going to be his job to review and digest the sworn testimony given to the committee and to distill it in to a report. He accomplished this with deftness and clarity, and in the fall of 1995, the committee produced its report containing the official committee report from the majority PC senators and a minority report from the government side, the Liberal senators.[5]

My role was to review all the documents produced for the hearing and prepare questions or lines of questioning for PC senators to ask witnesses. While that's a heck of a way to spend an Ottawa summer, I believe all of those involved, certainly from the PC side, were dedicated to seeing this through – and performed way above expectations in what was a long, complex set of hearings. My work was aided immeasurably by a lawyer from Toronto who was involved with the group that had signed the contracts to redevelop the airport. Gordon R. Baker, Q.C., became an invaluable source of information and relevant research, and along the way a lifelong friend and supporter, not only during the dark days of these hearings but also later in my life when other challenges arose.

Before these hearings began, I did not really know Senator Finlay MacDonald, except to exchange pleasantries. Unfortunately he, like Lynch-Staunton, is no longer with us, but I must say that the friendship we forged during this period lasted until his death in 2002. After a particularly bad day, at the beginning of the hearings, before we got our feet firmly under us, Finlay and I were walking back to his office in the East Block to commiserate. We passed a group of public works employees painting the fence on Parliament Hill. We stopped, looked at each other, and decided these guys had it made – show up, get a brush and a can of paint, get assigned a section of fence, and paint until quitting time. The brush and paint can go back to the shop, and you go home secure in the knowledge of a job well done. What's more – you didn't have to take home any fence to paint or worry about for the next day.

It was about then that Finlay asked the crucial question that would become the underpinning of our relationship until Finlay's retirement from the Senate: "Bruce, are you the kind of man who would be known to take a drink?" My enthusiastic, affirmative response was all Finlay needed. I quickly became a devotee of the senator's vodka martinis and Bloody Caesars.

The special committee sat through the summer and into the fall of 1995, hearing from public servants involved in the contractual process, constitutional experts and those appointed by the Chrétien government to advise on the contracts, and the principals themselves. It was as close as a politically adversarial parliamentary committee could come to a thorough airing of opinions, the facts, and a search for truth. And in my experience, it was as close as we have come in Ottawa to the kind of United States congressional hearings where witnesses are sworn, both sides are well prepared, and the committee itself has a real issue of importance to deal with and competent staff to support its work.

The final report of the Special Senate Committee on the Pearson Airport Agreements was exactly what the PC Party needed to begin to hold its head up once again. During this period, Reform MPs asked helpful questions in the House of Commons and lent what support they could to the cause. They knew that a negative report would tarnish all conservatives, regardless of party affiliation.

To top off the Pearson Airport hearings experience, Minister of Justice Allan Rock had introduced a bill designed to cancel the redevelopment contracts, to prevent lawsuits by aggrieved contracting partners for damages for breach of contract, and to take away any right the contracting parties might have to damages. Although the bill was opposed by the Reform Party in the House of Commons, it passed and was sent on to the Senate for deliberation.[6]

It failed to pass in the Senate on a tie vote. There were smiles once again among the small band of PC MPs and senators.

I believe the PC senators kept the lights on in the PC Party. They held the government to account and shared research resources with Charest's office, establishing as good a little working group as could be found on Parliament Hill.

While senators provided valuable work and resources, if the Party was going to make a comeback in the next federal election, it had to be fashioned around its leader in the House of Commons, Jean Charest. Two things needed doing before the next election. First, the Party needed a new constitution giving the rank and file, or grassroots, significant input into the running of the Party. Conventional wisdom at the time was that the Party leadership had lost touch with Party supporters, resulting in some of the more egregious decisions, which in turn resulted in the rise of Reform and in the 1993 election results. The outcome of the 1995 meeting was gratifying: after a day-long session of voting, a new Party constitution was adopted and Jean Charest's leadership of the party was confirmed.

The second matter that needed doing was policy and platform development for the next election. It was obvious that whatever the pluses of the record accumulated from 1984 to 1993, a series of new policy initiatives had to be developed. Parenthetically, one could argue, with the benefit of hindsight, that lack of policy and platform development beyond the Chrétien years of 1993–2003 is what really caused the downfall of the Liberal Party under Martin, Dion, and Ignatieff. The Dion Greenshift may have been a significant policy idea, but the introduction of a new tax and trying to explain its effect on the economy as the world headed for the worst economic recession/depression since the 1930s, compounded by an inarticulate message and messenger, resulted in the only significant Liberal policy initiative since 1993 being soundly rejected by the electorate. As is so often said in politics, "it is all about the timing." Recognizing the work that needed to be done, Leslie Noble and others from Ontario premier Mike Harris's team were engaged.

After the 1995 congress confirmed Charest's leadership and put a new constitution in place, a platform for the election had to be developed based on policies to be discussed at an August 1996 policy meeting to be held in Winnipeg. Thinking back to that period, it was not an easy time for Charest, as a "red Tory," to be leading a conservative party during the last half of the 1990s. The Reform Party was on the upswing, and provincial Conservative parties in Alberta and elsewhere were cut from the Manning cloth. In Ontario, Mike Harris had won a surprise victory in 1995, and there was no question that his views on public policy were more closely aligned with Preston Manning's than with Jean Charest's.

Nevertheless, Leslie Noble and others from the successful Mike Harris run at government were recruited to deal with policy and platform for Charest. Their views on many issues did not coincide with Charest's, and what ultimately ended up being produced as a platform was more in line with Charest's thinking than that of the group that drafted the original platform. Something similar occurred in Winnipeg, where the youth wing of the Party tried unsuccessfully to insert capital punishment in the policies of the party. This was opposed by Charest and was not included. The period 1993 to 1997 was not easy for Charest and the PC Party as the Party tried to define territory on the right of the political spectrum that the leader, PC senators, and supporters of the Party were comfortable being in, as fiscal conservatives driven by a social conscience.

The rebuilding of the Party – its structure, policies, and platform – was helped by Charest's increased stature across Canada due to the role he played in the 1995 Quebec referendum. From the vantage point of today, seventeen years later, reflecting back on that event, which could have led to the destruction of the country, one has to ask: What was the federal Liberal Party thinking at that time? For someone as politically astute as Jean Chrétien proved to be as prime minister, completely misjudging a situation that could have ended so badly for both Quebec and Canada was nothing short of astounding. It was clear that the federalist or "No" side spent a great deal of time getting ready for the campaign. As André Pratte pointed out in his 1998 biography, *Charest: His Life and Politics*, the organizing committee began to meet shortly after Jacques Parizeau became Quebec premier in September 1994.[7] It included representatives from the provincial Liberal Party, the federal Liberal Party, and the PC Party, those being: Senator Pierre Claude Nolin; François Pilote, a long-time Charest advisor and friend; and Jean Bazin, former senator, former head of the Canadian Bar Association, and friend of former prime minister Brian Mulroney. The Charest group attended all the planning meetings, so at that level, one cannot say they were left out physically.

The surprising part of the referendum campaign was PM Jean Chrétien's refusal to become involved and refusal to accept the fact that changes had to take place in Canadian federalism, in its relationship to Quebec, and indeed across the country. His stoic refusal to make promises or acknowledge that anything was wrong seemed to be a throwback to the Trudeau years. But even Trudeau became involved in the 1980 referendum. His position could also have been a reaction to Trudeau's strong but wrong and unprincipled stand against both the Meech Lake Accord and the Charlottetown Accord. Trudeau's opposition was all about ego; if he could not strike a constitutional deal with Quebec in the 1980–82 negotiations, no one was going to, and especially not a Conservative Canadian prime minister from Quebec, Brian Mulroney.

So Chrétien's judgment may have been clouded by constitutional battles of days gone by – the early 1980s, the Meech Lake Accord, and the Charlottetown Accord. However, this was 1995, and with time running out, the "Yes" forces, with Lucien Bouchard assuming the role of lead spokesperson, had a substantial lead in the polls. It may seem trite to point it out, but in a referendum as opposed to a "first past the post" election, every vote counts – so the polling results would be fairly accurate.

Although consigned to the less important "B" tour around Quebec, save for one day, Charest was very involved in the campaign. It brought him notoriety both in Quebec and across Canada. At that point, and in fact for many years after the 1993 election, the PC Party could ill afford the type of cross-Canada leader tours that national parties are supposed to, and are expected to, run. Crass as it may be to suggest it, Charest's participation in the "No" campaign not only saved the PC Party money but also achieved the same purpose as a cross-Canada leader tour: it got Charest into people's homes through either electronic or print media.

Charest, because of his youth, natural enthusiasm, love of the country, and love of campaigning, displayed through his words and actions that he could also be the agent of change. Jean Chrétien, reluctantly and at the last minute, on 24 October, offered Quebecers some hope for change: "We are keeping open all other avenues to change, whether they be administrative or constitutional." Charest was able to build on this opening: "The Canada Camp stands for change."[8] His presence and speech at the massive outdoor "No" rally in Montreal's Place du Canada was seen and heard across the country. For Canadians, I believe this was the "Charest" moment in the referendum. It showed him as a youthful, vibrant leader, a symbol of change, a strong supporter of Canada and Quebec within Canada.

It was what was needed if the next general election campaign was to be successful for the PC Party. It also put Charest in a place where Preston Manning couldn't go and demonstrated the different views of Canada held by the two parties.

The post-referendum activities of the two parties illustrated their different preoccupations. On the Reform side, MP Stephen Harper introduced a private member's bill that dealt explicitly with a referendum on separation. It was really the precursor to PM Chrétien's Clarity Act, passed in 2000.[9] Bill C-341, introduced by Harper in 1996, dealt with the clarity of the question as well as provincial and minority rights.[10] It reinforced the rule of law by stating explicitly that the federal government would not recognize unilateral declaration of independence by Quebec and would oppose it internationally.

On the PC side, after cross-Canada consultations, policies were developed that went to the Winnipeg PC policy convention in 1996. The party was en route to address Charest's second *R*. However, difficulties with the platform, as pointed out above, bedevilled election preparations. As Hugh Segal has pointed out in his work, *The Long Road Back*, it was remarkable and only due to Charest's superior campaigning skills that the PCs performed as well as they did in the 1997 general election.[11]

There are four events that stand out in that election. The first was the national leaders' debate where Charest always performed beyond expectations. It was after this performance that musing started in earnest about moving from two seats to Official Opposition status with most Progressive Conservative MPs coming from Quebec. The second event occurred when those on the ground in Quebec noticed a new phenomenon: Liberals turned on the spending taps in local campaigns. Only in 2003 did Conservatives, through the Report of the Auditor General and the subsequent Gomery Commission of Inquiry into the Sponsorship Program and Advertising Activities find out where the money was coming from.[12] The third matter, which has been written about extensively, is the Chrétien response to the question of whether a bare-majority referendum result would be enough to start negotiations for the separation of Quebec. His affirmative answer, and the lack of one for days from Charest and his team, hurt the PC Party cause in Quebec. Finally, while the election result wasn't exactly what was hoped for, it was good enough: twenty seats, and the regaining of official party status in the House of Commons.

A group of us met with Charest at Party headquarters the night after the election. After as much analysis as one could stomach twenty-four hours after the vote, we then discussed what it meant to be the leader of a recognized political party, under the House of Commons rules. After a lengthy explanation based on notes we had been given by the Office of the Clerk of the House of Commons dealing with such things as office budgets, the appointment of House officers, and staffing budgets, the leader's first question was: "Tell me about the car again." With only two seats in the House, this had been a nightmare for the Party since there was no budget provided for a car and driver. How to get the leader from place to place and back again was always a major issue. The president of Chrysler Canada, a Charest fan, had donated a car, but had died a few months later. Chrysler had no records as to why the PC Party had one of their cars from head office. It was good to have this situation resolved.

The 1997 election results put the Party back on the radar screen and established it as a recognized Party in the House of Commons, but they fell short of Charest's and the Party's expectations. After the leaders' debate, it looked like Charest would win as many as forty-five seats in Quebec. A resurgence in Quebec might help swing Ontario, and the Party knew that Atlantic Canada was solidly PC. With this optimism after the debate, the Party borrowed heavily to finance the final push. The end result was a respectable finish, something to build on, with still-solid support from the Senate side – at least it was a beginning. A debt-burdened beginning, but the Party was used to that.

On the Reform side, there was elation tempered with disappointment. It had become the Official Opposition, but still struggled east of the Manitoba–Ontario border. To make matters worse, Reform's lack of appeal in that part of the country gave centre-right voters no option but to vote PC, leading to its Lazarus-like revival. Jean Charest, taking the same position post-1997 election as he did prior to it, refused to engage in any conversation of merger or working with Reform. His attitude had not changed since his refusal in 1996 to attend the Winds of Change conference.[13]

Open Season:
Searching for Leadership of the Right

As the dust settled after the June 1997 election, it would have been hard to predict the turmoil that would occur in the period between 1997 and the next general election in 2000. Leadership change could not be ignored by either of the parties on the right. For the PCs, it was necessitated by a call to duty for national unity. For Reform, it stemmed from the continual goal of marching eastward, the need to win seats in Ontario through to and including Atlantic Canada – a goal denied until merger of the two parties in 2003.

But before going forward, we must go back and look at the work done by Reformers leading up to 1997. At the May 1996 Winds of Change conference, Stephen Harper argued in a speech to the conference that conservatism can only be successful by marrying traditional support in Atlantic Canada and Ontario with prairie populism and with support from the Francophone nationalists of Quebec, as done by Mulroney, Diefenbaker, and Borden.[1] While Reform had improved its seat numbers in 1997 to sixty and achieved Official Opposition status, it had not been able to bring together Conservative support in Atlantic Canada, Ontario, and Quebec. Therefore, it was time for the party to again look at what structural and personnel changes could be effected to achieve the goal set out in Harper's theory.

This challenge became the "United Alternative" project. Manning viewed this as an attempt to bring together all those who shared four fundamental principles: fiscal responsibility, social responsibility, democratic accountability, and reformed federalism.[2]

Because of the hope generated by the 1997 election results, fundamental disagreement over the status of Quebec, and just plain "right

The Provincial Leader. Jean Charest (right) led the PC Party out of the wilderness; Senator Michael A. Meighen, Q.C., (left) was part of the stalwart group of PC senators who helped keep the lights on. (Courtesy of Michael Meighen. Reprinted by permission)

wingism," Charest's and later Clark's attitude was to take a wide pass on the United Alternative movement. So the Progressive Conservative folks who joined Manning's United Alternative venture were mainly like-thinking provincial PCs who could have been labelled Reform and disaffected PC, Peter White, being the prime example.

Out of the United Alternative movement, a new political party was born: the Canadian Reform Conservative Alliance. The party was launched in late January 2000, and there was to be a leadership contest, designed initially as a coronation for the party's founder, Preston Manning.

While all of this was happening, the PC Party with its twenty MPs and still numerous senators was preparing to establish itself as the main federalist opposition party. During the 1997 campaign, a transition team had been formed, chaired by Senator Norman Atkins. It was composed of Harry Near, head of Earnscliffe Strategy Group; Senator Finlay MacDonald; Mike Allan, former Charest chief of staff; Christine Corrigan, Norman's assistant as team secretary; and myself. It was an interesting challenge: we knew we were transitioning – we just didn't know to what! We all believed that the Party would return to official party status in the election. Beyond that – perhaps post-debate – we dreamed of Official Opposition status. We recognized that posts would need to be filled in the House (House leader, whip, etc.) and critic roles assigned. And we recognized that, except for Jean Charest and Elsie Wayne, it was highly unlikely that a lot of PC MPs would have had previous House of Commons experience. In this we were pleasantly wrong; two MPs from the Mulroney era were elected, Bill Casey and Greg Thompson.

One of the major projects undertaken by the transition team was to act as the whip – Senator Atkins and I attended meetings with other party whips to deal with assignment of office space and getting human resources information about the pay and benefits for new MPs. Bob Kilger, a former NHL referee, represented the Grits at these meetings, and Chuck Strahl, the Reform Party. It was during these exchanges that Norman and I came to realize: if we ever thought we were not fond of the Reform caucus members, our feelings were modest compared to how Reform felt about the PC Party.

One anecdote to illustrate meeting matters. As leader of a recognized political party, Charest was entitled to an office in the Centre Block, as was Alexa McDonough, leader of the NDP. There was a suite of offices along the north corridor of the sixth floor that could be divided in two, creating the choice of a suite with an extra office and one with the washroom. After some deliberation we chose the one with the extra office. Alexa got her own washroom. Such is life at the bottom of the party numerical barrel.

The other main responsibility of the transition team was to design and run an MPs training college. Over two days, new and returning MPs would learn the ropes: everything they needed to know about being an MP, from the swearing in to collecting one's pay to Question Period to the opportunities available for MPs to advance causes near to their hearts. The "late show," where members can raise issues of concern to their constituents or hold the government to account on various matters; private members' motions; private members' bills; House committees; and the role of the Senate were explained by staff, but also by former PC MPs who were invited to be part of the faculty of the college.[3]

This PC MP training college was followed by a caucus retreat in Halifax. It was the custom in those days for the PC senators to hold a summer and a winter caucus planning retreat outside of Ottawa. Preparation for this one took place during the writ period and all was ready for August 1997. Fortunately, attendance increased by eighteen after the election. Traditionally, the retreats would deal with a couple of major policy issues, House planning for the upcoming session, and, in the summer, the annual golf tournament.

This one was different from those held since 1993. There actually was a House of Commons strategy to develop, as well as one for the Senate. The usual format for these meetings was followed, as senators and MPs met together and then separately to discuss what could be expected from the Chrétien government in the new Parliament. It was clear from the discussions that Charest and his new group of MPs were committed to building the PC Party itself and to continue taking on Reform everywhere. In the background, there was chatter about the political situation in Quebec, but at that point no one could have predicted the challenges to come in the next few months.

The return to Ottawa was full of optimism and energy. Charest had chosen his Commons officers well, especially Peter MacKay as House leader and justice critic. Others were either experienced or their personalities were a natural fit for their assigned tasks. One unnecessary dust-up occurred when Charest decided that as leader in the House of Commons of a recognized party, he would choose the Senate leader who would be the leader of the official opposition in the Senate. His argument was based on the fact that Brian Mulroney has chosen the Senate leader between 1984 and 1993; however, that person had also sat in Cabinet, so, of course, the leader/PM would make that selection. It was explained to Charest that after 1993, senators had started a new tradition: selection of their leader by secret ballot of the senators. Charest did not want anyone other than Lynch-Staunton. When Lynch-Staunton was unopposed for the leadership, the status quo prevailed, and this issue resolved itself.

But then things changed for both parties on the right.

The Ottawa-to-Quebec-City question had been in the back of Charest's mind for a long time. André Pratte in his biography of Charest recounts the outcome of a Charest–Bourassa meeting, where Charest believed Bourassa said that Charest would be premier of Quebec at some point.[4] A Charest-to-Quebec-City move seemed always to be lurking behind the scenes. It was raised at the Halifax summer caucus meeting as rumours persisted even into the new PC mandate that Charest would not see the job he had started in Ottawa through to completion.

This had an unsettling effect on caucus. Most, if not all, had decided to run in 1997 because they believed that a Charest-led PC Party could perhaps, after two elections, win the country. The Party could also regain the stature once held in western Canada during the Mulroney years. This is what they believed. This is why they ran. They believed Jean Charest owed his other nineteen MPs at least one more election. This is quite a contrast to parties and leaders in the second decade of the twenty-first century. The leader seems to be given one chance to win, and if it doesn't happen, the party is on to choosing the next messiah.

Despite the distraction, the PC Party, under the direction of House Leader Peter MacKay and with the help of question period coordinator Rick Borotsik, performed well in the House, punching well above its weight. And the PC senators continued to be relied upon for research support and advice, especially in dealing with analysis and criticism of government legislation. The important task was to outperform the Reform Party, to establish significant credentials on all issues. First, leave Reform behind in the dust; then take on the governing Liberals.

André Pratte's book, which basically ends as Charest heads to Quebec City, contains probably the most accurate, unbiased account of the machinations that took place in the winter and early spring of 1998.[5] Charest fundamentally resigned himself to the role of rebuilding the PC Party, regardless of how dismissively he was treated by Mike Harris or Alberta PC premier Ralph Klein. Getting a meeting with either one was a major task. But in December 2007, the expectation of Charest staying in Ottawa and rebuilding the PC Party started to unravel as rumours spread of Daniel Johnson's imminent resignation as Liberal leader in Quebec.

The problems facing Charest on the Ottawa-or-Quebec-City issue were largely brought on by himself – the first, unwittingly; the other a consequence of dithering over the decision. The former arose out of Charest's participation in the 1995 referendum. While it is argued that Charest's performance did not move the polls, he did gain nationwide acclaim as someone who could be in and of Quebec and put forward a credible Canada-wide view, persuading Quebecers it was well worth it to continue within Canada. This positioning and exposure obviously helped in the 1997 election – not as much as the Party wished, but Return, the third *R*, was always going to be at least a two-election process. So Charest was seen nationwide as someone who could deliver Quebec from the arms of the separatists.

This feeling in the country then combined with the problem Charest caused all by his inability to close and lock the door on this matter.

The matter was discussed near the end of February 1998 at the PC National Council meeting. Premier Johnson alerted Charest by phone of his impending resignation, and in the not-so-distant background were the hands of Laurent Beaudoin and former Prime Minister Mulroney, both creating a path that would lead to the National Assembly in Quebec City. The situation percolated while Charest conducted a House of Commons break-week tour of the West. Upon his return to Ottawa, and although he'd told caucus that he wouldn't go to Quebec City, Charest's mind was not made up and pressure was mounting. Canadians, once again, saw him as the saviour of Quebec and Canada. A pretty hard argument or plea to resist.

Two new points come up at this time. Pratte recounts PC MP André Bachand telling Charest that the Liberal Party in Quebec is not filled with people who would be loyal to Charest – it is no longer the party of Bourassa, who could envisage Charest as leader of the Liberal Party. Many others were corroborating Bachand's story. The other issue, created by Charest taking time to weigh all of the options, was what would happen if he turned Quebec down. A united Canada would be in jeopardy: Charest stays in Ottawa, the Parti Québécois (PQ) continues to form the government (which they did once more, even with Charest there), another referendum, the country splits apart – and it would be all his fault. Also, by turning his back on Quebec now, in the next federal election would Quebec turn its back on him and his party? What would his stock be in the rest of the country? It has been said that Canadians have short memories, and are forgiving. This may have been true in January 1998, but not so much in March 1998 when the question of Charest's future was still out there unanswered.

At a 10 March 1998 caucus meeting, Charest asked for yet more time to reflect on the implications of going or staying. This meant further pressures built, until finally on 25 March, he informed caucus, and on March 26 in Sherbrooke, he informed Quebecers and the rest of the country, that he was leaving federal politics and going to Quebec City.

So twenty became nineteen, and a Party still trying to deal with a substantial debt following the 1993 and 1997 elections was left without a leader. It was also left with a cumbersome and unexciting process for electing a new leader.

The leadership selection process ended in November 1998 with the Right Honourable Joe Clark once again at the helm of the PC Party. I worked with Bob de Cotret in support of Joe Clark in the leadership race.[6] We did policy and speech writing for the former PM and former minister of foreign affairs and minister of constitutional affairs in the Mulroney government. Hugh Segal, Brian Pallister, Michael Fortier, and David Orchard were the other candidates. There was a short-lived discussion about inviting Stephen Harper to contest the leadership. I got to know Harper in 1991–92, when I was working as the advisor to the Conservative side of the Special Joint Committee on a Renewed Canada. Clark, who was minister of constitutional affairs at that time, established conferences across the country on various constitutional topics. I attended on behalf of the committee and Harper attended as research director of the Reform Party. We renewed our acquaintance when he was a Reform MP. I actually thought he would make both an excellent candidate and leader, and should be invited to contest the leadership. However, the prevailing wisdom was that Harper had said so many negative things about the PC Party that this was just not on.

Clark's view, and the reason he was running – which both Bob and I bought into – was that from his days as a minister in the Mulroney government, he had a stellar reputation across the country, and he could translate that into support for the PC Party. Once it was clear to Canadians that Clark was back leading the Party, we would go to at least Official Opposition in the next election, perhaps forming a minority government, and certainly forming government in the election after that. In theory this looked quite promising and doable. Leadership debates were held across the country, and much to our pleasant surprise, there seemed to be no political rust on Joe. He performed well, in both languages in all of the debates.

Joe Clark was a treat to work with. He had run a government almost twenty years previously, albeit for a short period, and he had held two senior portfolios in the last Conservative government. His work between 1993, when he left politics, and 1998, when he returned, was such that he was in command of most policy issues, at least from his vantage point. As always, he was a quick brief, and the best speechwriter in the room.

Bob had returned to Ottawa from his sojourn at the World Bank and was on the faculty of the University of Ottawa Executive MBA program. While in the United States, he had maintained his interest in public policy, especially fiscal, economic, and social issues, so we set to work crafting policies and speeches. Joe, as anyone who has worked for him knows, has the ability to work countless hours long into the evening or night – though he's not so great at the up-early-in-the-morning stuff.

Entering the race, the idea was to win on the first ballot. Our policies, tour, and, most importantly, financing were all directed to the goal. I was preparing the briefing book for the Halifax debate to be held on Sunday of the Thanksgiving weekend, when I heard from Roy Norton,[7] who was keeping track of membership sales and everything else. He let me know that, given all the information he had at the time of the cut-off of membership sales, Joe was not going to win on the first ballot. He would be close, but would fall short. More importantly, someone had to tell him. That someone was me, since I just happened to be going to Halifax to brief Clark for the upcoming debate.

I had agreed to meet Joe in his hotel room on the Saturday morning. As is my custom, I went for a long walk prior to proceeding to the hotel at the appointed time, 10 a.m. Except I didn't know his room number. For security reasons, the hotel desk clerk wouldn't tell me, but put me through to the former PM's room. The great thing about a campaign done on the cheap is there are no aides or assistants to answer the phone. Joe answered, told me to come up – he was waiting for me, and hung up. I was none the wiser as to the room number, and the hotel clerk was still circumspect. I tried to call again and – of course – the line was busy. I kept trying with the same result. I finally got through and received the expected comment: where-the-hell-are-you-I'm-waiting-for-you. But this time before he hung up, I asked for his room number – which, of course, he didn't know!

I eventually made it up to the room. Always a believer in delivering bad news quickly and up front – that's where we started. I say: Joe, you are not going to win this thing on the first ballot. I should have anticipated his response: Why not? I tell him the votes aren't there. Again: Why not? Here I plucked up my courage, and hid behind someone else: I don't know – ask Roy. Needless to say, the briefing session, on whatever the topic was, was short, and then I travelled back to Ottawa – after alerting Roy that a call would be coming.

Clark went on to win. He took over a party much changed from
1993 and looked out over a political landscape that had also completely changed between 1993 and 1998. When Clark left the political
scene prior to the 1993 election, both the Bloc and Reform were in
their infancy. On his return they were well-established fixtures in the
House of Commons. And the Liberals looked forward to facing a
divided "right" into the foreseeable future, and to being perpetually in
government.

After Clark became leader, I believe we, the PC Party so-called brain
trust, with the concurrence of Clark, made a fundamental mistake.
Looking back at that period, it is hard to believe we were as stupid as
we were. It was the opinion of all of those involved, that Clark's time
would be wasted if it were spent in the House of Commons. So, there
was no need to seek a seat immediately in the House of Commons.
That said, when asked, Peter MacKay volunteered to give up his seat
for the leader, but the decision by the collective was that it was not
necessary at the time. So Clark spent what was left of 1998, all of 1999,
and the early part of 2000 roaming around the country, speaking at
federal and provincial party events, and drumming up support for the
PC Party.

During that period Reform was not sitting idly by waiting for the
next election. While the 1997 election results boosted Reform into
Official Opposition status, the party did not make the significant
headway in central and eastern Canada that Manning and his organization had hoped and planned for. In an attempt to broaden the appeal of Reform, Manning began yet another political movement,
another political party. At the Reform Party convention in London,
Ontario, in May 1998, Manning's idea of a United Alternative was
approved, and in February 1999, a convention was held in Ottawa to
see how this notion might work. The United Alternative was designed
to broaden the appeal beyond those supporting Reform. It could
become a home for PC supporters and perhaps PC MPs.

Out of the United Alternative movement came a new party, the
Canadian Reform Conservative Alliance Party. On the PC side there
was great hilarity at the first name change for the new party: the Canadian Conservative Reform Alliance Party (CCRAP). It was just another
indicator to PCs that the Reform gang, by any name, was just not, and
might never be, ready for prime-time politics.

A new party needed a new leader, and Manning resigned the leadership of the now moribund Reform Party to contest the leadership

of the new entity. Also vying for the leadership was Tom Long of Ontario, an organizer and strategist for Reform and for Mike Harris. Long was supported by Stephen Harper, who took a pass on the leadership, this time. The other candidate was the former provincial treasurer for Alberta, Stockwell Day.

A campaign based on one member, one vote boils down to selling memberships, and for that, Day had his tentacles into the Christian Reform movement. The first-ballot results were reported on 24 June 2000, and a second ballot on 8 July was a runoff between Day and Manning. Day won convincingly with 70,000 votes to Manning's 40,000.

For Day there was to be no waiting to get into the House of Commons. His instinct was to get there immediately and seize control of the former Reform MPs, who were now part of the new party. He engineered the resignation of Jim Hart so he could run in a by-election in the Okanagan Valley, where he was re-elected in many subsequent elections. Day's decisiveness forced Clark to move on getting into the House of Commons as well. Both MacKay and Scott Brison offered to resign. Brison's seat in Annapolis, Nova Scotia, was chosen, based on our polling that showed the riding as a safer bet for Clark to succeed Brison. The benefit was that Scott, no longer an MP, was available to help draft and assemble the platform for the next federal election.

The two by-elections were held on 11 September 2000, with both leaders winning and both entering the House of Commons on 19 September 2000. By delaying Clark's entry into the House for almost two years, the PC Party had squandered, what seemed at the time, a great opportunity to replace the Alliance as the sole party on the right. One never knows, but Clark performing well in the House of Commons for eighteen to twenty months prior to Day's arrival might have cast Day as even more of a novice than he actually was. Clark was returning to the place he knew and was comfortable in from 1974 to 1993. Day was making his first appearance in the major leagues, and he flubbed it immediately.

Day challenged Chrétien to call an election, which the PM was only too glad to do. However, Day had not considered how unprepared his party was to fight a national campaign and how the PC party, in debt and hamstrung by the 301 resolution passed at its annual convention in Toronto 1999 (to contest all ridings), was in no position to mount a significant attack on the Grits.

To make matters worse – or, depending on one's perspective, better – for the PCs, Clark had decided to run in Calgary Centre to demonstrate that the PC Party could be competitive in the heart of Alliance country. Usually a party leader is assured of electoral victory, but this was now not the case and considerable resources had to be targeted to this one seat to ensure victory for the leader.

To make matters even worse, Senator Gerry St Germain, a great believer in uniting the right, defected to the Alliance caucus in October 2000, four days before Chrétien called the election. This was not an easy decision for St Germain. He was, and is, fiercely loyal to Prime Minister Mulroney. While he held no personal animosity to Clark, he did not see Clark as the person who could unite the right and defeat the Liberals. St Germain had been party president during the Mulroney era. He believed Day was best positioned to unite the right and defeat the Grits; by joining the Alliance he could help. Prior to joining the Alliance caucus, St Germain met with Clark and Lynch-Staunton in the latter's Senate office. There was nothing that Clark could do or say to dissuade the senator. It was then decided to involve Mulroney, who at that point still did not want anything to do with even the successor to Manning, who Mulroney believed had destroyed the PC Party. However St Germain had his mind made up, and no one was going to talk him out of moving to the Alliance.

So just days before the 2000 election call, St Germain, on a caucus vote, was accepted into the Alliance caucus. True to form, if Gerry is with you, he is really with you; if he is against you, watch out. He was a great supporter of Stockwell Day. Even after the election campaign, when the Alliance failed once again to make much of a breakthrough east of Manitoba, Gerry stayed loyal to Stock. Gerry's view, post-election, was that Stock needed staff from the PC side, and Gerry and I met twice to discuss my moving from Lynch-Staunton's office to either take on the role of Day's chief of staff or a similar senior position in Day's office. Day rejected the idea, but for a few days it was flattering to know that this was being discussed and might happen. While I never met with Day, I did meet with Gerry over breakfast in the Sheraton Hotel in Ottawa to hand him my resumé. I never did find out the reasons behind the rejection. In any case, I was happy in Lynch-Staunton's office, working with Clark, with whom I had a long relationship dating back to when he was minister of constitutional affairs.

For the PC Party that showed such promise following the 1997 election, the time since Charest's move to Quebec City had not been kind. Potentially the best performer in the House of Commons was kept out of the House of Commons. With Clark's return as leader we had all bought into the two-election scenario: we would be back, or at least would form a minority government. But Joe was not leading a group who felt any particular loyalty to him. So when divisive issues came up – and they did – he did not have a solid base of support amongst his House of Commons colleagues. I must say that Lynch-Staunton and the Senate caucus were loyal supporters – they knew Clark since many had worked with him in the Mulroney era.

Much has been written about the Clarity Act, and Stephen Harper's role in influencing its drafting and its presentation to the House of Commons by the Chrétien government in 1999. Clark, having spent his last few years in Cabinet trying to fashion a deal that would unify the country and allow Quebec to sign on to the 1982 amendments to the Constitution, including the Charter of Rights and Freedoms, was not in tune with post-referendum thinking. It was his view – to which I subscribed – that the Clarity Act, albeit not expressly in its wording, could be construed by separatists as providing a path for separation. To those who opposed the Clarity Act, the federal government had just set out the structure or rubric under which secession could occur. To Clark, the former minister of constitutional affairs, this represented the federal government giving up on Quebec, giving up on Canada, and creating a formula for the nation's destruction.

But there was a mood in the country, reflected by this bill as well as by the Alliance Party, that there was to be no more appeasement of Quebec. A clear question, a clear majority, and the federal government would start the negotiations and the constitutional amending formula would be applied to get Quebec out. So, it was through the lens of the Meech and Charlottetown accords that Joe Clark viewed the Clarity Act as The Act of Giving Up on the Country. However, this was not the view of many of his caucus colleagues, and it was at times like this when Joe most keenly felt that this was not his caucus.

I was in Toronto when the Clarity Bill was tabled. Clark called me for my opinion, perhaps knowing from the time we worked together that our ideas were quite similar. After he explained the bill to me, I agreed with him that we had to oppose any bill that set out a roadmap to secession. Initially the PC Party, lead by Clark, opposed the bill. However, Elsie Wayne and others thought it was about time we spelled things out for Quebec. So by virtue of necessity, Clark allowed a free vote on the Clarity Act.[8]

We have had the Clarity Act with us now for more than a decade. Only with the PQ minority victory in September 2012 have referendum discussions surfaced. The Clarity Act is on the books to offer a separation process. The thought of even contemplating discussions on the need for a "process guide" was and is an anathema to Clark and others who supported Meech and Charlottetown and the accommodation route.

On his return to the leadership of the PC Party, Clark brought with him the cachet of a former senior Cabinet minister and, above all, a former prime minister. When trying to decide how to deal with the Alliance, Clark was dealing with Manning and then with Stockwell Day, people who had never held a federal Cabinet post, let alone run the federal government. They did not have his experience, and mutual respect was lacking. So, if there was going to be talk of merger or co-operation or electoral "no fire zones," it would be on Clark's terms and no other. He attended, along with Manning, a conference convened by Peter MacKay and Ian McClelland of the Alliance on areas of co-operation. While there were discussions, there was no agreement. This was not surprising – Clark still thinking that with one election the PC Party, under his leadership, would be well on its way back to respectability.

Joe Clark's view of the future led him to insist on complete support for a resolution passed in September 1999 at the PC Party annual general meeting (AGM) that the Party would contest all 301 federal ridings. It was also important that Clark put his own stamp on the Party he had taken over, so a policy meeting was held in Quebec City in the fall of 1999. One of the main policies adopted was not to run joint PC–Reform candidates in federal ridings in the next general election. In his speech to delegates he invoked the picture of Chrétien fiddling while the country was almost lost in the 1995 referendum: he said, "I have seen our country whole and I have seen it torn. I have come back to make the country whole again."[9]

Millennium Makeover:
The PC–DRC Coalition

The results of the 2000 general election were disappointing to both parties on the right. Having dared the PM to call the election, Day, by his campaign and his conduct, especially in the leaders' debate, demonstrated why he needed to age at least a year as leader of the Official Opposition prior to forcing and fighting a general election. While the Alliance seat count improved slightly, the breakthrough in central Canada, save for three rural seats in Ontario, did not happen. At that point, Day had every right to believe he would get at least two shots at forming a government, but that was not to be.

The PC Party that Joe Clark took over in 1998 was very much Jean Charest's party. Most, if not all, of those elected in 1997 were fiercely loyal to Charest. There was no question that the group was quite willing to give Charest at least one more general election, if not two, to rebuild the Party. There was little personal loyalty to Joe Clark. Yes, there was tremendous respect for what he had accomplished in the past, but he did not inspire the loyalty of PC MPs. So when it looked like the Party would be mired in opposition and when MPs' electoral chances looked better if affiliated with another political party, they left. From Newfoundland, Charlie Power resigned and Bill Matthews joined the Liberal Party in August 1999. In April 2000, André Harvey, who had served as party whip, left to sit as an independent; then on 12 September 2000, with David Price and Diane St Jacques, he joined the Liberal Party. If Stephen Harper was reluctant to force an election in May 2005 after losing Belinda Stronach to the Liberals, one can imagine Clark's dismay as he presided over a shrinking caucus with a possible election looming. The only redeeming feature in all of this

The Coalition. The PC–DRC coalition, led by Joe Clark,
provided an opportunity for PC MPs and senators to work
with Canadian Alliance MPs. (Courtesy of Brigitte
Bouvier/*Ottawa Citizen*. Reprinted by permission)

was Angela Vautour, an NDP MP from New Brunswick who joined the
PC caucus in 1999.

The 2000 campaign for the PC Party began against this dismal backdrop, so there was genuine elation and excitement that party status
had been maintained. It was a far cry from what Clark had hoped for
when he re-entered federal politics by winning the PC leadership in
November 1998. The two-election strategy was blown up. There was
no Official Opposition status upon which to build to take over government. The promise held out to PC supporters at the time Clark won
the leadership seemed to have evaporated. The other part of the 27
November 2000 result, which was tragic for all on the right of the
political spectrum, was a third consecutive Chrétien Liberal majority
– with an increase in seat count from 1997.

If the period 1993–2000 had been a time of warfare on the right –
to see which of the two parties would survive – the period 2000–03
was a time of tactical manoeuvres – with party leaders trying different

approaches to either kill off the other party or set up a structure within which to work together, or at least foster co-operation.

The first sign that some co-operation between the PCs and Alliance might occur emerged from the discussion at the PC winter caucus retreat held in London, Ontario, in January 2001. It was as upbeat as any majority government caucus meeting would have been. There was a feeling among participants – and there were attendees from Ontario, Manitoba, and Alberta provincial conservative parties – that something was about to happen on the right that would benefit the PCs. The positive attitude in the meeting was almost beyond comprehension, giving the results of the general election less than two months before. I suppose this was a case of the excitement generated when very low expectations are met or slightly exceeded!

On the other hand, the Alliance had a real expectation that the year 2000 under a new young, vigorous leader would be its time in the sun. Having failed to meet them in the 2000 election, these high expectations were quite impossible for Day to endure over an extended period going forward. A number of members of his caucus were not willing to be patient and give him the time to mature in his relatively new role. For example, the 2004 election results obtained by a merged new Conservative Party were not that much better than what Day had provided in 2000.

Day, to his credit – and probably subsequent detriment – encouraged his MPs to work with and set up discussions with PC MPs. Following the successful PC caucus retreat in London in January 2001, a dinner was held in Ottawa near the end of February. Sanctioned by Clark and later endorsed by Day, it included leading MPs from both caucuses. Bill Casey, Peter MacKay, Rick Borotsik, and Loyola Hearn attended from the PCs; Jay Hill, Gary Lunn, Chuck Strahl, Monte Solberg, Val Meredith, and John Williams represented the Alliance. The February meeting was followed by another in June after the House rose for the summer. Again it was off the record, with no publicity, and with party representatives meeting and finding out neither group had "horns and a tail."

All of this played out nicely for the PC Party. For Clark, it was like losing the election in 2000 would not matter if he could win the takeover war, and that is what he set out to do. Clark was leader of a recognized party with the added benefit of respect earned as a former prime minister and senior Cabinet minister. He used this for all it was worth to entice Alliance dissidents to form some type of coalition with the PC Party. As a result of feelers put out by the DRC, a breakaway group of Alliance MPs, to the PC members, a conference was held in Mont Tremblant, Quebec, in August 2001. The fifty delegates that attended included both Alliance and PC Party members.

Loyola Hearn and Senator Lowell Murray were among the main organizers for the PC side. The purpose of the meeting was to seek ways of developing closer co-operation in the House of Commons and its committees. How could they work as a parliamentary group, and if recognized as such by Speaker Peter Milliken, what privileges would flow from that status? The possibility of evolving into an electoral coalition to successfully take on the Liberals was also discussed.

The result of all the meetings, intrigue, and negotiations was on display for all to see when the House of Commons started sitting again in September 2001. The PC–DRC coalition was led by Joe Clark, with Elsie Wayne remaining as deputy leader of the PC Party, Chuck Strahl as deputy leader of the DRC, and Deborah Gray as caucus chair, with all members of the PC–DRC caucus sitting together as a parliamentary group.

This caucus coalition worked together effectively in the House and on committees. As well, they sat together in joint caucus meetings with PC senators. My experience with this group was very positive. I worked with, and also had the Senate research staff work with and support, the coalition on various committees. We also shared our research products, such as reviews of government bills. My first-hand experience was with Jay Hill, defence critic on the House of Commons Defence Committee as it held hearings into a number of issues and problems encountered by Art Eggleton, minister of national defence. I believe Jay found the support he received helpful, and together we fashioned a minority report. It demonstrated to all concerned that the PCs and the DRC, and by extension the Alliance, were enough alike in political world views that working together in a common cause was not problematic. It also established a firm foundation for research support when the parties merged at the end of 2003.

Prior to resumption of the fall sitting of the House in 2001, a joint PC–DRC summer-retreat House planning caucus meeting was held in Edmonton in September. All eight DRC MPs attended. It was ominous, or perhaps prescient, that the gathering occurred on 10–12 September 2001. While events of what we've come to refer to as 9/11 dominated our thoughts at the meeting, folks got along. Gary Lunn was a reluctant joiner, but in the end, plans were made to work together in the upcoming session.

Committee assignments, House tactics, question period strategy, and policy issues due to come up in the fall were discussed without rancorous debate or serious disagreement. The DRC members also got to meet PC senators face-to-face over the period, realizing that there was a wealth of information and knowledge lodged in the Senate.

Because of 9/11, all of the flights out of Edmonton were cancelled. Since there were more flights going east from Calgary, a decision was made to travel south and set up camp there at the end of the caucus meeting. This informally extended our time together by a few extra days as we waited for flights out of Calgary, which helped establish some solid working relationships. Back in Ottawa for the fall session, the PC–DRC caucus settled into a functioning unit both in the House and on committees, while matters just seemed to get worse and worse for the Alliance and Stockwell Day.

There was, however, one significant issue relating to the coalition that remained outstanding and unresolved at the 10–12 September caucus meeting: the question of DRC members joining the PC Party. The idea was rejected by the DRC, and would later become a salient point when Stephen Harper called them home in March 2002 after winning the Alliance leadership. It was a major point raised time and again by PC Party deputy leader Elsie Wayne since there was no formal commitment by the DRC to the joint process. The DRC had no skin in the game. They had all the benefits of party status, research facilities to call upon for help, time in question period, and seats on committees – all under the PC ticket, with no formal commitment in return, other than contribution to the exchange of ideas, strategy, and tactics in weekly caucus meetings.

In not insisting on a formal merger structure, Clark was playing the long game. If his plan worked, the eight DRC MPs would have no choice but to formally join at some point. His theory was that, prior to the next election, they and many other disaffected Alliance MPs would be taking out PC memberships, and Joe Clark as their Party leader would be signing their nomination papers. This was the plan. As more and more Alliance MPs left the Stock Day–led party, Joe Clark and others in the coalition would be there to welcome them into the fold with open arms. And the plan was, in fact, working. The Alliance continued to be in turmoil, leading Day to resign the leadership on 12 December 2001. Unheeding of the lesson to be learned from the experiences of previous leaders Clark and Manning, he announced he would seek to succeed himself as leader.[1]

A development that Clark had not contemplated was the growing interest of Stephen Harper to return to federal politics as leader of the Alliance. Harper, working with others, penned his "Firewall Letter" to Premier Klein in at the end of January 2001.[2] While trying to ensure that Day and the Alliance Party did not implode, Harper spent the subsequent spring and summer positioning himself for something, if he ultimately wanted to pursue that something.

William Johnson, in his book *Stephen Harper and the Future of Canada*, sets out in detail Harper's concern to personally not hurt Stockwell Day, all the while trying to find an opportune time to announce his intention to run for a job that was not vacant.[3] Time and again during the summer and fall of 2001, Harper was setting out his vision of the country, the state of constitutional politics, and the inability of the opposition to hold Chrétien truly to account. Harper did a low-key launch of his campaign for leader on 2 December 2001 to the press gallery in Ottawa, and then officially declared his candidacy at Alliance headquarters in Calgary on 6 December.

There were others in the leadership race besides Day and Harper. Members of parliament Dr Grant Hill and Diane Ablonczy were the merger candidates. While backed by a number of MPs and so called heavyweights within the party, their campaigns were caught between the Day and Harper forces and never really got off the ground.

From the vantage point of Joe Clark, leader of the PC–DRC caucus, it was hard to tell what effect the Harper campaign was having on rank-and-file members.

Harper was laying out his vision of Canada, and on 19 January 2002, he set out his views of Canadian federation, which, ten years later, have found their way into the March 2012 federal budget.[4] His main theory of Canadian federalism is that the federal government should not intrude into areas of provincial jurisdiction. The central task of the federal government is to ensure that conditions are right for free markets and the private sector to prosper. He set out that Canada is an aggregation of very different regions with widely differing cultures and economic interests, which should be allowed to flourish without interference from Ottawa.

His views on Quebec, which he was able to state again in December 2005 during the election campaign, were that in a strict division of powers, Quebec would have autonomy in areas that matter to it the most. He also made it clear that any attempt at secession would have to take place within the rule of law and under the precepts of the Canadian constitution.

On 20 March 2002, Stephen Harper became the leader of the Alliance party with a majority of 55 percent on the first ballot.

All of Clark's comeback eggs were in the Day-as-Alliance-leader basket. Day was going to have the same group of supporters that he had when he beat Manning for the leadership. Watching the race, the PC side believed that was enough support to win. What the PC side did not realize was that Harper was outflanking Day in support and in fundraising. His fundraising efforts were widespread and effective. He also articulated a simple message that Alliance supporters needed and wanted to hear: smaller government, lower taxes, equality of citizens, rule of law, and national unity.

Clark and those who bought into the Day-winning line of thinking were doing what happens so often in electoral politics: they were fighting today's battles with yesterday's ideas and yesterday's information. The concept of Day not winning did not occur to anyone in leadership on the PC side. At our usual Thursday club-sandwich lunch in Lynch-Staunton's office, in the week prior to the Alliance leadership vote, all present were speculating on the size of the Day win – not whether he would win.

So, having made this miscalculation, what did Stephen Harper as leader mean for the PC–DRC coalition?

There was now more than ten years of disunity on the right of Canadian politics. The leaders who were in place for the PC Party and Reform in 1993 were long gone. The Liberal party had dominated the federal political landscape for this period, with no end in sight to its hegemony. Chrétien read the mood of the Canadian people well, so after the tumultuous Mulroney years, Chrétien was content to balance the budget with money received from the GST – a most efficient and productive tax – and keep the Canada–US Free Trade Agreement (FTA) in place in order to revive the economy. After the scare of the 1995 Quebec referendum, it was business as usual for the Liberals, with little relief in taxes, budget surpluses, and a low-dollar spurring on trade, but masking Canadian's lack of productivity and competitiveness.

Although the PC–DRC coalition had been effective, Clark had fixated on Chrétien's involvement in, and ethical issues surrounding, a golf course in Shawinigan.[5] Knowing Chrétien as we do now, it wouldn't have mattered what scandals were unveiled, he was just going to put his head down and carry on. Chrétien's biggest concern was not Clark or any accusations coming from the opposition benches; rather, it was Paul Martin's continuous campaign to force Chrétien out and convene his own coronation. Looking at the Liberal government from this perspective of the split conservative right, it was difficult to see how the Grits would ever be displaced.

New Alliance Sheriff in Town: Stephen Harper

It was 20 March 2002 and Stephen Harper had gained the leadership of the Alliance Party. For Joe Clark, all the work he had put into building up the PC–DRC caucus was for naught. The Stockwell Day leadership implosion meant that the steady-stream-becoming-a-torrent of Alliance MPs leaving to sit with Clark and the other dissidents was not to be. Plan A, moving to Official Opposition status or minority government in 2000, had not come to pass. Now Plan B, making the move through destruction of the Alliance Party, was stymied. For Clark there was no Plan C.

As senior members of Day's caucus called his leadership into question, Plan B just grew from nowhere – although one could also argue that the early steps at PC–DRC co-operation made it possible. However, it should have occurred to Clark and his team that Day succeeding himself as leader would be an almost impossible task, after all they had seen the tactic fail twice before, for Manning, prior to Day, and for Clark himself in 1983. There was also a fatal misunderstanding of the strength of the Harper leadership bid. After some initial bumps the bid was well-organized and -financed, and, as one might expect, had a strong policy base. The two other entrants in the race for leader, Grant Hill and Diane Ablonczy, were essentially sidelined, since both sought some type of merger with the Clark-led PCs. Alliance voting members wanted a strong, resolute leader first; after that, they would concern themselves with the PC remnants.

To his credit, Clark recognized the magnitude of the miscalculation and spoke to Harper about a meeting. The meeting occurred on 9 April 2002. Prior to that, on 28 March, two members of the DRC, Chuck Strahl and Deb Gray, along with Ken Kalopsis, former co-pres-

The Return. Stephen Harper's return signalled the end of the coalition.
(Courtesy of Colleen Kidd/*The Calgary Herald*. Reprinted with permission of
The Calgary Herald)

ident of the Canadian Alliance Party, put together an open letter to all
Conservatives from both the PC and Alliance parties in the hope of
initiating a new beginning. It praised the working relationship that
had been established with the PC Party under Clark's leadership and
proposed three elements of a path forward:[1]

1 joint party task force on policy
2 joint committee on developing a co-operative electoral strategy
3 working coalition in the House of Commons

It was their hope that Clark and Harper could work out a series of
compromises that would end the division in the Conservative movement that had, in reality, resulted in the election of three majority Liberal governments. It was time, Gray and Strahl believed, to stop
fighting each other and start fighting the government. Their perception was prescient: in a matter of months Martin would ascend the
Liberal throne, and the Martin juggernaut would sweep the country
– and in its wake, sweep the two parties on the right, or at least one of
them, into the history books.

The only meeting that occurred between the two leaders was not a success. It is not clear whether Clark anticipated what Harper would propose, but it is abundantly clear that Harper knew what to expect from Clark. As Paul Wells pointed out in *Right Side Up*, "Each man played to type. Clark suggested a process. Harper suggested a solution. Clark lost."[2]

Clark proposed setting up joint committees of both caucuses to discuss policy, electoral co-operation to stop vote splitting, and working together in the Commons and on committees. Harper, anticipating that Clark would be all about process – with no real preference for a particular solution, and fuzzy on the leadership structure and exactly how it would all work in functional terms – presented a very practical alternative that could be implemented now. The parties would begin to sit together in the House of Commons immediately. They would work together on House committees. They should also agree in principle not to run candidates against each other in the next election; the mechanism by which this would occur would be worked out, but the proposal was clear: vote splitting would end.

It was obvious to Harper how this parliamentary coalition would be led, and the thirty PC senators would not figure in the mathematical mix. Harper also insisted that, given the proportion of members, only one in six caucus or committee positions would be given to PC MPs; the rest would belong to the Alliance MPs. In Clark's opinion, this was no way for a former prime minister and former senior Cabinet minister to be treated by a newly elected rookie leader with less than three years experience in the House of Commons. This was also no way to begin a working relationship together. The meeting ended with nothing agreed upon and no plans to meet again.

One could say this was all about ego, all about ambition on both sides. But for Clark, this was also not the way it was supposed to be. He was not even supposed to be meeting with the Alliance leader. Had Stock Day re-assumed leadership, there would have been no need to meet: Day's caucus would be dissolving, and running into Clark's open arms.

Clark's failure to grasp the nature of the situation in the spring of 2002 was not unlike his failure to grasp the situations in December 1979 when the government he led was defeated or in Winnipeg in 1982 when he decided to resign as leader, forcing a leadership contest that he lost to Brian Mulroney in 1983. It was a failure to adjust to the

new reality and build a new plan based on that reality. This was not
Clark's long or strong suit. But it was Harper's.

Fallout from the fruitless meeting was immediate. Harper, believing he held all the cards, would give Clark and the PCs one last chance
to agree to his terms of union, which he set out in an op-ed piece at
the beginning of May. Harper would hold this view until the
Perth–Middlesex by-election.

Prior to the 9 April meeting with Harper, Clark had tried to shore
up the coalition caucus. But Harper was not Stockwell Day. Upon taking over as leader, he had extended an invitation to the dissidents to
rejoin the DRC. It was a one-time, time-limited offer. When news of the
Harper ultimatum reached Clark, it was decided to hold a caucus
meeting in Calgary on 2 April 2002. For convenience, it was scheduled
at the Delta Calgary Airport Hotel. Personally, I cannot walk into that
hotel without thinking of that meeting. Senator Lowell Murray and I
accompanied Clark. I was working as senior advisor to the PC leader
in the Senate, John Lynch-Staunton, a great supporter of Clark and
someone who had bought into the idea of a PC-DRC coalition. Jim
Prentice, the long-time treasurer of the PC Party and nominated PC
candidate in Calgary Centre, also attended the meeting. It had a fune-
real tinge. The issue on the floor for discussion was whether the DRC
folks would stay or go back, taking advantage of Harper's one-time
invitation to return.

Some, like Jay Hill, had already made up their minds. It had been a
great experiment, and hopefully the working relationship between
the two groups would grow, but Hill was going back to where he
came from, now that Day was no longer the leader. It was readily
apparent that the DRC members' quarrel was with Day, not any other
part of the Alliance program. The feeling in the caucus room was that
with Day gone, things could go back to normal – whatever that was.
I believe the Alliance members were genuinely surprised by the reaction of disbelief from Clark, Lowell Murray, and other PC members at
the meeting. Their surprise came from the very points that Elsie
Wayne had raised many times with Clark: the DRC had no commitment to the PCs, had not taken out PC memberships, had no skin in
the game. They had found a temporary home in troubled times. And
now that the troubles were over, they were returning home.[3]

It was left to Chuck Strahl to explain the DRC dilemma to Clark.
Strahl began as he had in his letter of five days before, by expressing
how much he and the other DRC MPs had enjoyed working with Clark,

the PC MPs, senators, and staff. They felt they had gained a greater understanding of Parliament and how it worked, and a greater understanding of the PC Party. This was all good. The "however" came down to electoral politics. Discussion about creating "ceasefire" or "no fire" electoral zones (ridings in which Alliance and PC candidates would not run against each other) had gone on at some length during this meeting, without any conclusion. The Alliance and DRC members did not want these zones because they believed that the PC Party was simply an Atlantic rump party – and would, if left to its own devices, probably disappear altogether after the next general election. Chuck's main point, and he made it as clearly as he could, was that he could not win his constituency running under the PC label. That was the crux of the issue in the opinion of the DRC: the PC Party was a damaged brand. The damage had occurred more than a decade before, and the brand had never recovered.

This was a bitter pill for Clark and the other PCs present to swallow. There was considerable discussion, trying to persuade some that, just as through hard work and determination Clark had won in Calgary in 2000, Strahl could win as a PC candidate in the next general election in British Columbia. The problem for Clark was that if the coalition caucus dissolved, there would not be another magic bullet: there was no Plan C. While no firm decision was made in Calgary, it became evident that the writing was on the wall for the coalition.

The last joint caucus meeting took place in Ottawa on 16 April. To their credit, the DRC members attended, and after saying their good-byes, left, with only Inky Mark of Manitoba staying in the PC fold. A very disappointed and discouraged group of PC MPs and senators watched the door close. There was no fallback position.

To make matters worse for Clark, Harper kept up the pressure by writing an op-ed piece in the *National Post* in early May. It outlined the deal, he had offered to Clark. Harper stressed that all it would take to make the proposal operational was approval of caucus and the parties. There would be joint candidate protocols and joint platform development, but dealing with each party's finances would take time. Harper indicated the offer would expire on the day the House reconvened in the fall of 2002, and an answer was required. If it was "yes," the caucuses would begin to sit together immediately under his leadership.[4]

These were dark times for the PC Party. Relegated back to survival mode instead of growth mode, it was time to do some soul searching and determine a path forward, if indeed any existed. A leadership review was scheduled as part of the August AGM in Edmonton. This had been put off as long as possible, and the information coming back from the delegates was not pretty: they were not going to support Clark. If Clark allowed his name to stand and his leadership to be subjected to a review vote, he might suffer worse numbers than he did in Winnipeg those many years before.

John Laschinger, who ran the 2000 election campaign as well as anyone could with no money and virtually all volunteers and few paid staff, was called in to test the waters for Clark and the Party. He was to look at the viability of going forward with the leadership review in August, and at Clark's and the Party's favourable and not-so-favourable numbers across the country. At the same time, Greg Thompson, the veteran MP from New Brunswick who would later serve as minister of veteran affairs in the first Stephen Harper Cabinet, was doing his own polling with caucus members and supporters.

On 6 August, I attended a morning MPs caucus meeting on behalf of Lynch-Staunton. This was the meeting at which the two blocks of information would meet. Greg wanted to speak first. Clark told him that if he waited, he wouldn't have to speak at all. At that point, Laschinger launched into his explanation of his polling number results. It was clear that Clark was personally popular across the country and trusted by the electorate. This led everyone in the room to conclude that Clark was staying, was going to tough it out, and would put his fate in the hands of the Party membership. But John continued. He then dealt with the issues affecting the party in the mind of the public – the party was not polling nearly as high as the leader on all questions. Putting together the two sets of data, the conclusion was that Clark, while personally popular, could not pull the Party with him. His positives could not turn the Party's negative numbers into positives. As he would say in a public statement: "The good news is that I am widely trusted and popular. The bad news is that we cannot translate those qualities into votes for the party."

At that point, Clark submitted his resignation as party leader, to become official at the Party's AGM later that month in Edmonton. The second Clark era was over. It was now Greg Thompson's turn to speak, and he expressed his agreement with Clark's decision on the basis of the research he had done. What could have been an acrimonious caucus meeting turned into a bit of a wake, with MPs expressing gratitude for Clark's service to the Party and to the country. All I could think of was that it was a blessing that Bob de Cotret was not alive to see his good friend, whom he had supported throughout his career, coming up short.

At the Edmonton meeting, the former prime minister made his decision official. It was also the meeting at which Bernard Lord gave the best speech of his entire political career.[5] On the basis of that speech alone, he became the front-runner in the yet-to-be-defined leadership race. I met Peter MacKay after Clark's resignation speech, and urged him to run, and then said something to the effect of, "we could do a lot worse."

PC Leader of the Pact:
Peter MacKay

Less than a year after the first major joint PC–DRC caucus retreat in September 2001, Clark's time as PC leader was over. We were back in Edmonton for the August 2002 PC Party AGM, and asking ourselves: Where does the Party go from here? And who would want to lead it to wherever it was going?

At the AGM, Bernard Lord, then premier of New Brunswick, gave what was generally acknowledged as the best speech of his career. It was like he was auditioning for the job of national leader – except he had too many problems to deal with back in New Brunswick. Whether or not he was auditioning, the last provincial election in New Brunswick had returned his government to power with only a one-seat majority, so he was on a downward spiral. It was not to be his time. So, if not Lord, were there sitting caucus members who would want the role?

Sometime after the 1997 election, I happened to be standing in the main rotunda of the Centre Block when Peter MacKay walked in. That day, we were starting what we called MPs training college, for new members, and he was attending. MacKay is everything good that people write and say about him, and more. He is bright, witty, well spoken, and, having grown up in a political family, deferential to those from whom he believes he can learn. We hit it off immediately and went on to work together on many projects, such as the Chrétien security bill. When he was appointed to the position of House leader, he asked me if I knew of an expert in parliamentary procedure. This was the beginning of John Holtby's return to the Hill, since being the chief of staff to the James McGrath's committee on reform of the House of Commons in 1984–85. I believed Peter would make an excellent leader.

The Merger. Peter MacKay's commitment to party and country provided the basis for merger. Here with Bruce Carson (left). (Courtesy of Peter MacKay. Reprinted by permission)

Scott Brison and André Bachand were the other members of caucus who came forward. Scott was, and is, a bright young man who has a great understanding of policy and has a tremendous sense of humour. I worked with him, Marian Fernet, and others on the 2000 PC platform. His major problem – and it is a good one to have – is that he has so many ideas it is hard to keep track of them. He was a treat to work with when he was on the PC side of the House and has always been a friend, even after the merger, when he joined the Liberals as Prime Minister Paul Martin's parliamentary secretary.

André Bachand, had he stayed in the race until the end, would have been a powerful force from Quebec. He, like MacKay and Brison, is bright and articulate. André is also very thoughtful about the role of Quebec in Canada and how he, as a leader, could rebuild the party both inside and outside of Quebec. He was close to Clark, as he was to Charest, and would have been a formidable foe for Paul Martin – and for that matter, Stephen Harper, for whom he now works.

Jim Prentice was the lone candidate from Alberta. He had stuck with the PC Party when others were rushing to Reform. He was treasurer of the PC Party during those dark days of the 1993 election and was the nominated PC candidate in Calgary South when Stephen Harper won the Alliance leadership. When Harper decided to seek the nomination in that riding, vacated (so to speak) by Ezra Levant, Jim also stood down, allowing Harper to run virtually unopposed in the 13 May 2002 by-election that brought him back to the House of Commons. I had only met Jim once before, when we both attended the last desperate attempt by Clark to keep the PC–DRC coalition together at the caucus meeting held at the Delta Calgary Airport Hotel. After the election in 2004 and throughout the years we were both in Ottawa, we worked closely together and tackled many difficult issues. Given what I know now about Jim, had he won, he would have made an excellent leader.

And then there was David Orchard. Why? I guess the PCs had him because the NDP wouldn't have him. Even though his anti–free trade, protectionist mantra would have fit in nicely with the NDP caucus, federally or provincially. He had run in 1998, when Clark won the leadership, and Clark had quite rightly called him "a tourist in the PC party." On a positive note – and I can find few of them to describe Orchard – he and his followers were doggedly determined and certainly had a message to deliver. It was not, as far as I was concerned, a PC Party message, but it was a message nevertheless. After the 1998 leadership, Senator Noel Kinsella had kept in touch with Orchard, and for MacKay's sake, thank goodness he had. Orchard's support on the last ballot contributed to MacKay becoming the leader. Senator Kinsella, with others, was instrumental in securing victory for MacKay over Jim Prentice through their dealings with the Orchard camp.

Oddly enough, given what transpired the few months immediately after the leadership convention – MacKay becoming a believer in merger, whereas from the very beginning, Jim was willing to explore merger and discuss it with Harper – did it really matter who won? I would like to think that it did matter, since Peter had a close connection with those who were initially involved in the merger discussions, folks such as Mulroney and Stronach. As with so many things, we will never know; but hindsight, the result would have been the same: merger. Suffice it to say that post-merger, both men have done much to serve the united Conservative Party in opposition and then in government.

I told MacKay that, even though I had moved to Toronto to work for Minister of Education and Deputy Premier Elizabeth Witmer in the Ernie Eves provincial PC government, I would help him with policy development, speech writing, and debate preparation. Because I wasn't in Ottawa, my role in the MacKay leadership was very much in the background, except when I got to Ottawa, which was fairly frequently, or when he came to Toronto.

I first met with Bill Pristanski, who ran MacKay's campaign, in Ottawa when we had to pick a slogan and theme. MacKay liked "Charting a new Conservative Course"; as we neared the convention, it became "Believe." We were all quite skeptical about the Conservative Course theme, thinking it sounded too much like we were building a golf course not the leadership of a recognized national political party. However, MacKay had the final say and felt this best articulated his approach. It was time to work on policies and on getting MacKay ready for the all-candidates, televised leaders' debates, the first to be held at the University of Ottawa.

The "New Conservative Course" was MacKay's leadership policy platform. It dealt with the economy, health care, international security, accountable government, quality of life (investing in people), and justice issues (enhancing public safety). It was a fairly comprehensive piece and could have formed the basis for a platform had the party merger not taken place. The key policies were:[1]

Economy – Laying the foundation for sound fiscal management and seizing opportunities for economic prosperity
• Legislated debt repayment
• Eliminate wasteful spending
• Cut taxes on workers – EI payments
• Streamlined bureaucracy
• Expand Canada's trading relationships – Europe and the Americas
• Attract foreign investment by an internationally competitive tax regime
• Eliminate interprovincial trade barriers
• Raise the basic personal exemption on income tax
• Raise the married or equivalent spouse deduction
• Eliminate capital taxes

- Eliminate reduction on equalization payments for five years for provinces with new sources of offshore revenue

Health – Securing and protecting the future of health care
- Ensure stable funding
- Work with the provinces to ensure that the delivery of health care is secure
- Promote healthy lifestyles and wellness through tax incentives for those enrolling in sport and fitness activities
- Develop performance targets and goals for the health care system stressing healthy outcomes
- Experiment with private delivery of health care while protecting the single-payer principle

Security – Restoring Canada's role in the world
- Establish a Perimeter Security Agency to protect our relationship with the United States by combining the Customs Agency, revitalized Coast Guard, Port Police and Airport Security Agency to ensure the efficient and effective sharing of information, doing our part to protect North America
- Establish with the United States and Mexico a North America Security Perimeter
- Consult with our European allies and the United States on an appropriate role for Canada's armed forces
- Ensure our troops are well equipped and well resourced
- Ensure that the capital budget of our armed forces is sufficient to equip it with maritime helicopters and other much-needed equipment

Democracy – Making leadership and government accountable
- Leadership accountable to MPs
- Examine limiting a prime minister's term of office to two mandates
- Enforce ministerial accountability
- Make Ethics Counsellor an Independent Officer of Parliament
- Ensure senior government appointments are scrutinized by Parliament
- Ensure more free votes, especially on amendments to government bills

- Permanent and session-long assignments to House committees
- Consider lowering voting age to sixteen
- Make Senate more accountable by inviting provinces and territories to nominate potential senators with appointments being made only after meaningful consultation

Quality of Life – Investing in people
- Introduce a community contribution tax credit on the repayment of Canada Student Loans principal for the first five years after graduation. The tax credit would be based on an individual's voluntary contributions to charitable and community activities
- Eliminate the taxable status of scholarships
- Remove the GST from reading materials
- Ensure skills training is matched to the economy to enhance productivity
- Implement the Kyoto Accord by including province-by-province and sector-by-sector agreements, negotiated in good faith by the federal government
- Introduce a Safe Water Act – safe drinking water standards for all Canadians
- Introduce a Safe Air Act – acceptable air quality standards for all Canadians

Justice – Enhancing public safety
- Eliminate the long-gun registry
- Effective registration of DNA of convicted criminals and sex offenders
- Protect children from sexual predators
- Establish a victims ombudsman
- Ensure consecutive sentencing for those who commit multiple murders

It is noteworthy that most of the policy proposals advocated by MacKay have been implemented by the Harper government; others, such as border security, are in the process of being implemented. Those still outstanding, except for the Kyoto Accord, should be considered for adoption soon. The Kyoto recommendation is interesting in that we had no way of knowing at the time that the Liberals had done nothing and were never serious about implementation of the

Accord. However, even then, MacKay advocated some form of sector-by-sector approach to reducing greenhouse gases.

In addition to my involvement in policy, debates, and speeches, MacKay was supported by his assistant, Maureen Murphy-Makin, and Rick Morgan. Two debates were memorable: the first one, in Ottawa in March 2003, and one in Calgary in May. In both debates, but especially the first one, I believe MacKay did exceptionally well. He was knowledgeable on all the issues, and he was spending time improving his French. The issues discussed in the debate were much more extensive than they are now in the leaders' debates in a general election. The topics prepared for were: foreign policy, capital punishment, proportional representation, women in politics, regional development, gun registry, municipalities, taxes, guaranteed annual income program, free trade, environment, Canada–US relations, leadership, Progressive Conservative Party–Canadian Alliance relations, immigration, military, and transport.

In Ottawa, MacKay was the clear winner: he ended up being the centre of attention at the debate, as if he was already the leader, dealing with outside challengers. The Calgary debate was memorable for a number of reasons, not the least of which was the preparation that took place on the plane. I joined MacKay's Air Canada flight from Halifax when it stopped in Toronto. The short flying time to Calgary meant we had a lot to cover, and tight budgets meant Peter and I were in economy, in cramped quarters, trying to cover it all as quietly as possible. It was also great to see Harvie Andre when we landed. He had held many portfolios in the Mulroney government and was now a MacKay supporter. Calgary was Jim Prentice's turf, and while Mac-Kay did well, we had nothing to counter Prentice's continual references to his family, his wife, and three daughters. Prentice came across as a solid person seeking the leadership to make Canada a better place for his family and all families. This was a hard position to refute or argue against.

While Bill Pristanski looked after the day-to-day running of the campaign, John Laschinger, whom I knew from all sorts of old movies, acted as campaign chair and guru-in-whatever-we-needed. On a Sunday afternoon, 13 April, with John as chair, the entire campaign team met in what would be its only face-to-face gathering. It was such a treat to work with Lasch again, and he didn't disappoint. We were well into the campaign at that point, but we were not getting the traction that we thought we would get, or that we thought a candidate of Peter's calibre would attract. John took stock of where we were and the messages we were trying to get out either through Peter or on his behalf. I was asked to articulate our message and platform and what we stood for. I droned on, as John knew I would, and then he stopped me. His advice – and it is sound to this day – was that a campaign can articulate no more than three messages and have them remembered. "Everyone remembers 'Father, Son, and Holy Ghost.' No one can remember all ten of the Ten Commandments." Only John could combine theology and the fundamental policies of the MacKay campaign. We set about honing our message into three memorable sound bites.

Another participant in all of this was Barry McLoughlin. As well as being a communications expert, he is, above all, a political junkie – and by far the best person to work with on debate and speech preparation. While he is supposed to be policy neutral, he can't always stay away from giving policy advice. We needed all the help we could get, and everything McLoughlin did and offered was useful. His studio is in downtown Ottawa, and he is the definitive go-to guy for help in all of this – especially for a young candidate like MacKay in his first big venture seeking leadership. In debate prep, McLoughlin would act as moderator; I would come up with the questions and then sit in the studio and watch MacKay on closed-circuit TV. In addition, we taped each dry run so we could analyze and sharpen Mackay's performance.

In addition to the debates, Pristanski and Laschinger scheduled numerous speeches and a significant number of meet-and-greet receptions across the country. We needed a stock speech or speech module and key messages that could be delivered at these events. McLoughlin contributed in this area as well. I believe that he is, at heart, a PC – or at least a Conservative Party supporter – and that he quite liked MacKay, so he was helpful in every way he could be. Not to give away his secrets, but McLoughlin is a great believer in watching famous speeches being given, and he has them all on disk. The one he refers to most is Dr Martin Luther King Jr's "I Have a Dream" speech. He draws your attention to the technique that King used, lifting the words off the page, and then to the part of the speech near the end where King completely left the text behind. This is crucial advice, available from few others in my estimation. (And it usually came with plenty of cookies and Diet Coke.) From time to time McLoughlin's wife, Laura Peck, would be in the office, and we would have the benefit of advice from both of them.

At a certain point, as we moved toward the convention, I volunteered to write the convention speech and MacKay's thank you and acceptance speech. Both had to be kept under fairly high security, especially the acceptance speech. Lasch wanted MacKay's convention speech to be a real showstopper. Also, because candidates had a limited time for a demonstration and the speech – and in order not to run out of time, as Orchard did and as others have done at various leadership conventions, most notably Ken Dryden in 2006 in Montreal – MacKay's speech had to be short and punchy, with lots of applause lines.

At the beginning of May, I delivered a draft to Laschinger, and with other drafts submitted to him, he and I worked to bring together what we considered a final version at least a week or two prior to the convention. It continued to be reworked and by 28 May, we were on draft 16, and had something we could give to MacKay. McLoughlin, Morgan, Murphy-Makin, and I met with him in McLoughlin's studio to work on the speech. Knowing MacKay's penchant for adding text and alliteration, our instructions were to not allow him to make it longer and to maintain the major themes.

The main issue when working on speeches with bright people is the constant search for perfection. The right turn of phrase, the right expression, the most appropriate phraseology. While this is incredibly time-consuming, it is also necessary because the speech has to belong to the person giving it. I once wrote a speech for Senator Gerry St Germain that had the word *thus* in it. He let me know in no uncertain terms that if he lived to be 200 years old, he would never use that word in a speech. So the phraseology, language, and content, while written by others, have to eventually become the speaker's. And so it was with MacKay.

Beyond content, my main worry was length: the speech was long – time would be tight. MacKay, in addition to his fondness for alliteration, loves to add words and phrases to further emphasize whatever point he is trying to make. There came a moment, as we closed in on a final text, when MacKay started to add words. I grabbed the pen out of his hand and told him for every word he added, he had to delete a word (I should have said two words). He stared at me. And as we sat beside each other in McLoughlin's boardroom, I wondered if I was going to be the first speechwriter to be knocked out by MacKay. The punch never came, and additions and deletions were made.

We then moved the operation to Toronto, where the convention was to be held. Jeff Clarke arranged for a walk-through of the facility, which went well, and we settled into a final run-through of the speech with a new speech coach that Lasch had come up with on the recommendation of Jean Charest.

This experience was different. The coach wasn't really interested in the content – which was good. He was interested in how MacKay felt, his comfort level, and his breathing during delivery. While I am sure this was helpful, what MacKay needed was time alone, or with one listener, to learn the speech and how to deliver it. Eventually he got the time he needed. A common fault in the preparation of theses crucial speeches is that so much time is spent perfecting the text, the speaker never learns the text.

At this point, the text MacKay had was as good as it was going to be. It began by eviscerating the Liberals – Chrétien and then Martin – for their platform of patronage, privilege, and power at all costs. The Liberals were accused of downloading costs to provinces and municipalities to get rid of the deficit, gutting health care and our armed forces, and betraying our allies. Then he pivoted to the six priorities of the New Conservative Course. Establishing sound fiscal management, healing health care and promoting wellness, restoring Canada's place in the world by reinvesting in our military, making government accessible to Canadians, ensuring quality of life for Canadians through securing homes and communities, and ensuring protection of victims' rights. He then bridged into why he was running and that he would represent ordinary hard-working, tax-paying Canadians not the privileged, elite Liberal class. He finished with his request for support and his belief that he could lead the Party back to government.

Eventually, late in the afternoon on Friday, 30 May, I took my leave. I felt I had done all I could and was going back to Ottawa with my family for the weekend. I took the same approach with the Charest and Clark leadership campaigns. As the policy/writer person, I believe there comes a time when you depart and leave the result to the candidate and the voting delegates.

From all reports, the speech went well, was well received, and finished in the allotted time. The next day, and what happened, has been well chronicled by Bob Plamondon in both *Blue Thunder*[2] and *Full Circle*[3] and by Senator Hugh Segal in *The Long Road Back*.[4]

Not to beat a dead horse – and thank goodness for MacKay's wisdom and what transpired in the intervening years to make it a dead horse – but the question must be asked: Was the Orchard deal really necessary? MacKay was the logical home for Orchard delegates since he was the only non-merger candidate left on the ballot. Prentice's view, which ultimately proved to be the one implemented, was that some kind of working arrangement with the Harper-lead Alliance Party was necessary for survival of both parties, who were eventually going to face the Martin juggernaut.

In the end, it was obvious that if MacKay couldn't make the deal, Orchard was going to make it with someone – and it would have been Prentice, enabled by Scott Brison. Everyone also knew that wherever Orchard went, his delegates, loyal as can be, would follow. With that in mind, the deal with Orchard was struck. It must be appreciated: deals are the lifeblood of politics and political conventions. With the hindsight that only ten years later can bring, it wasn't so much that a deal was made for support; it was the conditions imposed by Orchard, which were specific in preventing any arrangement with the Alliance and requiring review of the Free Trade Agreement with the United States. But as Mulroney pointed out to Pristanski at the time: this deal with Orchard was not going to stop trade across the border.

The wording of the arrangement was actually pretty simple:

1 No merger, joint candidates with Alliance, maintain the 301 resolution.
2 Review FTA/NAFTA – blue ribbon commission with David Orchard with choice of chair with Peter MacKay's agreement, rest of members to be jointly agreed upon.
3 Clean up of head office including – change of National Director in consultation (timing within a reasonable period in future, pre election) and some of David Orchard's people working at head office.
4 Commitment to making environmental protection front and center including sustainable agriculture, forestry, reducing pollution through rail.[5]

When one gets into a leadership contest, the goal – and only goal – is to win. MacKay, the front-runner from the start, had run a good, credible campaign. He went everywhere and anywhere. He had put together a decent portfolio of policies – he was not policy-lite or an empty suit as suggested by Brison. (An aside: Having worked in the same policy, speech writing role with Bob de Cotret on the Charest leadership in 1993, with Clark in 1998, and now MacKay, I recall thinking at a certain point that I was getting pretty tired of the folks

I worked for being described as having no policies. I knew this wasn't true because of the attention and energy that went into our policy development.) MacKay had paid his dues. He knew if he didn't make the deal with Orchard, Prentice/Brison would, and that would be the end for him. No one should fault or criticize someone who is contesting the leadership of a major federal political party for having ambition and the guts to make a deal that secures a win. After you win, you deal with the fallout and criticism, and then move on to heal and rebuild. If you lose, you go home. MacKay chose not to go home and lick the wounds inflicted by a loss. He was a leadership contestant because he wanted to win and to rebuild the Party.

I spoke to MacKay by telephone on the Sunday afternoon after the leadership vote. I assured him as best I could that all would be well. He had won and that was all that mattered.

While the next few months were dominated by discussions with Stephen Harper that eventually resulted in merger, it would be wrong to think that MacKay had no plans of his own. It was always his intention to renew the policies of the PC Party, leading to the drafting of a new platform for the next election. In addition to the review of the Free Trade Agreement, which we knew would result in positive recommendations for its improvement, MacKay wanted to launch other task forces that would draw on the expertise of all members of caucus, especially senators, as well as external experts. In an 8 August 2005 memo to Rick Morgan, MacKay's chief of staff, I set out the terms of reference for these policy studies, with recommendations as to who might chair these studies. The subjects to be discussed by the task-force panels were varied. Sustainable Development and Environment would deal with clean air, clean water, the economic effect of Kyoto and provincial involvement and use of fossil fuels, especially in transportation. Post-Secondary Education and Lifelong Learning would look at the cost of education to students, funding of post-secondary institutions, and improvement of the education experience as well as ways to encourage lifelong learning. Seniors' Issues would look at unique financial and health needs of seniors, and review criminal law to determine how best to protect seniors from abuse. Public Government and Accountability would look at the role of the auditor general and of an independent ethics counsellor, adoption of whistle-blower legislation, independence of MPs, Senate reform, and scrutiny of public expenditures. Health Care would look into stable funding, private-sector delivery, and promoting healthy lifestyles. Foreign Policy, Defence, and Security would review issues in the context of a North America Security Perimeter, secure borders, and appropriate funding for Canada's armed forces. Future of the Economy and Canada's International Competitiveness would address the report of the Free Trade panel, legislated debt payment, productivity improvement, elimination of internal trade barriers, elimination of corporate tax, and attraction of foreign investment through an internationally competitive tax regime.[6]

Work began in some of these areas, and despite the agreement by the leaders to merge, the PC Party held a policy meeting in Ottawa on 1–2 November 2003. It was felt that the outcomes of that meeting would feed into the merged-party policy process, which MacKay eventually chaired.

By-election Wake-up Call:
Two Merge into One under Stephen Harper

If you lose, you go home.

In concentrating on winning the leadership, MacKay and those around him did not appreciate the full significance of what happened in the 13 May 2003 by-election in the sleepy Ontario riding of Perth–Middlesex.[1] Yes, it was recognized that Gary Schellenberger had won, demonstrating that the PC Party could still win in Ontario – which was great, and a tremendous boost for the Party going into the leadership convention at the end of the month. Schellenberger not only attended the convention but also gave his support to Mac-Kay. What went unrecognized was that, without any question, this was the single most important by-election in the history of the Conservative movement in Canada. It was the catalyst that led to the start of talks between MacKay and Harper and, eventually, to merger.

Stephen Harper, as leader of the Alliance, had made every effort he possibly could to ensure an Alliance win in Perth–Middlesex. The seat had been previously held by the Liberals; with the resignation of the ailing John Richardson, MP, it was up for grabs. Harper visited the riding himself five times. Many senior caucus members helped with the campaign. Ian Brodie and Doug Finley were brought in to help. This was the beachhead that Harper wanted to take to demonstrate to the party and himself that, under his leadership, the Alliance could begin to look at substantial gains in Ontario and farther east in the next federal election.

I was with MacKay in Toronto on the Sunday before voting day on the Monday. Elsie Wayne had committed one of her frequent gaffes, saying something negative about either gay marriage or homosexuals, and MacKay had to disavow her remark. But even with this, Schellenberger won by 1,000 or so votes. When the final results were in,

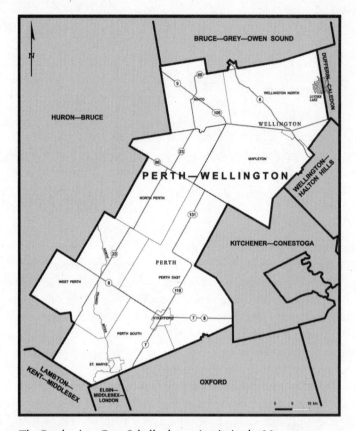

The By-election. Gary Schellenberger's win in the May 2003
Perth–Middlesex by-election provided the impetus for Harper to
consider merger. This reproduction is a copy of the version
available at www.elections.ca showing the riding after it was
redistributed and renamed Perth–Wellington in 2004.
(Reproduced with the permission of Elections Canada)

the PCs had won, Liberals came second, and Alliance was third. If not
for the efforts of Finley and friends, the Alliance might have finished
behind the NDP.

It was that night, on the basis of this result, that Stephen Harper
made up his mind to approach the new leader of the PC Party to effect
a working truce, a no fire agreement whereby the parties would not
run candidates against each other, and, at best, a merger. And it didn't
really matter what the terms of the arrangement were. There were to
be no more such Perth–Middlesex results – ever!

The merger talks are well documented in the books on this period by Bob Plamondon,[2] and are referred to by Senator Segal in his writings about the period.[3] Having worked with MacKay during this period and talked to Ken Boessenkool and Stephen Harper about it after the merger was a done deal, I have some background thoughts to offer.

I believe it is right to say that the PC side of the negotiation did not know or realize how determined, or even desperate, Harper and the Alliance folks were to get a deal. I think the underestimation is quite understandable. MacKay and those around him were dealing with a caucus that, at least on the House side, was fractured; in a small caucus, this is hard to paper over. There were those who had difficulty with MacKay's victory and the way it was achieved, through the deal with Orchard. This was not a unified group. The PC side was dealing with its new best friend David Orchard, who was making it clear that he wasn't going away and that he expected all of the conditions agreed to for his support of MacKay to be met. This meant trying to set up and run some kind of Free Trade review panel as well as clearing out the senior ranks of Party headquarters. And finally, the PC Party had won the Perth–Middlesex by-election and then, within weeks, elected a new leader – while merger, or some form of accommodation, was on our minds, it was not all-consuming.

Upon returning to Ottawa directly after the convention, there was the spring, or pre-summer, sitting of the House to get through and Orchard to deal with. Peter effected some changes at Party HQ, and collectively, we put our minds to the kind of NAFTA review that would meet Orchard's conditions – that is, come up with recommendations to improve the treaty – but that would not recommend it be scrapped. It was important to demonstrate to Orchard that we were serious about the review. Plus, MacKay was enduring enough criticism from others for entering into the arrangement with Orchard in the first place; he didn't need more of it from Orchard as well. For both reasons, MacKay undertook the actual organizing of this review himself.

We put together a Free Trade panel, and the first meeting took place in Ottawa at the Bell Canada building on Elgin Street on 23 October 2003. Those in attendance included Bill Casey, as chair; Bill Blair, who had an extensive business background; Joe Clark; Senator Kinsella; and Jim McIlroy, a noted trade lawyer. I believe it is important to note for the record the seriousness with which the group approached its work. The morning was spent trying to identify issues for discussion and resolving procedural matters. The group decided to accept written and oral submissions. In the afternoon, the group heard from witnesses – David Orchard, Tony Halliday, Elizabeth May, and Francis Shiller of the Canadian Lumber Remanufacturers Alliance.

Clark referred to the various dispute settlement mechanisms, wondering whether the United States believes it has a right to ignore World Trade Organization (WTO) decisions? Does the NAFTA provide sufficient market access to allow growth of exports? The effect of the involvement of the Canadian Wheat Board in the discussions was noted. Are there costs to giving US corporations the right to sue the Canadian government, and was this point ever ratified? And how do all the issues taken together affect Canadian independence? Clark concluded that we needed a permanent body with trade expertise, to which issues could be brought – but would this affect sovereignty?

In his submission to the panel, David Orchard talked of issues he had with the dispute settlement panel, arguing that it had no enforcement power; of access to markets being less secure than before, and of legal fees being enormous. He raised issues with softwood lumber and the Canadian Wheat Board, since the US wanted it gone. He criticized the energy section, as Canada can no longer maintain reserves. He believed that we needed security of energy supply in Canada; new investment into Canada should be restricted; and US agriculture production subsidies should be terminated. Water export was questioned, as was whether our continued involvement with NAFTA would result in Canada "going down the route of endangering our sovereignty." The solution for Orchard was to withdraw from NAFTA and then the WTO rules would apply.

The panel heard from other witnesses, including Elizabeth May, who criticized Chapter 11, stating that the investment provisions do not protect investors from expropriation of their investment without compensation and that water is vulnerable under NAFTA.

Summing up, McIlroy stated that trade and independence are linked; one does not trump the other. Trade, independence, and security are all in the public interest. The meeting adjourned with expectations of reporting after the Vancouver meeting, slated for mid-December, which would focus on youth and First Nations. But in reality, the successful conclusion of the merger talks and the subsequent ratification process overtook the Orchard/NAFTA review process.

The merger agreement was signed in principle on 15 October 2003 and had to be ratified by both parties by 12 December. The tight timeline was a two-edged sword for MacKay. It meant that a lot of logistical work had to be done quickly, in order to ensure an orderly vote on Saturday, 6 December. In addition, it focused him on the task of persuading two-thirds of the voting delegates to support the merger. However, the short timetable also worked in his favour: it gave less time for opponents of the deal to work to unravel it.

These were problems that Stephen Harper didn't have. The Alliance members, despite the terms of the agreement in principle – which totally resembled the PC Constitution – had long since bought into the merger and believed, with their superior numbers, that no matter what this was called in public, it was actually a takeover.

MacKay's problems also extended into his parliamentary caucus. Some members, both in the Senate and on the House side, still believed there was one more electoral fight to be fought and perhaps won. Senators LeBreton, Murray, and Atkins plus former leader Joe Clark, Deputy Leader André Bachand, John Herron of New Brunswick, and Rick Borotsik opposed the deal. Scott Brison was positioning himself to go either way on the deal, eventually voting for it and leaving within four days to join the Liberals as Paul Martin's parliamentary secretary. I wonder, as have others, if his position was based on reasons similar to those that compelled Trudeau to oppose Meech Lake: if I couldn't get it done, nobody is going to get it done, and I cannot support anyone who could get the merger done.

Senator Murray, in the 23 October *Globe and Mail*,[4] argued that the merger deal was messy and should have been an arrangement reached through joint caucus meetings convened to find common ground on divisive social issues. There is no question that Lowell had a point here, but it ignored reality. The reality was that time was tight, and Lowell's process could easily have lasted through the next election. It also fit well with the position taken by Joe Clark in his one and only meeting with Stephen Harper.

While MacKay and those close to him knew we were not going to get everyone in caucus to support merger, it was vitally important that he get as many as he could. For this reason, and because he had been a fan of merger since saying so at the May 2003 leadership convention, former prime minister Brian Mulroney was enlisted to help persuade as many as he could reach through his extensive Rolodex. First on the list was LeBreton who, like so many, was wary of the Reform/Alliance Party – what it stood for, especially in the social policy area, and its new leader, former Reformer Stephen Harper. It didn't matter that in 1998 consideration had been given to asking Harper to run for the PC leadership. I distinctly remember a meeting in Senator Atkins's office where this was seriously discussed. (No one could get past the hurt caused to the PC Party by Preston Manning and the negative things said about the Party and its leadership and members by Harper and his Reform colleagues. The idea of a draft-Harper movement was discarded.) So Brian Mulroney took on the task of convincing Marjory LeBreton, who had served as deputy chief of staff in his office and whom he had appointed to the Senate. He was successful, if only marginally so. LeBreton readily admitted at the time that she didn't like Harper and was quite concerned about the merger, since the PCs could be swamped on the social policy agenda by the social conservative Alliance MPs and supporters.

Prior to the Saturday PC vote, Harper announced the overwhelming support given by Alliance members to the merger. We weren't sure whether their merger enthusiasm would have a positive or negative effect on the PC vote. Another unknown was whether the technology that had been installed would work. Lack of time as well as logistical and financial reasons made it impossible to bring members together in a single place to vote. Instead, delegates gathered in various localities across the country. They would all be linked by telephone and computer technology in a virtual convention. There would be an opportunity for people to speak at each locale, and the vote would be taken across the country. As voting progressed, Michael Wilson, former minister of finance in the Mulroney government, spoke passionately in favour of the merger, as did others across the country. And so it went. By late afternoon, with no technical glitches, the voting was concluded.

I sat in the delegate room in Ottawa, working on remarks to be given by MacKay upon conclusion of the vote. It became apparent that the two-thirds threshold would be reached and merger approved. The question became, what would be the level of the final approval. MacKay felt he needed a strong mandate to counter all the negativity that surrounded and dogged him. Defecting or non-approving caucus colleagues, recalcitrant senators, David Orchard, and all the folks who vociferously followed Orchard were in that camp.

MacKay sacrificed a lot to get the deal done. He had campaigned relentlessly for months to attain the PC leadership. He had performed well at the convention, but the agreement with Orchard had unfairly brought his integrity and judgment into question. He had started to work toward fulfilling a number of the conditions in the Orchard agreement. And it is completely true that what started off as a series of meetings to discuss co-operation in the House and electorally, quickly morphed into a full-scale merger discussion – almost as if the discussions took on a life of their own. Not only was MacKay the subject of public scorn when he entered into the agreement with Orchard but he was also now getting criticism from the opposite direction, for reneging on the Orchard agreement, or at least the merger part of it.

MacKay had put party and country ahead of all else in making this deal with the Alliance. As Brian Mulroney said, when Paul Martin talks of a "democratic deficit," the real deficit is caused by the split on the Conservative side, by not giving Canadians a real choice to defeat the Liberals in an election. For MacKay, his work, his sacrifice, and the fact that he had negotiated a good deal with Harper for the PC Party needed vindication. And he got it, with a yes-to-merger vote of 90.4 per cent of delegates. The memorable line from MacKay's post-results speech was: "We have now become Paul Martin's worst nightmare." It was very apt. Little did Martin think that he would never attain a majority on his own, and that by 23 January 2006, his run would be over.

We adjourned upstairs to MacKay's suite – Peter Van Loan and his fiancée (now wife), Denis Jolette, Maureen Murphy-Makin, Rick Morgan, and others. One hurdle cleared, the next was a Sunday spent filling out paperwork and getting it to Jean-Pierre Kingsley, chief electoral officer, to formally register the new party with Elections Canada.

On Sunday morning, MacKay, Paul Lepsoe, the PC Party legal counsel, and others went to Stornoway to meet with Harper to discuss the logistics of the filing with Elections Canada and related subjects. An issue that arose immediately was that the new party needed a leader for the purposes of registration. This person would act in an interim capacity until a leadership convention was convened. There are some accounts that speculate that Joe Clark, as a former prime minister and twice leader of the PC Party and having a seat in the House of Commons, was the agreed-to choice by Harper and MacKay for this position. In the discussions that I was part of, Clark's name never came up. MacKay told me that when the issue of leader arose at breakfast, Harper had indicated Senator John Lynch-Staunton as his choice. Lynch-Staunton was the leader of the PC opposition in the Senate, had been deputy leader in the Senate when Mulroney was prime minister, was from Quebec and fluently bilingual, and, most importantly, had demonstrated credentials as a proven leader. The problem was that neither Harper nor MacKay knew how to contact Lynch-Staunton and neither felt he knew the senator well enough to make the initial contact to ask him to take on the responsibility.

I was to meet MacKay and the others in his offices in the Heritage Building behind the old Zellers store at Queen and O'Connor around noon. I got there before MacKay. When he arrived, he brought me up to date on what had transpired that morning and the issue of leadership. When MacKay told me of Harper's suggestion, I was floored. "I thought Harper hated appointed senators," I said. Whether or not he did, he must have eventually got over himself on this: he liked John Lynch-Staunton. The problem, as explained to me, was that neither felt comfortable making the initial contact, and, as I had known him for years, would I make the call? I was asked my opinion as to who would be a good second choice, should Lynch-Staunton refuse. We knew he supported the merger, we just didn't know how fiercely. I offered my opinion that Senator Michael Meighen would be a good choice. The grandson of a former Conservative prime minister, Meighen was fluently bilingual, had roots in Quebec, and was exceptionally bright and personable.

So, on Sunday afternoon, 7 December 2003, I placed the call to Lynch-Staunton. He was driving to Ottawa with his wife to attend the next evening's PC Christmas party when I got him on the phone. I told him immediately why I was calling. He told me he had better pull off the road and call me back – which he did within minutes. I repeated the ask – and told him the matter was of some urgency since we had to file the papers that evening with the chief electoral officer. We discussed why neither MacKay nor Harper could be designated at the time – either or both might run for the leadership. I told my usual story about all the support he would have from others and from me – which he knew was optimistic at best since I was still working at Queen's Park – and then he asked what I remember to be his only question: "Who else have you asked to do this?" I was able to honestly say: "No one. You are the first." Now, I know that might have made us sound really disorganized, but none of us had done this before and the positive PC vote was not yet twenty-four hours old – so, it was understandable that we were doing things quickly and perhaps not in the most organized fashion. Lynch-Staunton's answer was what we hoped for: yes. I said he would be receiving the formal request from MacKay shortly, and that was that.[5]

We had a new party and we had an extremely competent and experienced interim leader. Later that evening, the filings were made satisfactorily to Kingsley, bringing the new party officially, legally into being.

The PC Christmas party, by good fortune already booked in the Centre Block for Monday evening, was filled with an added degree of merriment. If there was ever any doubt in our minds that we had done the right thing by moving on the merger, it was dispelled by the supportive, celebrating crowd.

While one part of the work was completed, there were many miles to go before the new party was in any shape to fight back against the oncoming Martin juggernaut.

By the time the merger had been ratified, a considerable amount of work had been done on policy. Both legacy parties had their own policy statements and the "platform" that had been used in the 2000 election. There was a considerable amount of well thought-out policy already on the books of both parties. This is consistently true of Conservative parties. For example, the May 2005 Conservative Party policy meeting in Montreal was well attended, with delegates paying close attention to each policy matter discussed. Contrast that with the Liberal meeting that chose Stéphane Dion in December 2006: the Saturday policy session was gavelled to a close due to lack of a quorum. That would never happen at a Conservative policy meeting.

After the merger agreement was reached, MacKay and Harper each selected a person to represent them in policy discussions. Harper chose Ken Boessenkool, his senior policy advisor, and MacKay asked me to represent the PC side. Ken and I had not previously met, but doing this project with him – knowing how important it was that we get it right, supporting the party and leaders I cared about and respected – was one of the more enjoyable tasks that I have carried out in the field of policy development.

Shortly after being designated, I met with Boessenkool and Nancy Heppner, one of the Office of the Leader of the Opposition (OLO) staffers who worked with him on policy and question period preparation. Blending the policies of two legacy parties was not to be the pinnacle of Heppner's career. She left Ottawa in 2006 to contest what had been her late father's seat in the Saskatchewan legislature. She has been the minister of the environment and subsequently the minister of central services in Premier Wall's government.

Heppner and Boessenkool had spent some time and resources figuring out how we could get through the process as quickly and effectively as possible. As simple as their solution sounds, it was perfect. Heppner had placed the policy of each legacy party on various subjects side by side, shot slides, and then loaded them in a carousel for projection: half of the screen would display the Alliance suite of policies with the PC policies on the other half of the screen. The job for Boessenkool and me, with Heppner's help, was to decide which wording and context we liked best. Sometimes we would meld wording; sometimes it was obvious which was better, more appealing to a wider cross-section of conservative supporters; and sometimes, when we couldn't agree or thought we needed input from the leaders or caucus, we would set aside that policy and seek guidance or instructions. It was an interesting process for the three of us. What I found quite revealing was how easy it was for us to work together. After the first session, I went back to see Lynch-Staunton, the merged party's first leader. He asked me how my morning on the policy front had gone. I responded that it had gone better than I had anticipated, and "they don't have horns and tails."

From this rather rudimentary start, we developed a policy book or manual that MacKay could then take to the various caucus policy meetings. Meanwhile, we continued refining the policy base, which would also be the foundation for the new party's platform in the 2004 general election. As always, Conservative MPs and senators didn't disappoint; they showed up ready to discuss policy. The first draft of our labours was circulated by Dr Grant Hill, MP, the interim parliamentary leader, in a document dated 4 February 2004 and entitled "Areas of Agreement Conservative Party of Canada Partial Policy Statement." His covering letter (Appendix 1) explained the process, and I have included a few examples (Appendix 2) to demonstrate the end results.[6]

Once merger was approved, MacKay had to turn his mind to the question of whether he wanted to lead the new party that he and Harper had put together. It seemed to be a given that the latter would contest the leadership – but who besides him would sign up? I know that MacKay was getting a lot of advice to toss his hat into the ring. I also know that when giving or receiving advice on crucial career issues, a certain amount of self-interest can colour the give and take, and the advice. So, was MacKay getting advice from people who genuinely cared about his welfare, or from folks who were looking out for their own? Change leaders and a lot of jobs are up for grabs in the leader's office.

There was no question in my mind that MacKay could mount a credible campaign. There was also no question, as far as I was concerned, that he could do the job once elected leader. So why hesitate? Two main reasons, and then a third, will suffice. The first and foremost reason was financial. MacKay had escaped without any debt in his campaign for leader of the PC Party; he was not sure that would happen again. Second – and no PC supporter will ever know the answer – how much was he hurt in the eyes of party members by the Orchard deal of May 2003, and then by seemingly going back on that deal and working with Harper to merge the parties? Did the benefits of the merger itself, on substantially PC terms, obviate or counter the criticism for doing the deal with Orchard and then moving away from it. We will never know whether Jim Prentice, had he won the PC leadership, would have completed the merger and completed it with all PC principles intact. But we do know that if MacKay had not taken the Orchard deal then the Prentice/Brison group would have. One way or another, there was going to be a deal. And even though Mac-Kay had talked only of co-operation with the Alliance, his actions as PC leader resulted in, for the first time since 1988, an election to be fought in 2004 with only one party on the right of the political spectrum. Finally, as Brian Mulroney would say, it provided a real choice for Canadians. Was MacKay's crucial role in making this happen enough to make party members celebrate his candidacy and give him their support?

The third, and perhaps less important, reason was that MacKay had been pretty badly banged around by his own caucus from the time he was the leader, right through the merger process, and even after the merger was ratified. How much more would he be subjected to if he sought the leadership of the Conservative Party?

With all of this as background, MacKay and I met, and on a piece of yellow legal-sized paper made two lists – the yes list and the no list. Isn't this what our mothers always told us to do when approaching a big decision?

In the end – as it nearly always does – it came down to money. Pristanski, who had done such a great job with MacKay's campaign for leadership of the PC Party, assured him that the money would be there as soon as he announced. Ever the conservative Scot, Peter wanted to see the commitments up front. That was not to be, so MacKay sat this one out. Ultimately, I believe it was for the best. The two leaders of the legacy parties fighting for the leadership of their new creation might have irretrievably split the party. It was going to take a lot of work to blend together the two disparate groups, even though the MPs and senators came from basically the same conservative tradition. MacKay not contesting the leadership and instead working on policy and the day-to-day issues in the House of Commons helped bring together what might have been a fractious group.

With MacKay out of the picture, the leadership race was less divisive. Belinda Stronach, bringing her perspective to the discussions, had been involved as one of the midwives in the creation of the new party. She had assembled a star cast of advisors to run her campaign and to compensate for her lack of depth in the field of public policy. Tony Clement, with credentials as both a provincial PC in Harris's Cabinet and some notoriety as Ontario's health minister during the SARS epidemic, had been an executive with the Alliance Party. His candidacy for the leadership was a curious one, in that he had lost his last two electoral challenges, for leadership of the Ontario PC Party in 2001 and for his riding in the 2003 provincial election. Clement's intellect and knowledge of public policy added some heft to the campaign. But Harper was one of the founding fathers of the new party. The race was really his to lose. With basically the same team that ran his campaign for Alliance leader, under the steady direction of Tom Flanagan, he made sure that everything was done that could be done in order to ensure victory.[7] The real challenge was ensuring that overconfidence did not creep into the Harper team.

On 20 March 2004, the results were announced. Stephen Harper was declared the winner as he had over 50 per cent of the votes cast, to Stronach's 34.5 per cent and Clement's 9.4 per cent. With Harper solidly in place as leader, bigger tasks lay ahead for the Conservative Party.

Conservative Party of Canada

Message from the Parliamentary Leader of the Conservative Party of Canada

January 22, 2004

I am pleased to present an exciting new initiative – *Areas of Agreement: Conservative Party of Canada's Partial Party Policy Statement*. This document, which includes the Founding Principles from the Agreement in Principle to create the Conservative Party of Canada signed by Stephen Harper and Peter Mackay, is the first step in providing Canadians with a new vision for Canada; a vision that will unite conservatives from across the country.

This statement contains policy in areas where the Canadian Alliance and Progressive Conservative parties were in substantial agreement – as determined by common statements in documents passed by the grassroots members of both parties. As such, this document represents the common heritage of the founding parties of the Conservative Party of Canada.

For more than a decade, grassroots conservatives in Canada have been working toward speaking with a single voice on the federal stage. This statement achieves that goal by reflecting their views and beliefs.

At the Conservative Party's founding convention, this statement will be a catalyst for further discussion and policy development. We anticipate enthusiastic involvement and contributions from our committed, national supporters as well as our parliamentary caucus in that process.

The Conservative Party of Canada will succeed. We will succeed because of our vision and our distinctive policy. We welcome the participation and ideas of all conservatives.

Dr. Grant Hill, M.P.
Interim Parliamentary Leader
Conservative Party of Canada

Conservative Party of Canada

In future rounds of trade negotiations, a Conservative government will vigorously pursue reduction of international trade barriers and tariffs. A Conservative government will pursue the elimination of trade distorting government export subsidies within clearly established time limits. A Conservative government will seek a clear definition of what constitutes an export subsidy.

Inter-provincial Trade
A Conservative government will eliminate inter-provincial trade barriers in commerce, labour, and capital mobility through non-constitutional means.

TRANSPORTATION POLICY

A Conservative government will recognize the need for a safe, seamless, integrated, competitive transportation system for the continued economic growth of the nation and for facilitating both internal and international trade.

CRTC

A Conservative government will initiate an overall review of the relevance of the role played by the CRTC in Canada's communication and broadcasting industries.

ENVIRONMENT

A Conservative government believes responsible exploration, development, conservation and renewal of our environment is vital to our continued well-being as a nation and as individuals. A Conservative government will balance the values of preserving the environment and creating jobs.

Made in Canada Policy
A Conservative government will make protecting Canadian's health a key goal of its environmental policy by vigorously pursuing made in Canada policies that result in cleaner air, cleaner water and cleaner land.

Single Window Approval

A Conservative government will introduce single window approval authority for environmental matters to ensure the smooth operation of environmental and related legislation.

Endangered Species

A Conservative government will ensure that endangered species legislation is based on the principles of co-operation, coexistence and partnership. Endangered species legislation must provide adequate and fair compensation for any group or person forced to surrender land or income-generating capital to protect endangered species.

SOCIAL PROGRAMS

The Conservative Party of Canada believes that social programs should be designed on the premise that responsibility for the well being of citizens rests first and foremost with the individual and family.

Provincial Role in Social Programs

The Conservative Party of Canada believes social programs should be designed so the level of government closest to the people being served manage and deliver those programs. A Conservative government will respect the constitutional jurisdiction of the provinces in the delivery of social programs.

Healthcare

The Conservative Party of Canada believes all Canadians should have reasonable access to quality health care regardless of their ability to pay.

The Conservative Party of Canada believes spending decisions and setting priorities within the health care funding envelope should be left with the provinces.

A Conservative government will provide a stable level of federal funding for health care and will work with the provinces in a co-operative and constructive manner.

NATIONAL DEFENCE AND SECURITY

The Conservative Party of Canada believes that Canada's defence policy must reflect the global environment by balancing fiscal constraints with issues of collective security, participation in peacekeeping/peacemaking missions and an appropriately structured military that is sustainable and sufficiently flexible to react to future needs.

Military

The Conservative Party of Canada takes pride in Canada's military and its traditions.

A Conservative government will restore and maintain a Military Force that is appropriate to the needs of Canada as a modern democracy. Our top priority will be to ensure the operational effectiveness of the Canadian Forces.

A Conservative government will fund, train and equip the Canadian Armed Forces to be combat capable to fulfil the multi-purpose role of the Army, Navy and Air Force.

Reserves

A Conservative government will enhance the role of, and support for, the reserve forces.

Security Agencies

The Conservative Party of Canada believes that Canada has a direct interest in a less turbulent, less dangerous, more secure world. Our government must be positioned to deal with real international political, security and development issues.

A Conservative government will ensure better cooperation among Canada's intelligence and security agencies to more effectively protect Canadians against internal and external security and economic threats in a changing and unstable global environment. Canada must not be a safe haven for international terrorist operatives.

Party Launch, 2004:
Official Opposition, Springboard Platform, and Housecleaning

Spring 2004: The new party was in place, the new leader was in place, there was a policy book, and Ken Boessenkool was beginning to work on a platform. Because of our joint work on the melding of policies of the two legacy parties, Ken called for my help in reviewing drafts. I was still working in Toronto for the Provincial PC Party, but was fortunately able to do this. The platform had to address two issues. First, it had to contain a series of forward-looking policies that would demonstrate to Canadians what the united centre right of the political spectrum had to offer. Second, it had to fulfill a defensive role.

We knew that the attacks levelled by the Grits against the Alliance Party were not going to stop just because the Alliance merged with the PC Party. In fact, one of the new party's challenges came from within since some PC MPs and senators refused to work with the new party, clinging to the now-defunct PC label. The main reason they gave for their position was that the new party, even before it had Harper as a leader, was an extreme social conservative political party. Having Harper, a former Reform MP and Alliance leader, at the Conservative Party helm made matters worse in their minds by an order of magnitude. All of this was in spite of the work MacKay and others had put into the merger so that the founding documents reflected PC principles and the policy book reflected PC policies whenever there was a contradiction (the default position was to go with the PC policy formulation). Bottom line: If Don Mazankowski, former Mulroney deputy prime minister; Bill Davis, former iconic PC premier of Ontario, who personified "middle of the road"; and Brian Mulroney himself supported this party, then why couldn't senators Murray and Atkins as well as former leader Joe Clark? I remember saying to Atkins before and after the

The Defection. Belinda Stronach's defection to the
Liberals in May 2005 prevented the Conservatives from
forcing an election for which they were unprepared.
(Courtesy of Chris Mikula/*Ottawa Citizen*. Reprinted by
permission)

2004 election that the Conservative Party platform could easily have
been a PC Party platform that Clark would have been proud to run on,
in a campaign that the senator could have easily managed. All this to
say that the platform as developed had to be both an offensive and
defensive document, and it was.

The main themes of "Demanding Better"[1] were designed to shift
the public policy debate in Canada toward the right. They included:
accountability, lower taxes, less onerous economic regulation, stricter
enforcement of the criminal law, and a strong military.

The first theme was "Better Accountability" and dealt with solutions
to prevent anything like the Liberal Quebec sponsorship scheme, as
revealed in the auditor general's report, from happening again. The
auditor general's powers would be increased, and there would be an
independent ethics commissioner as an officer of Parliament.

The "Better Economy" theme included the middle-class tax break that involved raising thresholds on tax brackets and reducing rates. It also featured a $2,000 per child tax deduction; reduced EI premiums; investment in infrastructure through transfer of at least three cents of the gas tax to the provinces; and a registered lifetime savings plan, to provide a more flexible savings plan for Canadians, which would come into being in the first Conservative mandate. A policy that got us into trouble and had to be addressed post-election was the elimination of corporate subsidies and regional development agencies.

"Better Health Care" supported the public system and proposed to the provinces a federal catastrophic drug program as well as the designation of part of the health funding to support physical activity, which eventually became the sport tax credit.

Other "Betters" dealt with "Better Communities" and "Better Security." The main environmental measure was the commitment of $4 billion to clean up contaminated sites such as the Sydney Tar Ponds.

The campaign team was basically the Harper leadership group, so they had experience in national leadership campaigns – and they were going to gain valuable experience in a national election campaign. (And invaluable lessons learned meant that in the 2005–06 campaign almost none of the 2004 mistakes were repeated.) For reasons known best to him, Martin waited two months after becoming Liberal leader before dropping the election writ on 23 May 2004 for an election day on 28 June. While this gave the Conservative Party more time to get ready than it thought it would have, for a new party the lack of preparation time is an unforgiving enemy, especially in relation to candidate training and discipline. Others have documented in great detail the first national electoral campaign run by Harper as leader of the Conservative Party, including both Tom Flanagan,[2] the campaign manager, and Bob Plamondon, in his historical work *Full Circle*.[3]

I was proud and happy to contribute in whatever role was thought beneficial by those running the campaign. Initially, I helped with the platform, mainly to ensure it was a good defensive document. I had not been part of the Flanagan-Boessenkool-Harper discussions as to the promises or commitments that were made, but I could be helpful determining whether they were consistent with party policy, such as it was then, and whether the PC side of the family would find anything objectionable.

Because of my familiarity with the policy/platform part of the campaign and because Boessenkool and Flanagan were fully engaged elsewhere, I was asked by Michael Coates,[4] who headed up the debate preparation, to help in that area. I had known of him for years, and likewise, he of me, but we had never met. In fact, I would reach a point in discussions with others on various topics when Coates's name would crop up, and I would be asked if I knew him, how long I had known him, and similar assorted questions. As I said to Mike, I inevitably started telling folks that I did know Coates because it was almost embarrassing to be involved in the Conservative family and have to admit to still not knowing him. We finally met in his office, well in advance of sessions with Line Maheux, who is a communications expert and had been involved with the Reform Party. She was going to act as moderator when we engaged in the mock debates.

The first thing Coates had us do was a SWOT analysis – Strengths, Weaknesses, Opportunities, and Threats – of the four leaders who would be on stage on debate night: Martin, Duceppe, Layton, and Harper. This was an interesting exercise, as it required us as a team to honestly assess Harper in relation to the others. The results of this analysis led into the debate narrative we were trying to construct. While few elections have absolutely turned on, or been won or lost in, the debates, our goal was to present Harper as thoughtful, with a full grasp of all the issues. He could present himself as an agent of change and a safe alternative offering honest, competent government. Despite all the campaigning that Harper had done in the period between deciding to re-enter federal politics and the dropping of the writ for the 2004 election, he had never participated in a nationally televised leaders' debate in a general election. The stakes for him were high. He had to show he was knowledgeable, and not scary – especially, not scary. Coates was well aware of this and pulled Harper off the road for about five full days, including the two debate days, for preparation and the debates themselves.

Coates had rented a television studio at Algonquin College so that the rehearsal format came as close to the real debate format as possible. He also recruited people to play the other leaders: Brian Mitchell as Jack Layton, Richard Decarie as Gilles Duceppe, and Walter Robinson as Paul Martin; each was charged with knowing the platform of the party he represented. We knew the general topic areas, and it was not difficult to figure out the questions. Coates and Maheux would ask the questions. My task was to develop Harper's debate binder and get whatever research was needed, draft the sample questions, and help him with answers, if necessary. The subjects were health, economy, and public finance; governance, which included accountability, ethics, leadership, and democratic process; justice and social issues; globalization and Canada's place in the world; environment; crisis management; and immigration. Boessenkool assured me that I would have the full co-operation of the research unit led by Mike Donison, and that was, indeed, the case. While we may have taken Harper off the campaign trail for too long, causing us to dip in the polls, I believe, as did everyone involved, that the time spent in preparation was worthwhile. It served us well in these debates and formed a solid foundation for future debates.

Having done debate preparation on a number of occasions, it is always heartening when the French debate is first. A lot of the time in preparation is taken up by getting the right terminology for the names of organizations, concepts, or acronyms in French. By comparison, preparation for the English debate is much easier – the terms and acronyms are well known and the focus is more on nuance.

The SWOT analysis laid out that, since only Martin and Harper had a realistic chance of forming a government, our main opponent in the debate would be Martin and his Liberal Party. Harper had to focus on Martin and Liberal policies, and show the contrast between the two parties' policies. The French debate is actually about policy approaches as they relate to the province of Quebec. Therefore, it was necessary to nail, in French, issues of equalization, government granting programs, and even somewhat obscure local Quebec issues that might be the subject of questions. It was also Duceppe's time to shine, as the debate drew a large audience in the province of Quebec, home of the Bloc.

The English debate has a different dynamic since Duceppe is not campaigning, nor does the Bloc have any candidates in the "rest of Canada." However, Duceppe may address issues that come up from his strategic viewpoint, either relating them to Quebec issues or not, depending on how he is feeling. In the English debate, Martin was the clear target. We wanted to demonstrate, through Harper's approach, how scattered Martin's thinking was and how his grasp of issues, other than economic, was superficial at best. Layton, always a good campaigner and debater, would invariably go after the Liberals in order to attract Liberal support to the NDP. In this series of debates, he basically left Harper alone.

The key to debate prep, as with question period or any other situation involving questions, is to anticipate the questions and prepare the answers. The last thing you want to hear from your candidate is, "Gee, what a great question. I wish I had thought of that. Unfortunately, I have nothing to say." With Harper, it is almost a certainty that that would not happen since he is by far the brightest and best informed on all issues of public policy. But an obtusely phrased question might get him, or one on social conservative issues, which is where we thought the questions would go. We had to wait until the English debate in Vancouver on 5 December, during the next general election, for such a question to arise. In Ottawa, in 2004, Harper was well briefed and remained calm throughout the debate while others flailed around. He did not seem scary; he was articulate and knowledgeable. When he began to prep, he acknowledged that one of his weaknesses in debate is that he does not want to interrupt or jump in or raise his voice to be heard or to make a point. While we first perceived this to be a definite problem, in the end, it was actually a plus. Harper seemed in control, knowledgeable, and, to a certain extent, above the fray as Martin and the others confronted each other.

While Harper may not have won the debates – although I thought he won the English debate – he established a solid knowledgeable presence on the national stage. He showed he belonged as a leader and had important things to say about each question he was asked and in the back and forth amongst the leaders. He did not embarrass himself, and when you are the new guy, that is important. The polls showed the new Conservative Party solidly in the lead coming out of the debates. There was no question in my mind, as I drove overnight back to Toronto and my day job, that we would win this election. A couple of days later, the picture of Harper in a Blue Jays warm-up jacket, throwing out the first pitch at an evening game in Toronto, appeared on the front page of the *Toronto Sun*. I saw it for the first time when I was coming out of the Toronto subway with my daughter Sara, and I told her that Harper was going to be Canada's next prime minister.

A sufficient number of negative factors came together to prevent this from happening, and the people of Canada told us: not this time – let's see about next time. But there were also sufficient positives to the campaign and to Harper's role as leader to put an end to any further thoughts of a Martin juggernaut.

While it was important from a historical and strategic viewpoint that we know what these negative factors were, it was vitally important that we know how Harper should address them, in order that they never be repeated. While there will always be things that go south in a campaign, the object of the exercise in the remainder of 2004 and all of 2005 was to minimize the risk of failure, minimize the risk of unforced errors, or errors at all.

The first item was candidate control or discipline. Right from the start we had been put back on our heels by caucus members either freelancing or making statements that were taken out of context – which will happen – that were damaging to the party. Another item was the platform. It had to be costed by a credible, independent agency. Also with the platform, given that we now had some time – or at least we thought we did – before the next election, the next platform had to be as comprehensive as possible, addressing specific issues, with specific promises and related actions. The last issue was scripting: it had to last throughout the campaign, with some new nuggets every day. We almost got it right in 2006, but did it right in 2008 and 2011.

The issues that erupted from caucus members during the 2004 election campaign were predictable given the lack of time to prepare candidates properly for the guerrilla war that is a federal campaign, especially a Conservative campaign. I am sure all other campaigns feel they never get a break from the media, but those involved in a Conservative campaign really do believe the party is held to a higher standard than the others, and closer scrutiny.

For example, Canada is officially bilingual at the federal level. One doesn't muse out loud, especially if you are the official languages critic, on changes that might be brought to official bilingualism when the Conservative Party forms a government. The issue of abortion will be a part of every Conservative campaign. If by some fluke, candidates avoid the controversy, the media or the opposition will speculate about it. In 2004, it became an issue, then it got tied to our policy of allowing MPs to pursue their own interests through private members' bills. I remember trying to find a way out of this quagmire with Ken Boessenkool and Mike Coates. I tried to make a virtue out of our policy on private members' bills and private members' motions and voting one's own conscience or as constituents direct on matters of social conscience. No matter what we tried, it didn't work. We learned not to say "In my first mandate" as a modifying phrase. Abortion was raised by more than one of our candidates either directly or by the media resurrecting old stories. It is simply a fact of a Conservative campaign and being a Conservative government that abortion will always be on everyone's policy agenda, lying in wait to be posed as a question to a candidate when it is least expected. Being gay or same-sex marriage are, for the most part, no longer issues at the federal level, but in the Alberta provincial election held in 2012, the Wildrose Party found these matters can still come up, and anti-gay remarks, if not completely disavowed by the leader, can prove fatal to a party wanting to form a government.

Other issues arose in the campaign, and while we had taken a perfectly reasonable conservative position on them, we found we were on the wrong side of public opinion. Matters like regional development agencies and industrial subsidies had become so ingrained in Canadian culture after being in place for so many years, we found that it was extremely unpopular to say we were not in favour of them without doing a little more thinking about how they should be replaced.

We also had to address the issue of childcare. Martin was announcing enormous sums to be spent in this area. This was taxpayers' money that would go to the provinces to supposedly pay for daycare spaces. The program was described as creating universal, accessible daycare for Canadian families and their children. Who wouldn't vote for this! The problem with the program was that it really didn't produce any increases in spaces – it provided the provinces with money to pay the salaries of existing daycare workers. Instead of the Martin monetary commitment creating spaces, it was a provincial subsidy or transfer – the federal government using its spending power to interfere in, or subsidize, a provincial area of jurisdiction.

Finally, we needed to come to grips with our views on the Charter of Rights and Freedoms. As we headed into the last week before the election, I was in pretty close communication with Boessenkool. The "Martin and child pornography" situation had occurred and been dealt with, and even though the overnight poll tracking numbers were close, Boessenkool explained that we had invested heavily in first identifying our voters, then getting our vote out, so not to worry. The plan was that I would come up to Ottawa on Friday morning to meet with him and Flanagan. When we won on Monday, I would take over Boessenkool's position since he was going to stay out west to take a break before either coming back or moving on. He wanted someone (me) on the ground in Ottawa for Tuesday, to start doing what was necessary in the policy area in the transition from opposition to government. All of that changed with the release of the Randy White anti-Charter interview on the Friday morning. Harper was headed west and in the air, unreachable when this happened. There was precious little that could be done other than state that White, who was not running again, did not speak for the party. When I got to Ottawa, I walked into the middle of the Randy White crisis, and it wasn't pretty.[5]

The Liberals also did an excellent job on that weekend of door-to-door drops around the country designed to convince Canadians that Harper and his Conservatives were on the wrong path, they were scary, and to keep the Canada you know and love, vote for the Liberals.

The end result was: Liberals, 135; Conservatives, 99; 37 per cent of the popular vote to 30 per cent. While disappointing, from the vantage point of nine years later, it was almost predictable. It was going to take a monumental effort to unseat the Liberals on our united first attempt, especially with their new leader, Paul Martin, a known quantity on the Canadian political scene. The Conservative Party, while a merger of two existing parties, was still new and unproven. It's birth, while enthusiastically supported by members from both sides with over 90 per cent approval, had a number of detractors, particularly from the PC side, who were successful in their attempt to characterize the new party as possibly, if not probably, extreme. This defining of the Party by others as socially conservative – not mainstream – slowed progress: the Party was just getting its feet under itself and had not yet defined itself.

There was also the question of time. As Flanagan has pointed out, the Conservatives did not expect to get two months from the time the Liberals selected their leader until the call of the election, so that was a bonus. But a year would have been a lot more advantageous. The main problem with the short timeline, as demonstrated throughout the writ period, was that it exposed cracks in candidate discipline. When combined with increased media scrutiny, this created a perfect storm within which controversy could and would arise. The Liberals, although they called the election and, therefore, should have known when it was coming, did not seem organized with any coherent new platform or positive message. This helped the Conservatives initially, and they rose in the polls. However, the increased support reflected in the polling numbers for the Conservatives put the party in the lead – and from time to time, a substantial lead – which led to increased scrutiny of the platform and candidates. Too many things went off track in the post-debate period, which the Grits took advantage of because they played into the stereotype that the Grits were using to define the Conservatives. Abortion; the pornography incident with

Martin; Premier Klein's musings about changes to health care delivery, which might violate the Canadian Health Act; Randy White against the Charter – all combined to feed into and confirm the Grits' definition of the new Conservative Party.

Numerous stories have been kicking around for years now alleging that Harper decided it was not yet time to form a government and for this reason deliberately contributed to the "polling free fall" of the week leading up to the election. This is nonsense. Harper is a winner and wants only to win. In politics, there is no prize for second place, no silver medal to clutch to make you feel good about yourself. You either form a government, with the opportunity to implement your platform, your style of government, your work ethic, your approach to federalism – grabbing the levers of power and using them to direct the state in your direction – or you don't. If you don't, all you get is to sit in the bleachers and say, as all losing teams do, "wait till next year." Given the effort and personal sacrifice involved, Harper wanted to win. As many leaders have discovered, especially in the last number of years both federally and provincially in Canada, a loss in the first attempt may mean no opportunity for a second attempt.

Were there some positives in this losing venture? Yes, there were, but we could only take advantage of them if the negatives were addressed and corrected. And yes there were positives that just needed some work with slight course corrections. Like sports teams that almost win the prize, we were only a few players short in the personnel department – perhaps the addition of a few who had won the prize previously, at either the federal or provincial level, would help. Budgeting and spending based on the budget had been kept under control and within the allowable limits. Advertising expenditures would increase next time, but within the spending envelope with adjustments elsewhere. The voter identification and get-out-the-vote program in the last week, prior to the Randy White incident, was effective and worked well. The rest was a matter of tweaking – added staff on the tour, timing of announcements, and the use of candidate colleges led by Finley, Flanagan, and others.

The main questions that had to be addressed head-on came in the policy and platform areas – areas where the Party was weak and was exploited by the other parties during the election. The leader knew the areas; the challenge was how to address them so that they did not cause problems again.

In mid-August 2004, I was asked to come to Ottawa for a meeting with the Conservative Party leader. It was the first time we had talked since the election, or perhaps even since I congratulated him on his performance in the English debates and headed back to Toronto. I must admit that I had always liked Harper, his sense of humour and his encyclopaedic knowledge of public policy issues. After a discussion about the state of affairs nationally and in Ontario, he asked if I would consider joining his office in Ottawa as director of policy and research, with responsibility for developing the platform for the next election. He told me he wanted me with him for two reasons. First, I was older than he was and, as he said, had more experience and had seen it all before in many different movies. Second, I was slightly to the left of him – at that I laughed out loud and said something to the effect of, "You can bet on that." As sometimes happens in conversations, one blurts out stupid, inane comments. Mine was, "That sounds like a full-time job." His response was equal to it and in the affirmative – and repeated my words: "You can bet on that."

I told Harper I would think about it and get back to him. Later that afternoon I spoke with Phil Murphy, Harper's chief of staff, who told me that Geoff Norquay,[6] whom I knew well, had worked with before, and quite liked, would be joining the OLO as director of communications. Murphy described us as the "dream team." I'm not sure about that. On many occasions, we were just a nightmare.

I officially joined Harper's office in September 2004, while Boessenkool was vacating and Martin was entertaining the premiers at the Ottawa Conference Centre and dealing with the supposed health care "fix for a generation." As Harper and I sat on the couch in what was still Boessenkool's office, he said these prophetic words: "When I become prime minister, this will never happen again." Time has demonstrated he meant that the unbelievable bidding contest Martin had gotten himself into with the premiers would never occur on his watch. No amount of money would suffice and no strings were to be attached to actually improve the delivery of health care across Canada.

Harper faced a number of challenges that fall. He had to get ready for a new session of Parliament with all that entails. He wanted to work with Layton and Duceppe to lay down some markers for the Martin government. He wanted to let the governor general know that the opposition was ready to form a government if Martin lost a confidence vote. He had to address the issues that had disrupted the last campaign, and he had to supervise and approve the development of a new platform that we agreed had to take the form of a rolling platform, adjusting to address issues as they arose. But we needed a platform almost immediately, because we never knew when Martin might get fed up with running a minority government and ask for dissolution or engineer his own defeat, or if, perchance, the opposition parties might bring down the government either on purpose or by accident – all of these possibilities existed all the time.

Before we could draft a platform, the issues or challenges from the 2004 election had to be addressed. The questions were how would that happen and who would do it. Harper had the solution. Those with the most skin in the game were the MPs returned by the electorate in the 2004 election. It would be they who determined how contentious issues arising out of the campaign and deficiencies in the platform would be addressed. Harper isolated the topics; in some cases, he put one caucus member in charge, and in others, he set up a caucus committee with a chair he would name. The committees were to be supported by the party research service and would report to the leader and me. They could hold meetings, hearings, or whatever, as long as they came forward with a report addressing the specific issues and setting out recommendations that could, with some editing, be put into the next platform. This undertaking was a priority, as it had to be done before we got into a situation where an election could be imminent. On the basis of the work carried out by caucus, we would be prepared.

COSTING THE PLATFORM

While a couple of accounting/financial firms had looked at the numbers in the 2004 platform, it had not been formally costed. It used Department of Finance numbers, so we were not overly concerned as long as the numbers added up. The problem was that during the debate prep, it became evident that we could not point to a credible outside source as having gone through the platform in depth, ensuring that our predicted costs made sense. The other issue was that the middle-class tax cuts were to be at least partially funded by cuts in spending. This became the "black hole" in the platform, readily exploited by the Liberals once the platform was released. In addition to the question about where the money would come from, was the

related question of which programs and services would be cut. Therefore, it was imperative that we engage the services of a credible entity
with which we would work as the platform was assembled. We wanted to be inoculated against criticism of the numbers – projections of
revenues, spending, and savings – that would be set out in the platform. Murphy had retained the Conference Board of Canada's former
chief economist, Jim Frank, as our economic advisor in the OLO, so it
made sense to use the Conference Board for this task. The arrangement was made, and Jim was to ensure that the various versions of the
platform, especially any economic promises, were forwarded to his
contact at the Conference Board. They would be able to keep a running economic tally of what we were proposing. We used the government financial tables as the economic baseline upon which the platform would be constructed.

TAX PROVISIONS OF THE PLATFORM

During the 2004 campaign we promised a large personal income tax
cut, partially funded through reduction in spending. We did not want
this to negatively affect the overall financial health of the country. In
keeping with Harper's desire to have caucus and staff work together
on troublesome issues from the last election, Monte Solberg, the
finance critic, headed up a team that included Jim Frank; Patrick Muttart; Ian Brodie, when he became Harper's chief of staff in the summer of 2005; and Mark Cameron. The goal was to reduce taxes since
the government was running a large surplus. For Harper, a government running a large surplus meant a government taking too much
money from taxpayers.

From the fall of 2004 until the end of August 2005, this group, with
Solberg's guidance and Frank's support, looked at numerous combinations that would result in less tax paid by Canadians. The alternatives ranged from moving the income tax brackets to eliminating one
of the brackets and/or to changing the rate of taxation within one or
more of the brackets. Raising the minimum threshold for paying tax
was also on the table. The genius of working with Harper and these
committee members was that we all paid income tax, deducted at
source. We had all lived through Martin's biggest income tax reduction in the history of Canada, and no one had noticed any appreciable increase in take-home pay. Why? The reduction became effective
1 January. This is the date when paycheque deductions for annual CPP

and EI contributions kick in once again, so the decrease in income tax was offset when these deductions became applicable again. No wonder no one noticed Martin's tax cuts.

We had to design a system whereby Canadians would actually experience the reduction in tax and recognize where it came from. Frank and Solberg came up with a number of proposals, all aimed at the loosely defined middle class. Each proposal cost the public purse somewhere around $5 billion – revenues it would not receive because of these cuts. We set aside a Friday afternoon late in August 2005 for a conference call to settle this. I was driving to Toronto to watch an evening Blue Jays game; Harper, Muttart, Frank, Solberg, and Brodie were in Ottawa. I pulled off the road at Kingston to start the call around 1 p.m. After about an hour, I realized that it was going to take forever to go through all the Solberg/Frank variations – and I had better get back on the road if I wanted to make Toronto, let alone the game, by nightfall. No matter which scenario we used, it would cost the treasury a lot, with taxpayers seeing only a few dollars less tax deducted on their pay stubs and a slight increase in take-home pay. This did not satisfy Harper's desire to make the tax cut meaningful and noticeable for low- and middle-income Canadians. As I reached the top of the Don Valley Parkway, we had still not reached a consensus, so we adjourned.

I was back in my office on Monday morning, when Harper came in and said that he had been thinking about the tax discussion all weekend. He had decided we were looking in the wrong place to save Canadians tax – we should be looking at the GST. It made perfect sense for what we wanted to do. We wanted to reduce taxes for all Canadians in a meaningful and noticeable way. Harper knew better than I that economists and think tanks would disagree with this idea – they love consumption taxes because they are very efficient – but that was fine with him. He didn't care if the financial elites didn't like it; he was sure Canadians would. This approach also put the Liberals in a bit of a bind because they had promised in 1993 to scrap the GST.

We looked at it from a number of angles: It would help people at the lower end of the economic scale since it is the only tax they pay. The refund or adjustment process by which lower-income earners get a GST refund paid to them would still remain in full effect. We also realized, without the need of a larger focus group, that getting the GST down to 5 per cent was the magic number, and it should be quite doable at some point in the first mandate.

We now had our tax policy for Canadians, which would also help Canadian businesses. Because this proposal was so different, we were concerned it would leak out before we were able to announce it in the campaign – but it did not, even when there was considerable pressure in late summer to put out the entire platform.

CHILDCARE

We needed some response to Martin's multi-billion dollar so-called universal, accessible daycare program. We knew it was really only a fiscal transfer to the provinces and territories. It created few, if any, new spaces and was bogged down in federal-provincial negotiations. For the most part, the Martin daycare plan would help the provinces pay the salaries of existing childcare workers. It had nothing to do with creating spaces, or to be cynical, even daycare – it could have just as easily been part of the health and social transfer.

Harper established a caucus childcare policy committee that was chaired by Carol Skelton of Saskatchewan. Rona Ambrose, who had experience in Alberta working on federal–provincial issues, served on the committee. The committee's mandate was to develop an alternative plan to the one espoused by Martin in the last election. One part of the plan was to focus on what we normally regard as daycare and the other on helping the private sector create spaces. The belief was, and numerous studies indicated, that businesses were moving more and more toward providing on-site daycare for children of employees, which was a good solution for all concerned. If Martin could subsidize daycare in the public sector with federal dollars, then surely the Conservative Party could provide support at some level for those businesses in the private sector providing on-site daycare and in some measure relieving pressure on the public model.

Again, many different permutations and combinations of incentivized daycare were considered. At the January 2005 caucus retreat in Victoria, B.C., Skelton made a presentation to caucus as to the thinking of the committee at that time. It was a combination of a number of models, put together after analyzing the cohort of children, and the parents who needed and used daycare for their children. After listening intently, the leader and caucus decided that they now knew what they didn't want. The question was: what they did want?

We started to look at what we could do with the $5 billion that Martin was going to spend on his program. To help quantify the issue facing us, we got statistics on the number of children in Canada between the ages of 0 to 5 and 0 to 6. Then we made the public policy decision to give the money to parents rather than bureaucrats. This decision was based on our conclusion that the money the Liberals were going to spend did not create any spaces; by giving this money to parents of school-age children, we weren't reducing the number of spaces being created, but we would be helping parents address some of the costs of raising young children. With that decision made, a discussion, similar to that on the GST, took place – how much money should be allocated, how much would be effective, how much would the monthly amount have to be to show we were serious. Anything less than $100 per month per child would not wash, but it would be taxable. Since many of the recipient parents were on some form of social assistance, we also had to ensure that this money would not be clawed back against their income or against financial support from programs provided by the provinces such that they would lose other forms of social assistance. We did not want any clawbacks. We were pleasantly surprised with the co-operation we received from the provinces in this matter.

We knew that advocates of public daycare would line up against this proposal, so it had to be presented in a way that demonstrated that Conservatives support families. When we were putting this together, we never thought that the Liberals would use the beer and popcorn argument against it in the 2005–06 election, making the claim that recipient parents would just squander the payment and not use it to care for their children. We were so fortunate.

BILINGUALISM

Harper is bilingual and there is no question of his support for official bilingualism and the French language. In the early Reform days, a great deal had been made out of the perception that unilingual anglophones should not apply for jobs in the federal public service – they would be automatically disqualified. Reform was going to make changes in this policy when it formed a government. However, the merger between the Alliance and PC parties was based on the principles of the PC Party, which was supportive of the federal official languages policy.

Early in the 2004 campaign, Scott Reid, the Conservative Party official languages critic or spokesperson, announced – without clearing it with anyone – that when the Conservatives formed the next government, there would be changes to the Official Languages Act. In addition, late in the campaign, correspondence was released dealing with Air Canada and official languages. Harper believed that, since the Conservative Party was a national federal party, it had to once and for all wrestle its position on bilingualism and official languages to the ground. He established a caucus committee on official languages policy and structured membership in such a way that all points of view would be expressed. It was ably chaired by Guy Lauzon, MP, a fluently bilingual Franco-Ontarian. Since we had no MPs from Quebec, Senator Pierre Claude Nolin became a member. Representing a different perspective – those unconvinced of the value of official languages policies – was Brad Trost of Saskatchewan.

The issues before this group were fundamental and had to be resolved if this new party was to be considered mainstream and was to have any chance to grow in Quebec. The reality is that Canadians across the country will not support a party that is seen as anti-bilingual, which meant anti-French. That was and is a fact of life, and certainly a political fact of life. There may be areas where the Official Languages Act could be improved or adjusted, but it has to remain in place and be supported. The discussions were fascinating and heartfelt as each member of the committee recounted experiences with the policy and shared views on what it meant to be a national political party in Canada. In the end a report was written, with the unanimous support of all members of the committee, supporting the Official Languages Act.

INDUSTRIAL POLICY

One of the hold-over views or policies from Reform days that lasted through the Alliance period, merger, and directly into the 2004 platform was that industrial or corporate subsidies had to end. This was a laudable goal. Either we live and believe in a free market economy, where goods manufactured are produced for a free market and that the marketplace functions at its maximum capacity and to maximum efficiency without government interference, or we don't. It was that simple. Except that it wasn't that simple.

Over the years, the federal government, through the use of its spending power, had created federal agencies to provide support for industries in economically depressed parts of the country. The Atlantic Canada Opportunities Agency and the Economic Development Agency of Canada for the Regions of Quebec are perhaps the best known. It is not a big leap then to subsidize corporations or industries that are centres of employment, but believe they need government backing to compete. Canada is not a large country with a large population base. Sometimes corporations needed government help to survive and compete on an international scale. When looked at through a conservative political lens, this activity was seen to be more along the lines of Liberal governments propping up corporations that had deep Liberal ties. As far as Reform was concerned, this was Liberals wasting tax dollars to entice the political and financial support of corporations – an unending downward spiral. The conservative view was that if a company could not compete internationally, then its business model needed changing, with no requirement for the infusion of taxpayers' money.

This is good policy, but really bad politics, especially when at least one of the competing political parties is in favour of regional development programs and industrial subsidies. The 2004 platform had made it clear that business subsidies would end, or at least be phased out. The problem with the platform policy was in its application. When Martin toured the Ford plant in Oakville, Ontario, he could promise government money for research, for the introduction of new technology, or anything else for that matter. When Harper toured the Ford plant, all he could do was pat the company executives and workers on the back and get back on the campaign bus. Industry and workers had become so accustomed to the subsidy message that not hearing it became a real problem in the 2004 campaign.

Harper tapped James Rajotte to head up a caucus committee to review the party's industrial and regional development policies and come forward with recommendations for the next platform. This was quite a task for Rajotte and his staff, who fundamentally believed industrial subsidies were unnecessary and a waste of taxpayers' money. The best example of the educational value of the work of these caucus committees, and especially this one, came on the morning when the senior executives from Bombardier appeared to explain how the airplane manufacturing business worked in Canada and elsewhere around the globe. And of course, how the end of government subsidies would mean the end of the airplane-manufacturing business in Canada, mostly located in Quebec, and the end of hundreds, if not thousands, of jobs for highly skilled workers.

In the United States, Brazil, France, and other airplane-manufacturing countries, the research and development costs for military aircraft were run through the plane manufacturers. This created a large government subsidy for Lockheed Martin and other manufacturers in United States, Embraer in Brazil, and Airbus in France. As Canada did little to no military aircraft R&D, this put Bombardier at a distinct financial disadvantage. The caucus committee also learned of state and municipal relocation subsidies offered in the United States and elsewhere to entice businesses to locate in particular areas. No longer could one induce a major manufacturer to locate on the strength of a competent workforce alone. Tax incentives, free land, servicing, and the like were the order of the day in today's competitive marketplace, where all jurisdictions are looking at job creation as the measurement of economic and political success.

The report of the committee on this difficult subject, which ultimately recommended government subsidies, especially in the area of scientific and technical research and development, and continuation of regional development agencies found its way into the 2005–06 platform.

HERITAGE AND CULTURE

This was more of a defensive category and, unlike the others, saw an individual not a committee take this on. Bev Oda, former chair of the CRTC, was asked to come up with policies that would address culture and the arts. Her report, which found its way into the spring 2005 version of the platform, was largely omitted from the 2005–06 election platform. However, it did provide good thinking on broadcasting and communication. As indicated, it was important to demonstrate that the barbarians at the gate – as some viewed the conservatives – had at least some sense of arts and culture.

ENVIRONMENT

On this subject, Bob Mills, MP, was the lead. A great believer in environmental protection and enhancement, he was eager to fill the gap in the 2004 platform on environmental issues. If the party is not going to support Kyoto, then, to be at all credible, what is it going to say about the environment?

Mills's environmental program was based on "Clean Land," "Clean Water," and "Clear Air." Clean land was the promise to clean up government toxic waste sites such as the Sydney Tar Ponds. Clean air meant an attack on air pollution, and clean water was to ensure that Canada's many lakes and rivers would not be further polluted, with the government embarking on a program of cleaning up Canada's polluted waterways. The clean water version of Mills's environment proposal was extended to prevent bulk water exports. As we went along we realized that, if we were to concentrate on pollution and not greenhouse gases (GHGs), it might be worthwhile using the tax system to promote the use of transit. Out of this came the policy announced in the summer of 2005: tax deductibility of transit passes.

CANADA'S ARMED FORCES

Gordon O'Connor, a retired army general, was given the task of developing both our foreign and defence policies. O'Connor, like those working in the other areas, took this on with considerable enthusiasm. He delivered a procurement and manpower list delineating what needed to be done after thirteen years of Liberal neglect, which started with cancellation of the EH101 helicopter contract in 1993.

Not only did O'Connor's work make it into the platform in both the May and December versions, but it formed the basis of the campaign announcement outlining what the Conservative Party would do to rebuild the Canada military both in procurement and in the addition of personnel in the regular service and in the Reserves. This was part of the Winnipeg announcement on the Party's approach to the North, made just prior to Christmas in the 2005 campaign.

QUEBEC

Harper agreed with Prime Minister Mulroney that we had to do something about the Conservative standing in Quebec through a very targeted approach to Quebec. The 2004 election had seen the beginning of an alignment that had always supported and elected Conservative governments – support from the West; the thin blue line, as MacKay termed it, in Atlantic Canada; the beginnings of a revival in Ontario – but nothing in Quebec. There was simply not enough time to put in place the people and platform that would speak directly to Quebec.

Immediately after the 2004 election, Harper brought Josée Verner, the highest vote-getting candidate in Quebec, to Ottawa to be part of the shadow cabinet, to bring the voice of and perspective of Quebec to its deliberations. It was a good beginning, and it got better through the summer of 2005 with the addition of Lawrence Cannon. Verner had the benefit of advice from Denis Jolette, former president of the PC Party prior to merger, and Paul Terrien, Harper's speech writer, especially for speeches in French, and she successfully brought a Quebec view to shadow cabinet discussions.

While Harper's first speech on "open federalism," built on the Belgian federalism model, was given in the fall of 2004,[7] it was not until Cannon joined the OLO as deputy chief of staff in the summer of 2005 staffing shakeup that we really started to make progress toward a Quebec-centred set of initiatives. I realize that Harper's initial speech on a Belgian-style federalism was not well received by the media. It was mocked because of all the difficulties the various language groups in Belgium were having in dealing with each other. Harper's point, which the media chose to ignore, was that there are many kinds of federalism, and a more flexible view would probably serve Quebec and Canada better than the Trudeau/Chrétien-Martin rigid status quo. Harper phoned me the morning of the day he was to give the speech. I told him I didn't know much about the Belgian model, but that I believed new ideas, especially those rooted in flexibility, would be welcome. We were both taken aback by the vehemence of the criticism, but we both believed we had made a start in the right direction, which in itself was important.

Cannon's insight into the traditional grievances of Quebec regarding the federal government was invaluable. We were also fortunate to be facing a prime minister who had no difficulty dumping wads of cash across the country, but who did not recognize the fiscal imbalance vis à vis Quebec. I suppose this is the problem that results when the long-serving finance minister ascends to the position of prime minister: an inability to recognize either past mistakes or new realities from the chair of prime minister, not the chair of the finance minister. Martin's intransigence, especially on Quebec, made our job easier.

Cannon set to work with Verner and Terrien to develop the Charter of Open Federalism, which found its way into the 2005–06 platform and formed the basis for Harper's historic speech in Quebec on 19 December 2005.

IMMIGRATION; SAFE STREETS AND
HEALTHY COMMUNITIES; AND AGRICULTURE

To round out the caucus policy process, Diane Ablonczy led a task force on immigration and refugees, which addressed issues such as methods to attract immigrants needed for Canada's job market, family reunification, and recognition of professional credentials. Jim Flaherty and Russ Hiebert co-chaired a task force on safe streets and healthy communities. Its numerous recommendations were divided into three parts: protection of society, prevention of crime, and rights and needs of victims. And Diane Finley led a task force on agriculture, since it was important that agriculture be seen from an eastern or more Canada-wide perspective.

All of this policy work was done within the caucus, feeding specifically into the rolling platform process. Parallel to this internal policy process, we were trying to move ahead on other tracks.

There was the platform track. In addition to the issues being dealt with by the caucus process, which would eventually feed into the platform, the spring 2004 platform needed to be revised and updated. Harper's idea was to have a platform virtually ready to go at any time, should the government precipitate an election or actually fall, perhaps even by accident. This required a complete review of the 2004 platform to isolate deficiencies and determine how the world had changed so we could adjust. For example, even in 2004–05, Harper was concerned about the security of our border with the US and security of the North American continent from intrusion from abroad, so we started to put together a chapter dealing with Canada–US relations, the border, and perimeter security. In "Demanding Better II" (the working title), this was the introductory chapter, but as time went on, it moved further back and was eventually dropped as President Bush became more and more unpopular with Canadians.[8]

Then there was the parliamentary track, which began with amending the Speech from the Throne (SFT). Two other important government initiatives were the bill to recognize and legalize same-sex marriages and the 2005 budget. After listening to the September 2004 SFT, it was decided that it did not address a number of issues, so we worked with the House leaders of the NDP and Bloc to bring amendments to the SFT. The amendments dealt with Employment Insurance, tax reductions for low- and middle-income families, providing independent fiscal forecasting for parliamentarians, review of our electoral system addressing all options, and ensuring Parliament would have the opportunity to review all public information related to strategic missile defence and to vote on government decisions relating to missile defence. As a precursor of things to come, we did not know until the last possible moment whether the Martin government would, in fact, vote in support of the changes to the SFT that we believed it had already agreed to. After passing of the SFT, the budget was the next big confidence vote for the government. The same-sex marriage bill was an issue that Harper knew we had to oppose – he could live with civil same-sex unions but not the bill. We knew the bill was going to pass since both the NDP and Bloc supported the government on this issue. It was one of the few times in all my years working on public policy issues that I was confronted with the party I worked for taking a public position that I disagreed with. In over thirty years, I guess I was pretty fortunate that it happened as rarely as it did.

There was also the Policy Convention and Leadership Vote Confirmation Meeting track taking place in Montreal on 17–19 March. Fortunately, this track was in the hands of Gary Lunn, MP, who did a stellar job working on this from a caucus perspective, as did Ken Boessenkool and others. Since at least some parts of the platform would be informed by the decisions at the policy convention, this was not just another track. It was of vital importance if the Conservative Party was to lay claim to being a moderate, centre right, and mainstream political party.

The last and, obviously, most important track was Election Preparedness. The campaign team would be led, much as it had been in 2004, by Tom Flanagan and Doug Finley. Harper had put everyone on election preparedness or readiness footing early in 2005 for an election that could come along at a moment's notice.

I found my role and my responsibilities in all of this really confusing, especially when compared to our efforts later in 2005, when we brought in a motion, supported by the other two opposition parties, that brought down the government. In the winter of 2004 and spring of 2005, there were a lot of moving parts – all moving at the same time, but not always in the same direction and not always congruently with each other. In the normal course of election preparation, at least some of the tracks or variables are nailed down before work begins on the others. But this was the challenge – and opportunity – presented by a new political party, which we all believed was the government-in-waiting.

Dealing with each of these challenges, the caucus policy committee process moved along, fortunately with reports that, after some editing, could be plugged directly into an election platform. Obviously, as of spring 2005, the Quebec piece would not be completely finalized nor contain the level of detail it eventually did when Cannon joined the OLO in the summer of 2005. With regard to the taxes etc., we would just have to land on one of the many scenarios prepared by Frank and Solberg. But there would be sufficient material to construct or pull together a conservative, economically sound platform.

On the parliamentary front, Harper decided initially that the Martin budget was good enough, that it was not necessary for us to precipitate an election. This opinion would change as the Gomery Commission evidence was made public. There aren't a lot of funny, or sort of funny, stories to tell, but I recall one situation. I was in the opposition lobby when the Martin government's first budget was tabled. I had the opportunity to go through it while Harper sat and listened to the budget speech. When he came out of the Chamber, I was ready with my analysis – and for some reason forgetting where I was and to whom I was speaking, I started to explain the budget to Harper. He put his hand on my shoulder to stop me and, looking right at me, calmly said, "You know, Bruce, I am competent to read this." Right. As far as Harper was concerned, the budget did no harm, and in some places, like the armed forces, had actually increased the expenditure allotment. It was decided to let it pass.

On same-sex marriage,[9] knowing the legislation was going to pass, Harper put up a credible effort at opposition, and we landed on wording that would be suitable for the next platform. Upon forming a government (which everyone believed would be a minority), the Conservative Party would bring in a motion asking the will of the House on re-opening the issue; if that motion failed, that would be the end of it. In conversations with Harper after the same-sex marriage issue was put to rest, in opposition and then in government, he expressed relief that Martin had tackled this subject. If Martin had not, pressure would have continued to mount and we as government would have been dealing with opposition private members' bills on this subject. In a minority, on a free vote, they would have passed with the support of some government members – less than an ideal scenario for a Conservative minority government.

The March Policy Convention and Leadership Vote Confirmation Meeting was the next parallel track. As noted above, from a caucus or OLO perspective, Lunn managed this as well as anyone could and put in an inordinate amount of time and preparatory effort during the run-up to the convention. He worked tirelessly with the convention team to ensure that the results we wanted were realized.

Immediately prior to the convention, Lunn, Geoff Norquay, and I decided to brief the media so that they would have a better understanding of what was going to take place in Montreal. We should have known better – and I suppose in some ways, we did – but we thought it was worth the effort. During the week prior to the convention, we invited the media to a briefing in the Centre Block OLO boardroom. It is a beautiful room with a large, yet long and narrow, table. The OLO is well-appointed office space, and it is easy to see why, at one time, the fourth floor of the southwest part of the building was the prime minister's Centre Block office.

The briefing was well attended. After a few introductory comments by Lunn and myself, Norquay, as communications director (with a huge policy background), started to explain what was in the policy book and how the meeting in the Montreal would proceed. After a few minutes, he was interrupted, and we never got any further. There was only one issue on the collective mind of the media: What were we going to do with the resolution that would ban abortions? How were we going to handle this fundamental social conservative issue? The plan, we explained, was to make the party leader's wishes known, and then the motion would be defeated. But what if it passed, what would we do? The leader's position was reiterated. Why did we not just keep it off the agenda? We replied that we could not do that – it arrived here as a result of a democratic grassroots policy process in a democratic political party, and we would ignore the issue at our peril. And on and on it went. Few of the other policy resolutions were the subject of discussion.

If nothing else, the media briefing demonstrated where the media were going to focus. Coming out of Montreal, we would need to decide which of the policies adopted would find their way into the platform. As with most political parties, the leader is the final determinant as to what will be in the platform.

The policy convention in Montreal was a success on all fronts. Harper's speech was the best he had given to date as leader of the Official Opposition. The mid-80s percentage vote of support of his leadership put Harper clearly in command and control of the Party. The plenary policy session gave us a set of mainstream centre-right policies to work with, and the motion dealing with abortion was defeated.

I never did understand the dust-up between Peter MacKay and Scott Reid on the proposed change to the leadership selection criteria dealing with delegates sent by a riding to a convention. It was unclear to me why a change had to go forward at this convention, so soon after merger and so soon after Harper and MacKay had agreed upon the original rules. On the other hand, it was a minor change that would affect only a small number of constituencies where we would have less than a hundred members. But it was the subject of great debate, accompanied by hurt feelings, statements of betrayal, and kicked chairs – and it gave the media something other than abortion to write about. It captured the headlines on the Saturday morning, potentially overshadowing and hurting Harper's attempt to show unity and a party ready to govern. On this occasion, I missed out on the kicked chair (thrown debate briefing binders made up for that as we moved through the year), and all I knew as I left the hotel to drive back to Ottawa on Sunday afternoon was that I was to produce MacKay in Harper's office first thing on Monday morning.

Coming out of the Montreal policy meeting, the track was to update the rolling platform and begin to finalize the scripting, in the lead-up to a time when there would be an election. This is where, for me, the maximum amount of confusion occurred. Perhaps it was due to the other track that had existed all through 2005 and over which we had no control: the Gomery track![10] It played out in the background all through this period, providing fodder for question period, both on what the Liberals had actually done and on the issues of accountability and transparency.

We had an observer at the hearings, and we were being given information regarding the testimony of certain key witnesses; however, it was not until Mr Justice Gomery set aside his own publication ban on testimony that the full purport of the sponsorship scandal became known. On a Sunday afternoon, after the Jean Brault testimony had been made public, I recall receiving a call from Harper. I believe he was travelling out west at the time, and he wanted to know if what he was hearing was really true. I told him it was. The Chrétien government had funnelled monies set aside for sponsorship into the Liberal campaign in Quebec in the 1997 and 2000 federal elections. With the help of various Liberal advertising agencies, taxpayer monies had been used to fund various election campaigns in the province. We didn't know whether Martin knew what was going on; we just knew the actions and activities and how the money was spent. Harper's response was predictable: This was a political party and a government that had lost its moral authority to govern. It had to be defeated. A general election would be forthcoming.

For Harper and Conservative MPs, there were two related questions: when, and over which issues, to defeat the government. While we had "the" issue, and favourable polls, we were nowhere near ready for an election from a policy/platform/scripting/messaging point of view. On other fronts – those managed by Finley and Flanagan – we were in pretty good shape. That is, Finlay was ensuring that candidates were in place and that office space and all the technology needed to run a war room were either ordered or functioning. The plane and buses were on order, and Flanagan and Mike Coates had been dealing with Perry Miele on advertising. In fact, we had ads featuring the Harper team already in the can. But we were still missing the main part of the campaign: the messaging, the articulation of a reason as to why we were doing this – bringing the government down.

I suppose the last track in all of this was the Belinda Stronach track. It was a short, yet important, and in the end, not very pretty, track. Those of us leading campaign preparedness, who had been to Montreal and had been in shadow cabinet meetings, knew that Stronach was not at all times a "happy camper." There were at least two instances where Harper had confronted her, and he was just generally fed up with her need to be in the spotlight, usually contradicting or questioning the opinions he held or positions he had taken. I remember conversations with Harper about her. His view was that she would not remain in public life for long, and that she had no real feel for public policy issues. She believed, given where she came from in the private sector, that she should be in a position of leadership. However, with Harper receiving a conclusive confirming vote, the leadership of the Conservative Party was not going to open up any time soon. What surprised me, and Flanagan refers to it in his book *Harper's Team*, was her attendance at the candidates' college/workshops during the weekend of 14–15 May, immediately preceding her defection to the Liberals. If the stories are correct, during the day, she was attending our meetings, and at other times, she was meeting with former Ontario Liberal premier David Peterson and Martin's chief of staff, Tim Murphy.

On Tuesday, 17 May, no one was more surprised than me when Ray Novak, then Harper's executive assistant, knocked on the door where we were holding the 8 a.m. question period (QP) prep meeting, to tell me that the leader wanted to see me. I did not think it was of great importance so I remained in the room discussing the proposed QP lineup with Jason Kenney, who chaired the meeting, and Keith Beardsley, when Novak approached a second time, quite emphatic about Harper needing to see me. On the short walk across the hall to Harper's office, I tried to think of all the things I had done wrong and that I was going to be in trouble for. I never anticipated what I was about to hear. "Stronach is going over to the Liberals. We have to go upstairs and see Peter. He is a mess," said Stephen. As we went up to MacKay's sixth-floor office, Stephen briefed me on what had happened, and why, since I was Peter's closest friend in our office, it would be good for me to be there for support. The three of us sat in Peter's office while he recounted what had happened and that there was no way to stop it – not that we would have wanted to anyway at that point. It is one thing to muse about the loyalty of a caucus colleague, quite another to discover all those bad thoughts you had about lack of loyalty and lack of being a team player were actually true.

Arrangements were made to get Peter out of town, back home to Nova Scotia. He was hurt and he was angry.

The vote on the motion designed to defeat the government was to take place on the Thursday afternoon. If Cadman voted with the Conservatives, the government would fall by one vote. If Cadman voted with the government, it would be a tie vote, with Speaker Milliken casting the deciding vote to affirm continuation of the status quo, resulting in no election. Cadman was an interesting character. He was part of the original Reform crowd, a real law-and-order guy. He lost the nomination for his riding in the lead-up to the 2004 campaign, but ran as an independent and won. He had terminal cancer, and even as the vote approached, it was obvious that he was quite ill. While he had supported the Conservatives and voted against the Liberals on most issues, it was doubtful he would vote to force an election that he would be too ill to contest.

In the week prior to the Thursday, 19 May, vote, Flanagan, Finley, and I met in Harper's office to take stock of where we were. Flanagan and Finley wanted permission for one last meeting with Chuck Cadman to try to convince him to vote with the Conservatives, his natural political home. Harper told them to go ahead, but he was sure that Cadman, who was dying (and who, in fact, died shortly after the vote), would vote in his own and his family's best interests – to support the government so that all his insurance and death benefits would remain intact, and not be subject to the vagaries of an election. The other message that ran through this meeting was that Harper had lost interest in forcing an election at this time. He said that he would never want to go into an election on a downward spiral, and Stronach's defection had created that downward momentum. One last thing that needed to be done was to get MacKay back from Nova Scotia in time for the vote. During the post-QP debrief in his office on Wednesday, Harper asked whether anyone knew if MacKay would be back – he had to return. I volunteered to call him and went back to my office. I got Peter on his cellphone; he was on his way to the Halifax airport and would be back.

The Belinda Stronach floor crossing was a gift. Firstly, we believed she was going to defect at some point, probably during the course of an election or during some crucial policy debate in order to gain maximum attention and exposure. Now, that worry no longer existed; the defection had happened. If she defected again, it was not our problem.

Secondly, it saved Harper and the Conservatives from an election we were not completely prepared for. We had not been able to land all the moving parts in the timeframe available. The tracks that I have described were actually a number of parallel lines of work. As we moved toward and beyond the policy convention in mid-March, and then through the lifting of the publication ban on Jean Brault testimony to the Gomery Commission, the various tracks stopped running parallel and began intersecting with each other. In some way it could be characterized as a collision – sometimes controlled, sometimes not so much.

The Montreal convention had approved a set of policies, but that did not mean we automatically had a platform. For the most part, policies are aspirational guides, from which we then hoped to fashion a platform with specific promises for Canadians. It was great to have the policy book – and also great to have it without including any of the issues Harper was concerned about – but it was only a guide. The caucus policy development process, while it had delivered some preliminary findings, was still in the middle of consultations and deliberations. Some of the findings and recommendations could be incorporated, but we were not near completion. This left us at a considerable disadvantage. We knew that corruption, stealing taxpayers' money, and Liberals being unfit to govern would be the overall theme, but what did we have to offer, other than we weren't Liberals? What was to be the ballot question – the negative one regarding the Grits and the positive one regarding what Conservatives had to offer Canadians? It would be relatively easy to script the first week of a campaign and, if we were lucky, up to the debates, but where would we go after that? There is also a very practical problem: as soon as we forced the call of an election, we would lose a considerable number of staff to the leader's campaign tour, secondary tours, and election-issues management in the war room. While not insurmountable, it was a problem nevertheless – especially questionable when you are the party forcing the election. Flanagan, in *Harpers Team*, accurately refers to this period as trying to force an election while not being ready to actually run an election campaign.[11]

At the end of the day, the important result of all this was that lessons were learned. For the most part, the mistakes of the 2004 campaign and the deficiencies in the run-up to the May 2005 non-campaign were never repeated again.

Priming for Election 2006:
Strong Research, Targeted Platform, and a Few Lucky Breaks

I believe it is fair to say that on 19 May 2005, when Speaker Milliken voted to continue the debate and thus maintain the governing Liberals in power, with perhaps the exception of the Bloc, there was a feeling of general relief among members of the House of Commons. But the relief was short-lived for the Conservatives.

We now faced the fact that Martin's Liberals had been out on a full-scale poaching mission prior to that vote. Some Conservative MPs, especially the Grewals,[1] were out meeting with the Liberal leadership trying to get their "thirty pieces of silver" for their vote – a Cabinet position. The Grewal affair and the duplicity around it was the last straw for Norquay, Harper's director of communications. Spending hours and days of his life poring over tapes of conversations, sometimes in Punjabi and sometimes in English, perhaps missing crucial points, was not his, or anyone else's, idea of a productive use of talent. Norquay was also under the impression that Harper had lost confidence in either him or the communications team that he had assembled. Harper did nothing to dispel this feeling, so a talented communications and policy resource departed. Harper had to confront not only some serious management and staffing issues but also the question of the looming summer with the House not in session. How would he fill the time in a productive manner?

Doug Finley had now joined the OLO as deputy chief of staff in order to address the staffing and other deficiencies that had surfaced in the winter/spring of 2005. Finley brought a sense of professionalism, knowledge, and a feeling of hope to a pretty dispirited team, and to a leader who at one time during the spring thought he would be

The Management. Ian Brodie, chief of staff for Stephen
Harper from mid-2005 to mid-2008, brought rigour,
drive, intelligence, and professionalism to the office.
Here with Bruce Carson (left). (Courtesy of Jake
Wright/*The Hill Times*. Reprinted by permission)

going into the summer as Canada's new prime minister, not continuing his role as leader of the opposition.

Perhaps this is as good a place as any to say that being leader of Her
Majesty's Loyal Opposition has got to be one of, if not *the* worst job
in Canadian federal politics. There is a car and driver, and a free house
to live in with accompanying staff, but that is where it ends. Caucus
members always believe they have better ideas, and better ways of
communicating those better ideas. At any time, there are usually at

least one or two planning your demise. Other than kicking someone out of caucus, there are few disciplinary tools. Sure, the leader could remove an MP from a much-desired committee position, but, really, how many fights does a leader want to pick with caucus members? All travel, unless the party wants to charter a private plane, is by car or commercial aircraft. (By way of contrast, as the newly minted prime minister, Harper invited the members of the transition team to 24 Sussex for lunch on the Saturday after the Cabinet was sworn in. On the preceding Friday, he was in New Brunswick on government business, addressed the New Brunswick PC Annual General Meeting in the evening, and was home and in bed by midnight. As leader of the opposition, that trip would have taken three days out of his life, which you don't get back.) The only benefit is that there is no protective bubble in which to escape public opinion. On one occasion, at a meeting of what Harper called his priorities and planning committee, comprised of the House officers from the House and the Senate plus the party whip, after Senator Kinsella had described what he perceived to be fairly negative poll results in the Maritimes, Harper responded. He told us of his day-before, late-night trip to Vanier Harvey's on Montreal Road for a burger (have I mentioned the junk-food issue and the weight problem?) and how everyone in line told him he was doing a great job and to keep it up. So much for polling!

To conclude on this issue of being leader of the opposition, most, if not all, of your time is spent planning your party's attack on the government during question period, knowing full well that beyond Wellington Street in Ottawa, Canadians neither watch nor care about what goes on in QP. The other part of your time is spent trying to devise policies that will provide the party with a winning platform in the next election. In all of these areas, caucus members, and in some cases party officials, believe they should have direct input – so virtually everything one does is *ad referendum* to the caucus. The only way to deal with this is to enforce strict discipline on caucus and to charge one or two senior staff members with the task of meeting with caucus members to gather their ideas and their complaints. Harper did this with a great deal of success, both in opposition and later in government. I was one of the staff persons, along with Ian Brodie, to meet with caucus members, gather their ideas, and relay them to Harper. This approach frees up the leader's time and allows for a frank exchange of ideas.

With that bit of context, back to what to do in the summer of 2005, when polling numbers were declining and Harper's opportunity to be prime minister did not materialize. The tour planning group put together several options, all giving Harper and his family some vacation time, out of the public spotlight. One June evening, at a meeting in Harper's office that included Carolyn Stewart-Olsen, Ray Novak, Doug Finley, and me, after he had rejected all the plans, I asked Harper, "What the fuck do you want to do?" His reply was quite telling as to his mood and the state we were in at that time: "I really don't know." One thing he did know was that he didn't want any time off. So with that instruction, the tour-planning group went back to work, eventually coming up with the endless-summer BBQ tour, which kicked off at the downtown Ottawa Convention Centre.

As with all things, time helps erase perceived defeats from our consciousness, and in politics one either quits or rises to fight another day. For Tom Flanagan, the sign of the turnaround came with Harper and MacKay tossing a football around on the front lawn of the Centre Block. For me, it was a morning later in June when Harper came down to my office, which was at the other end of the OLO fourth-floor office from his. He sat in a chair at the table (the couch had long since disappeared) and put his feet up on my desk, and we chatted about a number of things, including politics and Belinda Stronach. Harper had come to grips with what had happened and predicted, correctly, that she would lose interest in politics. It was his opinion that with leadership not an option in either the Conservative or Liberal party, she would seek something outside of politics. I could see the clouds had lifted from Harper, and we were ready to once again take the fight to the Grits.

Before Parliament started its fall 2005 session, we held two caucus meetings outside of Ottawa, one in Toronto and the other in Halifax. We also started to release parts of the platform. As has been noted by many commentators on this period, the OLO was reduced in size, but added three significant members, and became completely focussed on two areas: platform development and election readiness, and issues management centred on attacking the government.

On issues management and attacks on the government, long-time PC staffer Keith Beardsley had assembled a small but effective team with a huge database containing everything the Liberals, NDP, and the Bloc had ever done or said about public policy issues. Jason Plotz and Jared Kuehl were the keepers and updaters of this database.

On the platform–policy side, Patrick Muttart joined us on a full-time basis from Jaime Watt's firm, Navigator; Lawrence Cannon joined the Party and then the OLO as deputy chief of staff with specific responsibility for Quebec; and finally, Ian Brodie moved over from party headquarters to become Harper's chief of staff.

Politics is a lot like sports. Sometimes you are just one or two players away from putting together a championship team. And sometimes you have to quit playing defence and start playing offence. That is what these changes did for the Conservative Party. While their force and effect were felt immediately, they were in full swing when the House commenced sitting again in September. We would be ready the next time the opportunity to force an election came along.

Even though Harper was spending the summer criss-crossing Canada, getting out to meet Canadians, we decided to hold a summer caucus meeting in the media centre of Canada, Toronto. The party had not done well in major metropolitan centres in 2004, so the thought was to showcase the Party and perhaps one or two of its policies that were relevant to urban dwellers. It was decided that the proposal to allow transit pass users to deduct the cost of their transit pass from their taxable income seemed like the right policy to announce in the right location. Just that one announcement taught us a lot about how prepared we had to be; how to withstand and answer questions from a skeptical media; and how careful we had to be in the scrutiny of our announcements from the point of view of communications products such as press releases, backgrounders and caucus talking points, and prepared Qs and As. This announcement was almost like a pilot project or dry run for bigger announcements to come. We were questioned as to its effectiveness. Would it really take people out of their cars? What were we going to do for businesses that encouraged carpooling by paying for downtown parking, or for people who could not use transit but carpooled? How much would the proposal cost? How would we police it? What level of proof was required? Was this a proposal to address Canada's Kyoto commitment by taking cars off the road and thereby reduce GHGs? And we also learned a lot about staging events in a big city – Harper was to board a streetcar and then get off at a later stop and make the announcement, but with lots of media around and about, we lost him for a while.

Other summer issues revolved around the fact that we actually did have a platform; it was long and very detailed, more defensive than offensive, but a platform nevertheless. We were also in the mid-20s in the polls with the newly invigorated Liberals riding high. I was approached by a number of caucus members about the possibility of a mid-summer release of the platform. The usual, and somewhat compelling, argument was that Canadians did not know what we stood for, and the platform would provide an answer as well as a hoped-for sizable bump up in the polls. I spoke to Harper about this, and we had quite a conversation. He was convinced it was a bad idea. But I still wasn't. I went home to think about it. I was out walking the dog that evening (Cory, our border collie, knew more policy than some MPs), when it occurred to "us": What if we release the platform and no one cares? What if the polls remain stagnant? It is the middle of the summer and no one is paying attention. What if nothing happens, and then we have nothing left for a pending election because the platform is already out? I informed Harper the next morning that I completely agreed with him, and we stonewalled caucus on this issue until the election.

The OLO changes were in full effect as we moved into September, and a caucus meeting was held in Halifax to plan the fall session. I believe this was the first parliamentary caucus meeting and Senate caucus meeting attended by newly minted Conservative Senator Hugh Segal. It was great to add one more senator to the depleted Conservative Senate ranks; that Segal chose to sit as a Conservative senator was especially important in keeping some positive momentum going. He probably never realized what a morale boost that was. Senator Segal epitomizes links to the Red Tories and to the Progressive Conservative part of the merger. There is his relationship with Bill Davis, former PC premier of Ontario and one of the PC emissaries in the merger, as well as his personal and former business links to Senator Norman Atkins, who has eschewed the merger. No one would have been surprised if Segal had self-designated as a Progressive Conservative senator. The surprise was that he not only told Martin of his intention to sit as a Conservative but also followed it up with a call to Harper and immediately joined the caucus, bringing a wealth of provincial and federal experience and his policy background to the party. This is how it started, but by mid- to late 2013, senators led by the same Segal were bucking the government whip and instructions from the PMO. Segal has announced that he will be leaving the Senate in 2014.

As we headed into the fall and away from the debacle in the spring, the only items on the agenda coming out of the caucus meeting in Halifax were election preparedness and the questions of how and when to bring the government down. The Gomery Commission continued its work, with the interim report coming later in the fall; it would include the comments of the Commission on the testimony of Jean Brault and other similar witnesses. Under Brodie's leadership, we were going to be ready when the time came to bring down the government. We were not watching the polls; we were working on our priorities and the messages we wanted to convey to Canadians: policies and messages that differentiated Conservatives from Liberals.

The spring platform was large, too large – I had put it together by incorporating the available commentary and recommendations from the various caucus policy committees. It was more of a policy buffet than a tightly focussed platform. Realizing the vulnerability of the Party to attacks of being extreme, the platform presented a wide, diverse, middle-of-the-road policy buffet for Canadians. It would be hard for the PC part of the Conservative Party to disagree with any of it, and there were no holes where controversial or divisive social conservative policy issues could creep in, especially when taking into consideration the results of the recent policy convention.

Muttart went to work, trimming down the platform document that I had produced and Flanagan had tried to edit back in May. It became clear that there needed to be an overall theme. We determined that the platform would begin with accountability – spelling out in detail the contents of the Conservative's signature piece of legislation, the Federal Accountability Act. This proposed legislation, referred to many times by Harper during the fall of 2005, would deal with the ethics of public office holders, strength the Lobbying Act, ban secret donations to political candidates, clean up procurement, provide real protection for whistleblowers, establish a Parliamentary Budget Authority, strengthen the role of the ethics commissioner, and create a director of public prosecutions position.

With the main theme decided, we needed to determine what ideas or proposals, what policies or sets of policies would go into the platform to appeal to Canadians who were already Conservative supporters or were within the Conservative Party universe. But first we had to find out precisely who those voters were. One of Muttart's strengths was his ability to slice and dice our polling information. Once this was done, we could identify our core support and others who might be open to Conservative policies.

On the Saturday of the Thanksgiving weekend of 2005, Harper, Doug Finley, Patrick Muttart, and I met in the boardroom of the OLO to be treated to a slide show the likes of which we had never seen before. Doug started the meeting by telling both Stephen and me that we actually did not know any of the core supporters of the Conservative Party personally. We told Doug and Patrick that this was ridiculous – we knew lots of people who voted for us, or said they did. But Doug and Patrick persisted and insisted that they were right. What Patrick had done, and this was as much to benefit the advertising folks as the policy platform developers, was categorize and name various Canadian family groups as to their propensity to support the Conservative Party, or not, and what they would need to see in a platform for the Party to actually gain their vote. We knew they were leaning to the right, but we had to seal the deal with policies directed to their needs. I realize this has been written about many times, but here are some of the names and categories of possible supporters, as well as those we believed were beyond our reach.[2]

1 Dougie: We loved him. We didn't know any Dougies, unless of course one of our kids became a Dougie. He was a tradesperson; worked at a physically demanding job; and lived, for our purposes, in a small town. He didn't usually vote because politics were irrelevant for him. But if we made it relevant to him and his job, he might vote; and if he did, it would be Conservative.
2 Zoe: She was the other favourite. She was a single woman in her late twenties living in a big city, like Toronto – probably in a condo; loved bistros; and would never vote Conservative.
3 Mike and Theresa: They moved from downtown to the suburbs; mortgage, two kids; one of the parents had a college degree. Boutique tax proposals would appeal to people like this couple.
4 Marcus and Fiona: The downtown couple – both university educated – who lived in a high-rise condo with no kids, didn't give to charities or volunteer, and were beyond our grasp.
5 Steve and Heather: Married, with Steve owning his own business; probably Protestant; with three children. They would vote with self-interest, depending on the party platform that best represented what they needed from a cost-of-living point of view.

6 Eunice: Widow, in her seventies, Protestant, living on a modest
  pension but owning her home. She was also reachable, by stressing economic issues, health care, home care, and criminal justice
  matters such as elder abuse.

Senator Marjory LeBreton had a good way of summing up our support: we appeal to the Tim Hortons crowd, not the group that goes to
Starbucks. So much for polling, just ask Marjory!

Having sifted through the research, which as John Laschinger and
others have said has to drive everything – Harper and I were fascinated. The question in my mind was, can we get Dougie into a polling
booth? And the quick and short answer was: never – unless we give
him a good reason that personally affects his well-being. Then he
might go there. Statistics showed that Eunice and her male counter-
parts vote. However, our busy families may decide they are too busy
to vote and politics is irrelevant to them. Again, it was up to us to
make it relevant and ensure through boutique, targeted programs that
they had a reason to stop by a polling station on the way to or from
kids' activities or work and vote Conservative.

The many small, but important and relevant, tax credit or deduction programs that have populated Conservative platforms from 2006
to the present came from this analysis. There was nothing really new
about this approach of research driving policy; what was new was that
Conservatives were doing it.

As we moved into the fall, a lot of the fuzziness around the caucus
policy process started to sort itself out and conclusions could be put
right into the platform. After accountability, we needed to focus on
personal income tax: change the brackets, eliminate a bracket (still
under consideration), and lower the rates. The totality of the options
could not be put on a bumper sticker. But the new tax reduction plan
could be put on a sticker in any shop window: reduce the GST from 7
to 6 to 5 per cent. Given the propensity of ideas to leak, it is quite
amazing that this proposal did not get out before it was announced.
It may have been the best campaign announcement ever made by the
Conservative Party as it was unique and caught everyone by surprise.
Reducing the GST would appeal to and be supported by all voters in
our catchment area. It would also find opposition among professional economists. This appealed to Harper since he enjoyed having his
policies opposed by what he considered to be elites. On reflection I

wonder if this should have tipped me off to the battles that would loom in the future with scientists and others, especially in relation to environmental policies.

Childcare headlined a whole package of family-oriented policies. Demanding Better, the 2004 platform, had a tax reduction per child – but it didn't help during the year, only helped those who pay income tax, and didn't reach anyone at the bottom end of the income scale. Knowing how much Martin was willing to invest in institutional daycare, our plan was simply to give parents $100 per month for every child under six. Also $250 million was set aside to help businesses wishing to establish on-site daycare. This seemed like a great way to support what was already being done, and to encourage businesses to accommodate their employees and their families in this way.

Muttart had studied the 2004 general election in detail and the platform of Prime Minister John Howard of Australia,[3] especially as it related to folks like Dougie, or parents trying to make ends meet yet raise and provide for their families. With regard to Dougie, Muttart compiled all the recommendations that Howard had put into his platform to help trades people get ahead. He met with Mark Cameron and me to discuss how we could propose similar recommendations to encourage and support the trades. This required some research since we knew little about the trades and, therefore, little about our core support. We had gone quite far off track.

But we recovered and set out the following niche platform promises for Conservative supporters:

- $1,000 Apprentice Incentive Grant to help new apprentices cover the high cost of tools, etc.
- Apprenticeship Job Creation Tax Credit
- Tool Tax Deduction of up to $500 for existing tradespeople
- increase from $1,000 to $2,000 the pension income tax amount eligible for a federal tax credit
- exemption of the first $10,000 of student scholarship income from taxation
- $500 textbook tax credit for students or their parents
- $500 tax credit to parents for registration fees and membership for physical fitness activities for their children – later expanded in the 2008 platform to include the arts and music to help counter the negative effect of the arts expenditure cuts
- federal tax credit for those buying monthly transit passes

All of these spoke to the real concerns of the supporters Muttart had identified. Each one became a message event for a day.

The report from James Rajotte's caucus committee on industrial policy and regional development agencies was convincing, so the platform embraced regional development agencies and was silent on business subsidies, not calling for their elimination as we had done in 2004. In fact, in 2006, $500 million over five years would be used to support university-based research to spur innovation.

The platform also spoke to health care, one of Eunice's great concerns. We knew we had to address health care, and we wanted to deal with it in a positive, not a defensive, fashion. There was no need to put more money into the system, but one of the things Martin did not do was put fences or goals around the money given to the provinces. One of the biggest issues in health care for Eunice and others, especially with families, was the possibility of interminable waits for important procedures. This was to be addressed in the Patient Wait Times Guarantee to be worked out with the provinces to ensure that all Canadians receive essential medical treatment within clinically acceptable wait times.

The most significant difference between the 2004 and 2005–06 platforms was that the latter spoke directly to Quebec. This started with Josée Verner joining the OLO and took off when Lawrence Cannon was recruited during the summer of 2005. He had one monumental task – through the platform, make the Party relevant to Quebecers. He used Harper's fall 2004 speech on Belgian or open federalism as the foundation for the Quebec suite of policies. Cannon kept in close contact with the main platform group through many conversations and meetings since he did not want any of his recommendations to contradict the main document. He and I also worked to ensure that nothing in the main document would set off problems for him in Quebec, that the main platform was at least palatable to Quebecers, and that the Quebec platform would not cost the party seats or create a backlash outside Quebec. (In the 2008 campaign, insensitivity to Quebec cost many seats, and there did not seem to be any particular gain or upside in the rest of Canada. The rest of Canada knew full well that the Conservative Party was the "tough on crime" party, regardless of whether one was a young or older offender.)

When a party has not been in government for a while, there is a certain freedom that develops. The party is not hidebound by its recent record in government or by past decisions that limit future actions. So it was with the new Conservative Party and Quebec. Cannon, and those working with him, were free to consult where and when they wanted, exploring all the social and economic issues that had troubled Quebecers over the last thirteen years in dealing with the Liberal governments of Chrétien and Martin. Because of his wonderfully engaging personality, his experience as a politician in Quebec, and deep family roots in Quebec politics, Cannon had ready access to Premier Charest and former prime minister Mulroney as needed. His task was to build and put flesh on the ideas set out in Harper's Belgium federalism speech.

As recorded in William Johnson's biography *Stephen Harper and the Future of Canada*, Cannon felt good enough about where all of this was going to give an interview to Alec Castonguay of *Le Devoir*, published on 17 October 2005.[4] His theme was that in the next election, the Conservative Party would be able to speak to the Québécois and project ideas that would resonate. The main political enemy at that time was the Bloc, and our argument was that it could not deliver anything for Quebec. But the target could just as easily have been the Liberals, since we were about to stand many long-term Liberal policies on their collective heads.

The foundation for the Quebec platform was the Constitution Act, 1867 and the division of powers set out in sections 91 and 92, supplemented sections 93 and 133 that allow for Confessional Schools in Quebec and the recognition of French and English as languages of the courts and legislature of Quebec. In reading Harper's early writing and speeches on Canadian federalism, it is obvious that he believes in a strict interpretation of the heads of power sections of the constitution and not in the aberration that the federal spending power has become over the years. Therefore, it was only right that a francophone secretariat be established within the Department of Canadian Heritage. Language is integral to culture and should be recognized as such. The Government of Quebec would have a seat at UNESCO, similar to their participation in La Francophonie. The implementation of this became somewhat problematic, since the questions back from Quebec were, "Do we have voting power? Do we have a veto?" Our response that it would be similar to La Francophonie was not helpful; we discovered there are no votes there – everything is done by consensus. Where provincial jurisdiction was affected in the negotiation of international treaties, the Conservatives would allow some form of provincial participation in the development of the Canadian position. The Official Languages Act was to be supported, and the government would work with the provinces to enlarge the opportunities for Canadians to learn both official languages (this from Guy Lauzon's caucus policy committee).

On the fiscal front, the fiscal imbalance between the federal and provincial governments would be addressed in a permanent fashion. This was one instance where we were free to make economic commitments we believed in because, unlike the Grits, we were not hampered by a governing track record. It was astonishing to us that, in the spring and again in the fall of 2005, when threatened by the real possibility of an election, the Martin government would engage in profligate spending promises across the country. And then advance the argument that the Liberals had to be kept in power or the spending promises would evaporate. But in all of the promises made – amounting to billions of dollars – Martin refused to deal with the federal–provincial fiscal imbalance, claiming it did not exist, and since it did not exist, there was no reason to address it. His policies as finance minister had created the imbalance, but he was not going to reverse them. This left the field wide open for the Conservative Party.

On the issue of federal–provincial jurisdiction, the Conservatives were again able to strike out on their own, making the commitment that there would be no new shared-cost programs within provincial-territorial jurisdiction without the consent of a majority of provinces. If not agreed to by the majority, any province or territory that wished to proceed with its own program in the area would be compensated as long as it offered a similar program with similar accountability measures.

All of the above was packaged in Harper's 19 December speech in Quebec City.

With the various parts of the platform put to bed, the election scripting under the direction of Boessenkool was in a much better position to draft media releases and speeches to support the announcement of the day. Realizing that the platform was a fulsome document with many announceables, the campaign team decided early on to set up a daily early-morning announcement process. There were to be no theme weeks, and we would not dwell on the sponsorship scandal, except in answer to questions in daily media scrums. Even announcements of the various parts of the Federal Accountability Act did not dwell on Liberal shortcomings; they dealt with the Conservative solution, just pointing out that these solutions would ensure a sponsorship scandal would never happen again.

The only matter missing was the election.

On 1 November, Mr Justice Gomery[5] released his interim report on the sponsorship scandal. The issue now was whether to force an immediate election or wait for Martin to keep the promise he made in the spring to have an election early in the new year. If at all possible, the latter had to be prevented. While the Conservatives had decided not to campaign on Gomery, it was to play as background music throughout the entire writ period. If nothing else, the NDP, the Bloc, and the media would constantly remind Canadians of the sponsorship scandal. Martin was trying to stall into the new year, possibly after a federal budget, which would give the Martin Liberals the opportunity to distance themselves from the corrupt Chrétien Liberals – remembering that Martin claimed he was exonerated by the first Gomery report.

The decision was made to force an election now – but how and with which party or parties in support? We actually expected Martin and Finance Minister Ralph Goodale to cave in to Layton's demands once again – this time on health care, protecting against privatization, and funding – and defeat any non-confidence motion. As with the argument on fiscal imbalance, the Grits were showering money across the land, so why not a few billion to keep Jack onside? However, when Layton's demands were spurned by the Grits, he had to make up his mind about what to do. And would his decision be supported by the other opposition parties, from which he had broken in the spring? On Harper's part, he did not want to try to force an election again with only Bloc support.

On Sunday, 13 November 2005, Harper reached a deal with the other two opposition parties. Ian Brodie and I were in the office that day. I was working on platform issues, and Brodie was directing traffic coming from and going to Harper's Centre Block office. Duceppe was wary of Layton and trying to make another deal with him. Duceppe's position was clear. The Liberals were corrupt, and he believed he could increase his seat count and popular vote total in Quebec at their expense. His goal was to get more than 50 per cent of the popular vote in Quebec.

Layton, as usual, had his own scenario that he felt compelled to play out. As we moved through years of governing, it became more and more apparent that on major decisions, until his last campaign, Layton believed he could not make a decision on his own but had to consult with and obtain approval from either his caucus or the NDP Party machinery itself (we were never sure which). It always seemed that Layton was getting pressure or strong advice from somewhere and did not have the luxury of making his own decisions – so a simple, straightforward plan was never in the offing.

This time Layton wanted to put a motion into the House calling on the Liberals to prorogue Parliament in January and to hold an election in February 2006. He thought this was a reasonable compromise to a non-confidence motion now and the Martin promise to call an election sometime in the New Year. That motion, put on 21 November, was rejected by the Grits. On 24 November, Harper's motion "that this House has lost confidence in the government" was tabled. It was voted on and carried on 28 November, and the election writ was dropped on 29 November for an election day on 23 January 2006.

We had forced an election even though we were ten points behind the Grits in the polls. The theory was that if we waited for the government to pick the date to dissolve the House, it would, for sure, not be a date favourable to us. Martin might decide after Christmas to bring in an early goodie-laden budget and use the tactics he had used before – if Canadians don't vote for us, the goodies will be lost. It would also give him an opportunity to respond to the Gomery findings, put more rules into Reg Alcock's web of rules, and pronounce that this would never happen again. He would also claim that he personally had been exonerated: it wasn't me; it was those bad Chrétien Liberals. We were not willing to take the chance that Canadians might buy that explanation. We also had a campaign plan that, for the most part, would see us through to the end on a policy track. Sponsorship, accountability, and trust would be the background music as the campaign played on.

The group travelling with Harper was bolstered by the presence of Ian Brodie, chief of staff; William Stairs, director of communications; and Senator Marjory LeBreton, who had many roles, including dealing with the media and keeping the leader positive and sharp. One of LeBreton's oft-repeated sayings in relation to bad press is that "yesterday's newspapers are used to wrap today's fish" – in other words, don't let one bad story bother you; it will be quickly forgotten.

The war room had been set up with Tom Flanagan as editor-and-clearer-of-everything-in-chief and Jason Kenney ready at all times to do media. I found it interesting that Kenney's constituents thought his not being in the riding during the election was okay. He explained that his constituents took a larger view. Since he was a known commodity and they were going to vote for him anyway, he should be out there trying to ensure the election of as many Conservative candidates as possible. He said his constituents get mad at him when they see him in the riding during the writ period. In addition to Flanagan and Kenney, Keith Beardsley had moved his rapid-response crew, mainly Jason Plotz, over to the war room so that the database of everything ever said by a Grit, Bloc, or NDP MP, candidate, or major supporter on every hot issue was at the campaign's fingertips to counter whatever mud Martin stooped to sling. I moved over from my Centre Block office to join the research rapid-response group to provide support for the war room and, through it, to Harper's tour. Boessenkool and his team looked after the daily and nightly scripting of media releases and speeches. Muttart basically liaised between scripting and advertising, helping with both. And Doug Finley ran it all.

The first day of campaigning saw Harper in Quebec City, making the announcement of the creation of the Office of the Director of Public Prosecutions. British Columbia had a special prosecutor in relation to certain matters, the Law Reform Commission had recommended the creation of this position over the years, and we believed it was one of many suitable answers to deal with the sponsorship scandal. It would take all of the prosecutorial heavy lifting, post-Gomery, off the backs of already overworked attorney general staff and provincial Crown prosecutors. The media were obtuse about it, and MacKay disagreed with it as a usurpation of provincial jurisdiction. And then Harper, with no notice that I am aware of to anyone, mused openly at the end of his media availability regarding what he was going to do about the issue of same-sex marriage after 23 January. He would bring a motion in the House to see if the House wished to reopen this issue. If the vote was in the negative, that would be the end of the matter. While it took us by surprise, it was a successful move to take that social conservative issue right off the table. No one thought the Conservative Party would form a majority government, so this would work as a method of keeping the existing same-sex legislation intact.

The campaign went on to the Maritimes then back to Ontario for the GST announcement. Surprisingly, it still had not leaked. The tax announcement – which everyone predicted would be, when made, a repeat of our 2004 platform, or a variation thereof – was unexpected. It was being made by a leader who was an economist, and it was so bold and different that it gave commentators pause. For our team, the reaction made us believe we could actually pull off a win here. With the childcare announcement of $100 per month per child under six years old, it made Canadians who were watching and listening, as well as the media, pay attention, and begin to realize that this was not going to be a repeat of 2004. This was an entirely new approach led by a very engaged Stephen Harper and his team, both on the road and back in Ottawa.

We knew from the start that the campaign was not going to be easy. We stumbled a bit on day one and some of our new communication equipment didn't work at the outset, but we were off to a good start. What did work well was the roll-out strategy and its implementation. The numerous conference calls from early morning to late in the evening kept communications flowing and mistakes to a minimum. The debates on these calls as to what to do and when to do it were always lively and, in retrospect, probably even entertaining – it just didn't seem so at the time. Harper would always do an announcement early in the morning, so that would give us an opportunity between 10 and 11a.m. to reconnect with him daily to determine how our announcement went and to discuss what our approach should be to whatever Martin was going to do. Usually we were all in agreement as to how Harper or Kenney or both should respond. However, on one particular morning we had been tipped off that Martin was going to make an announcement on gun crime. Not only was he going to make an announcement right in our wheelhouse but also he was going to announce a ban on handguns. Harper was anxious to get out in front of this because it was a bogus announcement, like so much of what Martin did and said. Handguns had been banned in Canada for decades. I convinced Harper that our information must be incorrect, that this must be a serious announcement that merited study and reflection before we ran out and commented. Much to my disappointment and with his usual great flourish, Martin announced that he would solve gun violence by placing a ban on handguns. I stopped making suggestions for a couple of days.

The main issue we faced prior to the leaders' debates in December was trying to figure out what the Liberal campaign was all about. Other than Buzz Hargrove embracing Paul Martin at the end of week one, a rehash of the 2004 childcare announcement, which would take the funding out another five years, and the mythical handgun announcement, there was not much in the way of policy coming back at us.

Our war room in the early going was having fun. While Martin and Dion were waxing on about climate change at the international climate change meeting in Montreal, we were putting out a reality check on the plane Martin was using – a fuel-guzzling Boeing 727. The biggest Martin gift in the early part of the campaign was the "beer and popcorn" statement made by Scott Reid, Martin's director of communications, and confirmed by Liberal commentator John Duffy, in reference to where Liberals thought parents would spend the Conservative's promised childcare allowance. The phrase "don't give people twenty-five bucks a week to blow on beer and popcorn" signalled the major difference in the approach of the two parties to virtually everything in the campaign. The Liberals knew best how Canadians should raise their children – in government-run daycare centres. Anything other than that, and parents would waste the money. The same with taxes – there was a stark contrast between an unrecognizable reduction in personal income tax and the lowering of the GST, which affected virtually every purchaser and was of great benefit to those at the lower end of the economic spectrum because it was the only tax they paid, and they would still get the rebate.

The ability to pivot off Liberal mistakes and use the intelligence gathered by Beardsley and his group is a tribute to Flanagan and Kenney. It's great to have the information in a database to counter the attacks or to jump on an opponent's misstatements, but the real genius is in knowing how and when to use it.

The next big event was the debates scheduled for 15–16 December in Vancouver.[6] We scaled back the debate prep considerably from what we did in 2004, but for the most part, we did take Harper off the road from the 14th through to the 16th. Our debate prep team joined the leader's tour in Vancouver and went to work on preparation for the French debate, which was scheduled for the evening of the 15th. In this debate, as in 2004 and, in fact, in all the debates, decisions are made in advance as to the broad subject areas. My job was to again work with Mike Coates to ensure that we had a large stockpile of questions on all of the areas in order to test knowledge and syntax in French. We also would spend a great deal of time on the French names and acronyms for government programs and agencies.

My primary task in all of the debates in which I participated was to put together the leader's briefing binder, which in most cases would become the binder he took into the debate with him to jog his memory. It would also contain the leader's opening and closing statements. The process for putting the binder together became a bit of a science, and we got better at it as we went along. A coloured tab separated information on each major debate subject, with that subject heading written on both sides of the tab, so it could be identified when the binder was lying open on the podium. On each subject and on each subset of each subject, the Conservative Party position, either from the policy book or from the platform, was placed on the right-hand side of the binder with the policies of the government, the NDP, and the Bloc on the facing page. The idea was that, at a glance, while others were debating or making opening statements, the leader could refresh his memory and anticipate what others might say. As would be expected, the opening statement was at the front, and the closing statement was the last section of the binder.

Doing debate prep is a lot like coaching a major league athlete. You want to ensure he doesn't get too tired, maintains his confidence, and masters all the intricacies of the subject matter. Sometimes this is harder to accomplish in French because of the jargon and pronunciation; it can never look like the leader is translating from English to French in his head before the words come out of his mouth.

A new twist in the 2005–06 debates were the questions on videotape from selected Canadians. If the leader, for whatever reason, doesn't understand what the questioner is trying to get at, there is no opportunity for clarification. Nothing like some added stress to an already stressful couple of days. We hit on a format for answering – probably not unique, but it worked for Harper. First, thank the questioner by name for the question. Second, show empathy with the issue brought out by the question; third, demonstrate some knowledge about the issue; and finally, offer the solution. If time permits, thank the questioner by name. The leader was also to use the questioner's name as often as possible.

Martin had a couple of good days preceding the debates. At the Climate Change Conference, he took some uncalled-for shots at the United States for doing nothing to diminish GHGs, which brought about a rebuke from US Ambassador David Wilkins, never one to back away from a fight or disagreement. Then Martin took another shot at the Americans in a lumberyard in Richmond, B.C. He was assuring Canadians that the United States was not going to dictate policy to him. What he should have been explaining was how the soft-wood lumber dispute between the two countries had spiralled down-wards and out of control under the Grits, and perhaps how he was going to resolve it.

And then the Liberals did what they always do before a debate: they find something obscure, and embarrassing, done by the Conservative Party or its leader, jump on it, and make the most of it to throw us off our preparation schedule. In Vancouver, it was a speech that Harper had given in 1997, when he was vice-president of the National Citi-zens Coalition. He referred to Canada as a "Northern European Wel-fare State in the worst sense of the term." He also told the American Conservative gathering, "Your country, and particularly your conserv-ative movement, is a light and inspiration to us in this country and across the world." It was helpful to know to expect something, so we were not surprised. I believe that, from beginning to end, we lost less than an hour of prep time over this. (I like to think the celebration of my birthday, near the end of the prep time, was more disruptive.) In response to the Liberals' attempted destabilizer, we had our own de-stabilizer in Senator LeBreton. By the time she was done explaining – the statement had been out there for a while; Stronach had tried to use it during the leadership contest; it was old news – wrap fish in it!; it did not represent the leader's views now; the Liberals should be ashamed of themselves – it got them nowhere.

In the English debate, Martin rather curiously went after Duceppe, calling him out for trying to destroy Canada. If he had really wanted to score points against Duceppe in Quebec, he would have raised this in the previous evening's French debate. But, of course, what he was trying to do – what Liberals consistently try to do – is paint them-selves as the only party that can stop the separatists, the only party that can save Canada. This was a direct appeal to the rest of Canada, since Martin and the Liberals knew they were going down in Quebec. This might have rallied a few Quebec federalists to the Liberal cause, but even that would soon begin to change.

The debates in Vancouver were pretty much inconsequential. They were too early in the writ period to have any lasting effect on voters' intentions. Coates and I believed Harper had done well in both the English and French debates. Our goals for the debates may have been different from those of the other leaders, but we believed Harper had to come across as knowledgeable, understanding of the issues, empathetic with the issues to be discussed, in control, polite, with an inner strength that one would expect from a leader. We did not want him shouting, bullying, trying to hog the debate time, being rude or disrespectful. It was only a year and a half since the Liberals' successful attacks at the end of the 2004 campaign that portrayed Harper as a really scary guy who would take Canada into the dark, as the leader of the Barbarians getting close to the gate. The last thing we wanted was for his debate performance to give credence in any way to these attacks.

From our point of view, Harper either did well or won. On a marking scale, we would have said, as we did in 2004, he surpassed our expectations. As stated, unless there was a colossal error by one of the leaders, this debate would not play a role in deciding the final outcome. It was too early in the writ period, and even if something needed to be corrected, the parties, including the Conservatives, had six weeks to do so.

But the fallout from the debate worked to our advantage. Martin's over-the-top performance in attacking Duceppe in the English debate resulted in Martin, in the usual media debrief that follows these events, challenging Duceppe to debate him anywhere, anytime. As William Johnson writes sarcastically, "No Mr Dithers he"! What Martin, of course, didn't expect was that Duceppe would accept the challenge, arrange TV time, and for the first few days, keep letting Martin know where he was going to be so Martin could find him and debate with him. Nothing happened, but after his successful Chamber of Commerce speech on 19 December in Quebec City, Harper said he would pick up the challenge and debate Duceppe.

The turning point after the Vancouver debates was Harper's 19 December speech in Quebec City. It built upon his debate performance, especially in the French debate, which gave him the confidence to fly to Quebec City and begin to turn the election on its head in Quebec and elsewhere. The words and the content of that speech were carefully planned. Looking back, it began being drafted shortly after the 2004 election, when Harper decided to put all the people who had varying opinions on bilingualism in the same room – over and over again, under the watchful eye of Guy Lauzon as chair of the caucus committee – until they had worked through all of their issues and decided on recommendations that supported the Official Languages Act and bilingualism. It also began with the naming of Josée

Verner as a member of shadow cabinet, representing the views of Quebec. And it moved along with an attempt to define a new relationship between the federal government and Quebec in a speech in the fall of 2004 that stressed open federalism. It picked up steam with the addition of Lawrence Cannon as deputy chief of staff and the beginning of the development of a Conservative platform for Quebec, drafted by Quebecers under Harper's leadership.

The purpose of the speech was to reintroduce Harper to Quebecers, emphasizing who he was – a family man who spent his early and teen years in Toronto, learned to speak French, moved with his parents to Calgary, became involved in politics, and cared deeply about the essential place of Quebec in the Canadian federation. The speech reflected the Quebec platform, and while written by Paul Terrien, it was developed under the watchful eye of Lawrence Cannon and Benoit Pelletier, Charest's minister of intergovernmental affairs. The speech hit on all major points that needed to be made, and then some:

1 Allow Quebec to play a role at UNESCO, as it did at La Francophonie.
2 Address the fiscal imbalance.
3 Define open federalism further, as closer to asymmetrical federalism.
4 Discontinue use of the federal spending power in areas of provincial jurisdiction without the consent of a majority of provinces, and with the possibility of a province opting out if it had a similar program and still being compensated.
5 "Quebec is the heart of Canada, and the French language an undeniable part of the identity of all Canadians"[7] – while not part of the platform rollout, this crucially important reference was part of the speech.

While the speech hit every note, it was the reaction to it that really cemented Harper and the Conservatives in the minds of Quebecers. Martin denounced it on two counts: there was no fiscal imbalance to be rectified – he had been finance minister and he knew better; and Canada would only speak with one voice at international meetings or on international bodies. This latter statement contradicted a position he himself had held in 2004. There was no reason for Martin to take either position. He could have killed the effect of the speech by simply saying that he thanked Harper for raising these points and that when his government was re-elected he would address them. But he didn't, and instead continued to quarrel with Duceppe, to the point where Harper, with his new-found Quebec confidence, offered to debate Duceppe. Duceppe declined. He only wanted the prime minister, and he wasn't about to give Harper any further platform time in Quebec to explain his policies. He could probably see the ground shifting ever so slightly away from him and the Liberals.

Following the speech, Harper took a shot at Martin for focusing on separatism and accused him of undermining Jean Charest, "the most federalist Premier in my lifetime," and hoping for a PQ victory in the next provincial election. This was calling Martin's game for what it was: setting up a straw man that only he and he alone could knock down. Martin took the usual offence, but this time the response from Harper was not what Martin was expecting. As detailed by L. Ian Mac-Donald, Harper said, "I don't go around asking for apologies, I can take a punch." I remember it more along the lines of Harper saying about Martin: "Can't you take a punch?"[8]

The Quebec City speech made an impact not only on those in the audience but also among the Quebec media. The Harper campaign unexpectedly had something to say to Quebec, and the media was ready to listen. As L. Ian MacDonald pointed out, one of them was iconic Radio-Canada anchor Bernard Delorme, who during a half-hour interview on 12 January gave Harper the opportunity to restate his message to Quebecers via one of Quebec's most respected political commentators.[9]

Ontario was also important in the mix that went into the 2005–06 campaign since that is where we really hoped to pick up seats. A factor that could hurt would be Premier McGuinty joining forces on the campaign trail with Martin. We had an interesting relationship with McGuinty while we were in opposition. From time to time he would come to Ottawa, and Martin would either be too busy to see him or have to postpone the meeting to a later hour, so McGuinty would meet with Harper and senior staff. This led to exchanges between Harper and McGuinty on the frustrations of dealing with Martin. During the campaign, there was a conversation between Harper and McGuinty wherein Harper agreed to address some of McGuinty's concerns over infrastructure funding should the Conservatives form government. While McGuinty wasn't silent during the campaign, these discussions led him to take a more neutral position.

The next major Harper announcement came in Winnipeg on 22 December. It was a military strategy for the North. Gordon O'Connor and his office, led by Aaron Gairdner, put together the armed forces part of the platform, in which the North figured prominently. Again, it was in stark contrast to Martin and the Liberals who had dined out on soft power for the last thirteen years. Conservatives would not only stand up to countries that would use and abuse our Northwest Passage without permission but also be able to back up their statements with real hard power. In Harper's announcement that day he stated: "You don't defend national sovereignty with flags, cheap election rhetoric and advertising campaigns. You need forces on the ground, ships in the sea, and proper surveillance. That will be the Conservative approach."[10]

As Christmas approached, the decision was made to keep campaigning to the greatest extent possible. We did not believe Martin would "down tools" through some phony holiday truce, so why be fooled. As it turned out, Martin's campaign was nowhere during Christmas, but by continuing on in small localities in British Columbia, with local media coverage, we kept the dream of winning alive and the team sharp.

During what was supposed to be the Christmas-break period, three incidents occurred that, when taken together, had a profound effect on the rest of the campaign. As Canadians sat down to Christmas dinner, the Conservatives still trailed the Liberals by 6 per cent nationally. We had come up, but not significantly, given the time and energy that had been put into the campaign.

Two of the incidents occurred on Boxing Day. Mike Klander, executive vice-president of the Ontario wing of the federal Liberal Party, resigned his position over offensive comments he had put on his blog about Jack Layton and his wife, Olivia Chow. Layton was described as an "asshole," and his wife was compared to a Chow Chow dog. This echoed the "beer and popcorn" attitude displayed earlier in December in response to our childcare announcement. It demonstrated a Liberal arrogance about their positions on issues and how they saw themselves. Later that day, the shooting death of Jane Creba, while she was out shopping on Yonge Street in Toronto, startled the nation. It was the most everyday of things to do on that day, and she died, the victim of a stray bullet in a gang war. If this could happen in Toronto, it could happen anywhere in Canada. The reactions of Martin and Harper were a study in contrasts.

Given its geographic size and population diversity, Canada is a remarkably safe country. Statistics published annually seem to illustrate a decline in the number of violent crimes. Arguments ensue among criminologists, police, politicians, and others about what these numbers really mean. For quite some time now, those on the left of the political spectrum have interpreted these numbers to show a more peaceful, law-abiding society, in no need of a "tough on crime" agenda. Those on the right of that same spectrum believe that violent crimes, especially in domestic situations, are very much under-reported. Also, they believe that many violent crimes are committed by serial offenders out on bail, on parole, or subsequent to their having secured a pardon for previous convictions. The right believes there is a place for rehabilitation in prison, but the overall view is that the Canadian judicial and legal system has for too long been soft on crime.

The Jane Creba murder occurred as this debate raged in the federal election campaign. Martin's was the knee-jerk reaction, representing the views of the political left. It would seem that when he spoke, he actually had not thought through his words and how irrelevant they would seem. Tom Flanagan says it was almost like Martin was sympathizing with the killers. "I think more than anything else, they [the killers] demonstrate what are in fact the consequences of exclusion. I was in Toronto not long ago and met with a number of members of communities in the Jane and Finch area ... and the young people talked to me about the void in their lives, and what hopelessness and exclusion can bring."[11]

Contrast this with the views expressed by Harper. He prefaced his remarks by saying that this was not the Toronto he knew or the Toronto he had grown up in. He then moved into his familiar critique of the criminal justice system, his words being more relevant than ever before. "There is nothing else you can do to deal with crime other than to make sure people who commit crimes are severely dealt with, and that we don't run a revolving door justice system. The problem is, this is the first government in our history that seems unable to enforce our gun laws, and I think obviously this is just the consequence of 12 years of lax criminal justice law enforcement."[12]

The debate was joined. Two very different approaches and this terrible incident focussed the spotlight on one area where the Conservative Party has a lot of credibility.

But we had to wait a couple more days for delivery of the best, late-Christmas present Harper has ever received. The NDP announced that one of their members, Libby Davies, had received a letter from the RCMP telling her that, as a result of her letter reporting what she believed to be some shady dealing around the 23 November announcement by the Liberals regarding the tax treatment of income trusts, the RCMP were launching a criminal investigation. This letter, which was unanticipated and came out of nowhere, solidly reinforced the background narrative that the Liberals were corrupt. Martin could no longer make the argument that scandals belonged to those other Chrétien Liberals and that the new Martin Liberals were squeaky-clean.

One question that has been asked many times but never answered is how could such a letter be written and sent out during an election campaign? Surely the RCMP would have known that it would become public and influence people's views on the trustworthiness of the various participants in this election. What had the Liberals done to the RCMP that we didn't know about that could result in this type of obvious retaliation?

There is no doubt that the release of this letter from the RCMP was a turning point in the campaign. Polling before and after the Christmas break was remarkably different. The Creba murder and the income trust revelations had had their effect. No one will ever know, but it is my firm view that the RCMP investigation on its own would not have been enough to turn the tide in favour of the Conservatives. The methodical, workmanlike campaign of the Conservatives from the very beginning of the election laid the foundation for this turnaround. As Marjory LeBreton said near the end of the 2008 campaign, which finished over Thanksgiving weekend, and Doug Finley said in 2005: when Canadians sit down to their holiday dinners with their families, they will discuss politics and the election, and they will talk about getting out and supporting Stephen Harper.

While all of this was going on, a decision was made to group and rank the policies already announced. This Conservative government would be a government of priorities, but not where everything was a priority – just five priorities. People can remember five priorities, especially if they are relevant to how they live their lives. It also provided a nice contrast to Martin, whom *The Economist* characterized as "Mr Dithers" for his failure to make decisions – and one could add failure to set priorities and address them.

So the five priorities – Accountability Act, GST reduction, childcare allowance, crackdown on violent crime, and patient wait times guarantee – were packaged together and re-launched at a rally on 2 January in Ottawa. The only tough thing to explain was whether anything else was a priority. This would be a constant question for the rest of the campaign. The answer was that everything else we had committed to, we would do, but these we would tackle first. It was also designed so that four out of the five priorities were totally within the jurisdiction of the federal government to implement. So we could say – although I don't believe anyone ever did – that all of these could be significantly addressed in the first one hundred days of a Conservative government. While the armed forces were important, implementation of that platform commitment would take time. In retrospect, we didn't realize how much time!

On the way to Montreal in January to begin debate prep for the second round of debates, we read a *Globe and Mail* report on another potential corruption story. Apparently, the Department of Canadian Heritage had asked the RCMP to investigate a $4.8 million grant made to Option Canada, a federalist group active in the 1995 referendum. Then, on the morning of the 9 January English debate, came the ultimate destabilizer for the Martin campaign, although we did not arrange for it. Two Quebec journalists held a press conference to release their book *Les Secrets d'Option Canada*. This would give Duceppe something to yell at Martin about, and Martin's debate prep team would be taking time away from what they were supposed to be doing in order to come up with answers. For us, the binder was pretty much the same as the one Harper had in Vancouver, with a few additions.

As I have said before, the main task in debate prep is to anticipate every question, every argument – but sometimes you just get lucky. On 21 December 2005, the Supreme Court of Canada announced a new definition of public indecency as it overturned the conviction of Montreal resident Jean-Paul Labaye,[13] who had been charged with keeping a common bawdy house. We did not agree with the decision. Harper called me while I was out Christmas shopping and asked whether this would be the opportune time to talk about invoking the "notwithstanding" clause of the Constitution Act, 1982. I told him I would get back to him on it. We agreed we should involve our justice critic, Vic Toews, in this discussion. So on Christmas Eve 2005, the three of us were on a conference call to discuss the case and the use of the notwithstanding clause. We all agreed that the decision on the subject matter was wrong, but the Court was simply interpreting the Criminal Code provision and had not invoked the Charter in the decision, so there was no opportunity to invoke the notwithstanding clause to cure the decision. Clause 33 of the Charter of Rights and Freedoms, the notwithstanding clause, only applies to certain sections of the Charter and did not apply here at all. As good as we thought our logic was, it wouldn't work in this case. Fast-forward a couple of weeks to 9 January in Montreal. When we finished debate prep, I sat with Harper for a few minutes and discussed the origins of the notwithstanding clause, how essential it had been to the Charter compromise, and while it might be nice to broaden its application, that would fundamentally affect the original compromise that led to the agreement that gave birth to the Charter. We had no idea what Martin was going to do that night, but Harper had been thoroughly briefed on this clause just before game time.

At his first opportunity in the debate, Martin enthusiastically said he would revisit Section 33 of the Charter and extricate from it the federal use of the notwithstanding clause, and dared the other participants to disagree. What he received from Harper was a very calm, logical set of reasons as to how the clause came about, why it was crucial to the Charter compromise, and no, he would not support Martin's argument on this. What Martin didn't know at the time was that Anne McLellan, his deputy prime minister and former dean of law at the University of Alberta, had no knowledge that he was going to do this, and disagreed. It is noteworthy that shortly after the Montreal debates, the Liberals stopped mentioning their notwithstanding clause promise, and it did not appear in their platform.

All of the leaders did well in the English debate, and Harper was able to come across as we always wanted him to: knowledgeable, calm, and – now an added phrase – prime ministerial, above the fray. In our debrief with Harper after the debate, we all agreed it had gone as well or better than anticipated. We knew the next night's debate would be tougher.

The day of the French debate, 10 January, was also the day of the Liberal gift of the over-the-top negative ads. Through the benefits of modern technology, the ads were on the Liberal website the day before they would be shown on national TV. But for that, we would never have seen them prior to the debate. All but one was the kind of negative ad one would expect: too close to Bush, too much like Mike Harris, and social conservative issues. But then there was the one ad – about Harper putting troops in the streets. It had briefly seen the light of day and then disappeared. But it was out long enough. Media outlets played the "troops in the streets" ad continually, demonstrating how low and desperate the Liberal campaign really was. We understood that the Grits never intended to use the ad, but there it was. We made sure Harper saw it before he went over to the studio for the debate.

The preparation went as it always does on French debate prep day – long and somewhat testy, but productive. We spent an inordinate amount of time on the opening and closing statements since this would be the last opportunity to talk directly to the Quebec audience on television in the campaign. As each version changed, I would insert it in the debate binder. After a whole day of questions in French and being continuously admonished for his pronunciation and syntax, Harper decided he had had enough and thought a bath and a rest would be more productive. However, he wanted to take the debate binder with him, and I handed it over. He flipped to the opening statement, only to discover that I had inserted the wrong version. The binder came flying back (yes, he did throw it at me, and what a mess – all the pages came out!), the right version was inserted, and we were back on schedule. It should also be noted that Jason Kenney played an integral part in the debate prep in Montreal. When we did the mock debate, Kenney played the role of Martin. He did it so well that it almost threw Harper off his game – and led Kenney to wonder later if his exclusion from the first Harper Cabinet was a result of this performance.

The French debate was really helpful for Harper in Quebec, again establishing his credentials and the reasons for Quebecers to vote Conservative. The other theme playing out was the context of the attack ads and whether Martin had approved them. From the start of the campaign, we had made it clear that at some point the Grits were going to go negative. We had prepared the ground as best we could, but this was beyond what we anticipated.

The last part of this string of good luck was the release of the Liberal platform, set for 11 January, the day after the debates. This was going to be another game changer for them. What they didn't know was that Finley had a mole inside the Liberal operation. He had told me a few days before we went to Montreal that he would be receiving the Liberal platform before its release, and we would need to get together a group of eager young researchers to pull it apart and analyze it. He also spoke to me about ensuring his source would have employment, post-election. I told him I saw no difficulty with that, but I am not sure what happened with that person.

Finley received the Liberal platform as promised, and I assembled a research team on the evening of 10 January to go through it. There was nothing there. It was a regurgitation of their pre-writ spending announcements, the main campaign promises to date save one (the notwithstanding clause), and a lot of white space with catchy phrases about how great Canada was and how lucky Canadians were to have had a Liberal government for these many years. And if Canadians were grateful and smart, they would elect a Paul Martin government and all would be well for the future. It was a real letdown and disappointment. Finley made sure the platform was distributed widely to media and other interested folks before dawn, and we provided the leader's tour with our analysis, such as it was.

With election day ten days away, the Conservative platform was to be released on Friday, 13 January. This was supposed to be a slam dunk. We had announced most of it; the launch was just putting it all together along with our financial tables. Unlike 2004, we had gone to great trouble and expense to have Paul Darby, chief economist at the Conference Board of Canada, go through every part of our program and certify that our numerical calculations and assumptions were correct. We had a letter dated 22 December from Darby to Stephen Harper describing our financial program and then stating: "In summary we found that the Conservative Party's economic platform is affordable in each from 2005–06 to 2010–11. In each year there is enough fiscal room to pay down at least three billion dollars in debt as in the fiscal plan."[14] The letter was attached to the platform when it was released.

The day started badly. I received an early morning phone call from Harper about a part of the platform that he had requested to be changed, which had been changed – and then changed back to the original statements. The rest of the morning got worse, since no one giving the background briefing to the media could give a detailed, yet simple answer to questions on the financial part of the platform.

Robert Fife of CTV News was the most critical. He has a penchant for the negative phrase like few others and a way of describing his take on things in words everyone understands and remembers. He called the costing of our platform "voodoo economics"; ten months later he would describe our Clean Air Act as "dead on arrival." Those phrases stick like glue. To this day, I am not sure how she did it, but Senator LeBreton took Fife aside after the media briefing, went through all the costing information with him, and after an hour, he was describing it all as "just a glitch."

Having gotten through the launch, we thought we were going to be all right. On the following Sunday, 15 January, a CP wire story by Dennis Bueckert came out claiming that Darby had backed away from his endorsement of our platform. There had been no costing for addressing the fiscal imbalance or for implementing the patient wait time guarantee. As we were going to run a surplus of $22 billion over five years, we didn't this was necessary. Also, if it was a concern, he should have addressed it with us before the platform was released. And what was Darby doing talking to the media and, as we later found out, doing an interview with CBC Newsworld on the day we launched the platform? We got Jim Frank to deal with Darby. Jim Frank's office was next to mine in the Wellington Building and Jim approached me, suggesting he talk to the media. This idea was met with a resounding "NO." As Tom Flanagan explained, we never did get completely on top of this, and had to issue our own statement about Darby's re-conversion.[15] It all felt eerily like 2004 all over again.

Then Buzz Hargrove helped us by endorsing the Bloc in Quebec as the only way to stop Harper. Having endorsed Martin at the beginning of the campaign, this took the heat off us, as Martin had to clarify the views of his new-found, sometimes-separatist-sympathizer friend.

Heading into the last week of the campaign, we had completed the policy rollout. I moved from the Wellington Building over to the war room for what was supposed to be the week when we closed the deal with Canadians. I had also started to receive briefing material from Derek Burney, head of our transition team. I had successfully persuaded Brodie that since I knew Burney and the platform, I could be useful as we fashioned mandate letters for ministers. I also had some experience working on previous transition teams, although, unfortunately, on none that ended up winning the big prize: twice for

Charest, in 1993 under Bob de Cotret and in 1997 under Senator Norman Atkins; and helping with various chores when Joe Clark became
PC Party leader in 1998.

It was great to be part of the war room in that final week – lots of
familiar faces and Finley made sure everyone was well fed from the
moment they arrived until the end of the day. He was the sparkplug
in any campaign he worked on. He knew the strengths and weaknesses of all of those involved, from the leader, through the war room
team, to the candidates. He perfected the concept of hiding candidates
whose views ran contrary to those expressed in the platform. You always knew where you stood with him; there was no mincing of
words. He also did not suffer fools, and that led to his fights with Elections Canada and anyone who questioned how he dealt with election
financing laws. Doug was a fighter, in elections and in life against the
disease that ultimately took his life. If he had a fault, it was his eternal
optimism, always thinking we would do better than we did in elections. His tenaciousness and his wit will be missed by all who had the
privilege of working with him.

Having gotten over the platform costing issue, we were faced with
another familiar problem: with the platform and the five priorities
out there, we had basically run out of new material for the leader, and
the media still had to be fed. On Tuesday, 17 January, trying to miti-
gate concern about electing a Conservative government, and perhaps
a majority Conservative government, Harper reminded Canadians
that there would still be many parts and members of the system in
place that had been appointed or created by the Liberals. The senior
ranks of the public service, the Senate, and the judiciary were all populated by Liberal appointees put in place over the previous thirteen
years. It was a good US division of powers, checks, and balances lecture. The Grits pounced on this, saying that Harper had no respect for
the independence of the public service or the judiciary. He responded
on Wednesday by further clarifying his remarks, but that just seemed
to keep the ball in the air. Later that day, Harper got into a bit of a
dust-up with Kevin Newman during an interview on the abortion
issue, but he stuck to the wording in the platform and got through
that one.

On Thursday evening, senior folks in the war room had a heated
phone conversation with Harper. We could see our support slipping
away, and we had to get back on message. We tried to get the point
across to him that we had a great platform, we had five priorities, and

we had it all costed – so let's just get on with this thing and nail it, as we only had three days to go. Harper was upset and responded that he had been left all alone out there with nothing to say, and that we had no appreciation of his position out among the people and the media with us not giving him anything to say. Eventually we agreed to get back on the main message. After the call was over, I said to the group that I thought it went well. "How so?" asked Jason Kenney. "As long as he's yelling at us, he isn't yelling at anybody else, and that is a good thing," I replied.

Also during the last few days of the campaign, when it started to look quite likely that the Conservatives would form a government, Jim Prentice received a call from Phil Fontaine, the national chief of the Assembly of First Nations (AFN), requesting a meeting. Prentice called me, and we thought there would be no harm in this. During the campaign, Patrick Brazeau's group, the Congress of Aboriginal Peoples, representing mainly off-reserve Indians, had endorsed our platform, and we believed Fontaine was simply trying to let us know that he was out there as well. We met in a boardroom at the Ottawa airport as both Fontaine and Prentice were stopping in Ottawa between flights. Fontaine brought his chief of staff, Bob Watts, with him. The meeting was friendly, and I believe Fontaine's aim to brief us on where the Assembly's agenda stood on a number of matters.

The first issue he touched on was the Kelowna Accord negotiated by Martin just before the government fell. Prentice had been at the meeting. We told Fontaine it was a great agreement in theory, but there was no money set aside to implement it. However, we agreed with all of its laudable goals, so if we formed a government, we would be looking at specific actions on housing, infrastructure, health care, clean drinking water, and education. Fontaine raised the residential schools settlement. He told us that he believed it had been to Cabinet and had been approved. Prentice explained that we don't get copies of Cabinet minutes and that we would deal with this when we knew its status. Fontaine then briefed us, in general terms, on the plight of his people and the need for government support. He also brought up funding of the AFN itself and the need for this to be increased. All in all, it was a pleasant and informative meeting. We all agreed to work together should Canadians elect a Conservative government.

On 23 January 2006 at about 10 p.m., when Paul Martin conceded and said he was stepping down, I realized I really would be going to meet Derek Burney and the others at 10 a.m. at the Wellington Street entrance to the Langevin Block to begin the transition from opposition to government. It was an incredibly proud moment, seeing the success of something to which I had contributed. No one at that point could envisage what we were beginning, how long it would last, or how it would turn out. We did know, as Ian Brodie expressed many times, that it is not often Conservatives have the privilege of forming government, so we should make the most of this opportunity.

Minority First Mandate:
A Cabinet Made with Green Timber

Canadians delivered a mixed-message verdict on 23 January 2006. The Conservatives had been given the most seats of any political party, but they would govern with a thin minority and on a short leash back to the voter. The Liberals were reduced to opposition. With Martin's resignation and an interim leader, there might be some breathing space for this young government. But as we all knew, strange things can happen in Canadian politics – none stranger than the resurrection of Pierre Trudeau in 1979–80 to fight yet another election and defeat the Joe Clark–led PC Party. So nothing is a sure thing. Also Bill Graham, the Liberal interim leader, was an entirely decent man, had long Cabinet experience, and was an able parliamentarian. So a "comeback" by the Grits or a coalition forming on the heels of a government defeat was never far from the minds of those setting up the Cabinet and trying to devise a parliamentary strategy.

It was vitally important in the mind of the new prime minister that he be seen as governing. Everything was to move along quickly. There was precious little time between 24 January at 10 a.m., when the Harper transition team led by Derek Burney began to settle in, and 6 February, when the prime minister wanted to present his Cabinet to the people of Canada. One other note to illustrate this mindset: the National Capital Commission, which looks after official residences, wanted the Harpers to delay their move into 24 Sussex Drive until renovations were carried out. The Martins had found the official residence cold and drafty. Harper's response was that the Martins were a lot older than his family, and if it got cold, his family would wear sweaters. The move from Stornoway to 24 Sussex was on. In all respects, it was necessary that the new government be seen as governing, even in the location of the prime minister's home base.

The Victory. Forming the government was the culmination of years of work for Stephen Harper and the team, and Harper's swearing-in as prime minister a historic moment for Conservatives. (Courtesy of Julie Oliver/*Ottawa Citizen*. Reprinted by permission)

The transition team was small in number, but long on experience. The tasks were divided into three groups: Cabinet making, drafting of mandate letters for ministers, and staffing ministers' offices. The team also had a communications person on board so that all decisions could be packaged and given to the media in a professional manner. Ian Brodie had already been asked to stay in his position as chief of staff, so while not an official member of the team, he was involved in the Cabinet personnel discussions and kept a watchful eye over all aspects of our work.

We had been on the job one full day in the east end of the fourth floor of the Langevin Block. The tables had been taken out of the lunchroom, and it was now equipped with computers and cubicle separators. As my youngest daughter, Emily, so aptly described it, "All that work and you get to sit beside the Coke machine." At the end of day one, Burney came and told me he was supposed to meet Harper in his office in the OLO around 6 p.m., upon his return from Calgary.

The problem was that Burney had no idea where that was and had no pass to get into the Centre Block. So over we went, to be confronted by the reality that becomes the routine in working for the prime minister: the constant presence of the RCMP. Arriving on the fourth floor and my key still able to open the main door, we walked in on a number of RCMP officers doing a sweep of the offices and two already stationed outside Harper's office in the OLO. We watched the motorcade come onto the Hill and were both beaming as, through the darkness, we watched the red lights of the police cars flash across the snow-covered roadways. As Derek said at the time, "This is a new reality." The question was, were we ready for it?

After greeting Harper, I left to go back over to Langevin, and Burney and the prime minister got down to the business of Cabinet making. There was a general realization that this group of elected Conservatives was short on Cabinet experience, and especially short on federal Cabinet experience. Not that prior Cabinet experience is a necessary qualifier, but it helps. Cabinet making in the Conservative minority government of Stephen Harper was no different than in any other government of whatever stripe. There are regional pressures, linguistic pressures, gender pressures, and perhaps even knowledge pressures.

With experience counting for a lot (unless you were Garth Turner), some positions were easy to fill, such as finance, health, justice, defence, international trade, and public works. The major piece of business to be done in the first months was the drafting and passage of the Federal Accountability Act. This was to be done out of the Treasury Board, and someone who had a proven track record handling difficult and complex files and who could get things done had to be placed there.

Harper faced a common problem of most prime ministers: too many competent MPs from one province – in this case, Alberta. (For former prime minister Mulroney, much as he might have liked to, he was not going to put both John Crosbie and Jim McGrath from Newfoundland into his Cabinet.) So, tough choices had to be made. This affected a number of Alberta MPs. Jason Kenney, Diane Ablonczy, and James Rajotte would have fit nicely into anyone's Cabinet.

Hard work combined with the need for regional representation got Gary Lunn into the first Cabinet. He had worked as hard as any caucus representative could to ensure the success of the Montreal Policy Convention in March 2005. Usually when MPs are named to be the caucus person on an ongoing or working committee, little is expected. With Lunn, the opposite was true; he was highly dedicated to the task, and his hard work was rewarded.

In the early days in government, being able to attract David Emerson and Michael Fortier was a mixed blessing. While Emerson brought both business and recent Cabinet experience, the unexpected public furor – he had been elected as a Liberal and crossed the floor to become a Conservative Cabinet minister – hurt his early effectiveness. However, he did recover and became a rock throughout his time at the Cabinet table. He was the natural choice to fill in as foreign affairs minister after Maxime Bernier was sacked, and he also chaired the Cabinet Committee on Afghanistan, a committee recommended by the Manley Panel on Afghanistan. Unfortunately, given the vagaries of electoral politics, Emerson only served one term in the Harper Cabinet, choosing not to run again in 2008.

Fortier's appointment, while no less controversial than Emerson's, gave us a representative in Montreal. It was never clear to me how this appointment came about. Co-chair of an election campaign is usually an honorific role, but Fortier seemed to be everywhere, which seemed odd to me at the time. Was a Cabinet appointment something he wanted? On the other hand, he made it clear that he was persuaded to accept the appointment by the prime minister. In whatever way he got there, he did bring an urban Quebec perspective to the Cabinet table, with a great deal of business experience. Unfortunately, as with Emerson, the appointment of Fortier created controversy – he had not been elected and would be sitting in the Senate, an institution we were supposed to reform.

Another portfolio that had every possibility of proving troublesome was Indian and Northern Affairs. With Fontaine at the head of the Assembly of First Nations, the Martin Kelowna deal a no-go, and no idea where the residential schools settlement stood, this department would need a sure and respected hand on the tiller. Throughout his time in shadow cabinet as critic for Indian and Northern Affairs, Jim Prentice had delivered thoughtful, reasoned opinions and advice to the leader. He had also kept a low profile, helping where needed, sure-footed all of the time. His business acumen as well as his experience as a claims negotiator and conciliator would be valuable not only in Indian and Northern Affairs but also as chair of the Operations Committee of Cabinet. This was the problem-solving Cabinet committee that grew in prominence during the Mulroney years when ably chaired by Don Mazankowski. Its task was to review the communication plans on thorny subjects; in reality, it reviewed the strategic deci-sion-making on major issues, with communications almost as an afterthought. In a government where there was only to be a chief of staff, with no principal secretary and no deputy prime minister, Pren-tice came as close as anyone to fulfilling this latter role of deputy prime minister, at least until just after the 2009 budget.

House and Senate business strategy would need experienced hands. Rob Nicholson had experience, although brief, in a federal Cabinet and had served with Jay Hill as part of the House leadership team in opposition. He had years of experience in Parliament, knew how things worked, and got along with everyone. Jay Hill, a former Reform-Alliance MP and for a brief period a member of the PC-DRC coalition, had served as whip during the opposition period; in a minority, his strength and indefatigable work ethic would be essential. From the Senate, there was no other choice: Marjory LeBreton had demonstrat-ed the importance of institutional memory and consistent support through the election campaign. Not as a reward for her help, but in recognition of the qualities she demonstrated during the campaign, she would be the government leader in the Senate, responsible for energizing a group of tired Tory senators into shedding their tradi-tional opposition role and supporting government initiatives, includ-ing Senate reform. The enormity of this task, and the task ahead for the Conservative senators, should not be underestimated. They were out-numbered in the chamber and on all Senate committees. Conserva-tives did not chair many committees – it was all based on numbers. But the Conservative senators had two things in their favour. The Liberal senators were fighting the Liberal leadership race – not only the upcoming 2006 one, but the one before it and the one before that, when Chrétien beat Martin. Also, the Liberal senators were led by Sen-ator Dan Hays of Calgary, who had been a government leader in the Senate and Speaker. He had great respect for the Senate, and enjoyed great respect from all senators.

The rest of the Cabinet rounded itself out. In most cases, the prime minister was simply looking for people who have demonstrated lead-ership skills, the ability to master complex subjects, and some ability to work with others, as well as geographical balance. The caucus poli-cy committees, which Harper struck when in opposition, provided a good demonstration test of those qualities.

If we made a mistake – and I believe we did – it was in the envi-ronment portfolio. There was nothing wrong with putting Rona

Ambrose in charge. The problem was in not giving her the support she needed and not anticipating that environment, in a growing and flourishing economy, would become a major issue, one we could not ignore. The poisonous atmosphere created by leaving Samy Watson as deputy minister was compounded by moving Cassie Doyle, who was virtually the deputy minister after Watson had been sidelined, to natural resources. She knew the environment file and could have been a great help to Ambrose. Having moved Doyle and Watson, Michael Horgan, who is extremely capable, took over as the new deputy minister. A few weeks later, Horgan's mother died in Prince Edward Island, and he spent most of the summer down there dealing with her estate. It just seemed that from a staffing point of view, Ambrose received little or no help, and even a bit of a hindrance, but more on environment later.

The people of Quebec had come through in the 2006 election and that had to be recognized by more than putting Fortier in the Senate on the condition that he would run for the House of Commons in the next federal election and giving him public works. Lawrence Cannon, who led the drafting of the Quebec platform, was involved in the 19 December Quebec speech, and had been deputy chief of staff in the OLO, would now be the minister of transportation, which would include the government infrastructure programs. Harper liked to say that Cannon always looked like he knew what he was doing and was completely on top of all the issues. The PM would say, "You can turn the sound off when he is on television, and it still looks like he knows what he is doing." Max Bernier, former head of the Montreal Economic Institute and a free market libertarian, had won the seat in his father's former riding of Beauce and took over at industry. It seemed to be a good fit. Jean-Pierre Blackburn, a returning MP from the Mulroney era, would take on the position of minister for the economic development agency of Canada for the regions of Quebec.

Greg Thompson, the only PC MP to support Harper in the Conservative leadership contest in 2004, would become the minister of veteran affairs. I remember Thompson as being a great guy, and a tenacious person to work with. When he believed he was right, there was little or no chance of changing his mind. He was, however, a great supporter of Canada's veterans.

The last person to make the cut was Monte Solberg. It was the weekend before the Cabinet was to be sworn in. I was to call him on his cellphone, and if I couldn't get him, then leave a message that he call Derek Burney – which is what happened. Derek and I had agreed that when Monte called back, I would answer, which I did. I told him that I had no idea why he was calling and that no one here wanted to speak with him. There was a long pause on the other end, and then we let him off the hook and Derek took over. Transition-team humour – not very good, but all we had.

Obviously, the most important task was putting the right ministerial team in place. But the newly minted Cabinet ministers had to know what they were to do. This would be set out in detail in the ministerial mandate letters, the second major task of the transition team. This all circles back to the view that the government could be brought down early, and if we had no track record to show for whatever time we spent in office, the question for voters would be: do we give these Conservatives another chance or reject them as having promised a lot but delivered very little?

The easiest way to establish goals and track progress was to go straight to the platform. If the platform was not sufficiently detailed, I had all the preceding drafts, which might have more detail. The released platform was a radically pared down version of the May 2005 effort, with a number of changes as our thinking crystallized in various areas. For example, Canadian heritage in the January 2006 platform was limited to maintaining the CBC, Radio-Canada, and a mention of the CRTC. Previous versions were more fulsome, so those points would be added to the mandate letter. In order to help the new minister, staff, and deputy minister, items were prioritized, so there was not only a road map but also mileage indicators along the way to ensure progress on the most important items. Ministers couldn't tick off three or four easy things at the beginning of their term and then sit back saying they had accomplished more than half of the things required of them.

The public service had done a remarkable job analyzing the Conservative platform. Briefing binders had been prepared on 8½" × 14" paper under the various subject headings and promises contained in the platform. These were very helpful, as not only did they address the platform promise, but also the implementation of the platform promise. As a rule, the public service was cautious when addressing new ideas. I said to Brodie that the five sections under each commitment followed a pattern. After first congratulating us for proposing a particular new initiative, there followed sections on: implementation; problems that could be foreseen with implementation; possible Charter issues that the proposal might attract; reasons why it might not be prudent to proceed with the proposal at the present time, or reasons to proceed with caution; and finally, the suggestion to establish a committee to give further study to the proposals. All of this was help-ful in providing a counsel of caution, signalling the pitfalls that might await an inexperienced group as we moved forward.

The mandate letters themselves all had pretty much the same begin-ning and end. The middle part, taken from the platform, was the only matter that varied. Even though the Federal Accountability Act was in the early formative stages, we had a good idea what it would contain. Therefore, every letter made reference to it and the expectation of high ethical standards in government. The role of the deputy minis-ter was spelled out, as was the need for the minister to consult and work with the deputy and the Public Service. The letters were review-ed and signed by the prime minister. The idea was that they all would be ready and put into the hands of ministers on the day Cabinet was sworn in.

The third major aspect of transition came with the staffing of the var-ious ministers' offices. This was extremely difficult since we had to wait until the Cabinet was firmed up before dividing up the resumés we had received since the election according to who might be a good staffing fit for which minister. The first task was to review all of the resumés and discard the ones that, for whatever reason, were deemed not suitable – usually on grounds of lack of experience. The Conservatives had not formed a government for thirteen years, so staff with previous federal ministerial experience were in short supply; however, there were numer-ous staffers who had made positive contributions in opposition and should be given the opportunity to be a part of the new government. We were also aware that those named as ministers would probably want to keep some or all of their existing staff. So, we were predominantly looking for resumés from people who could handle the job of chief of staff or senior policy advisor, or administrative positions – and, very importantly, were available immediately. No small task, but for the most part it worked well, with only a couple of chiefs departing early. Most ministers found the arrangements suggested to their liking.

While these three main tasks were being pursued, the day-to-day work of governing also had to be attended to. We did not take over a regime in a vacuum; there were decisions to be made that would affect governing down the road. For example, the financial part of the platform – revenue and expenses and projected surplus – was based on the promise and premise to effect savings in all departments except Indian and northern affairs and defence by limiting future growth of spending in federal grant and contribution programs. The savings projected were modest – tied to the rate of inflation plus population growth – but they needed to be achieved to maintain a surplus in order to keep spending promises and the commitment to pay down the debt. Those projected savings had caused no end of consternation when the platform was released. What programs would be affected, and would public servants lose their jobs?

The first meeting to discuss the implementation of this economic-savings platform promise was held in the clerk's boardroom near the end of the first week of transition. Burney was supposed to attend, but couldn't, so I was sent. It seemed like a pretty straightforward assignment, and I would report on how this platform promise was to be accomplished when the transition team met the next morning. It is amazing what one doesn't know about government finances when in opposition.

Alex Himelfarb, Clerk of the Privy Council, chaired the meeting attended by the Deputy Minister of Finance Ian Bennett, the secretary of the Treasury Board, and a few other officials. There were binders all over the boardroom table. The meeting began with the usual comments about the need to control the increase of government spending and how great it would be if that actually occurred. However, programs and grants were calculated to increase, and we had to level out the increases before we could implement the inflation and population-growth part of the platform. It was not that the senior public servants were refusing to implement the campaign promises; it was simply impossible to implement them in the short term.

There was another financial matter that Burney charged me with: fulfilling a promise to get aid cheques into the hands of farmers at the earliest possible time. For this I had to deal with Yaprak Baltacioglu, one of the best public servants you could ever encounter. She let me know that between Department of Agriculture and the Privy Council Office (PCO), they had figured out the amount of the cheques, and that the cheque run would be done in Winnipeg. Again naively, I had no idea how long it took to do a cheque run of this size and get them in the mail. Burney wanted 100 per cent delivery by the end of February; we managed approximately 90 per cent, and I felt I had pushed the bureaucracy as far and fast as I could. Everything was a learning experience.

One of the more humorous moments in these first few weeks came in a meeting of the prime minister; the clerk of the Privy Council; Mark Cameron, senior policy advisor in the PMO; and me. The premiers and territorial leaders were in Ottawa for a Council of the Federation meeting on post-secondary education and skills training, and Harper had invited them for dinner on the evening of 24 February. While this was to be an informal meeting, he knew that eventually the discussion would focus on money. During his months in office, Martin had made numerous financial commitments concerning his cities and infrastructure agenda. There had also been a number of spending promises both preceding the May 2005 non-election and in the run-up to the non-confidence vote in November. Harper believed he needed some details quickly, as the 2006 platform committed the government to maintain in force the existing federal infrastructure agreements with the provinces and municipalities. He informed the clerk about the dinner meeting, and his apprehension regarding infrastructure funding. His premise was that each one of the provincial and territorial leaders would know what was promised in infrastructure funding by Martin. Harper wanted to know what the federal government numbers on that subject revealed. Seemed like a simple enough request, but it wasn't. The exchange went something like this.

"Alex, can you tell me what the previous administration committed to each province and territory for infrastructure?"

"No, I can't, Prime Minister."

"Alex, can you tell me how much each province and territory received for infrastructure from the previous administration?"

"No, I can't, Prime Minister."

And so it went. There had been so many promises, so many commitments, so many plans, so many initiatives that the public service had given up counting – and that is not a criticism of the public service. On short notice, it was impossible to come up with answers. Cameron, who has an encyclopedic mind, tried to list off the programs, hoping that would help. It didn't! So what was Harper to do? The clerk promised to do his best to compile a summary, but could not guarantee its accuracy. He also acknowledged that the prime minster was right in assuming that the premiers would know to the penny what had been promised and what had been paid.

In the same vein, I was told that under Martin, the agenda in the morning was not the agenda in the evening. The agenda and priorities and expectations changed so often during the day that the public service had basically downed tools until it got a sign that a final decision had been made and that the government would stick with it. No wonder our five unchanging priorities were looked upon as such a blessing.

As well as finding and designating Cabinet ministers and dealing with mandate letters and staffing, we had to look at establishing the various committees that would undertake the work of the Cabinet. Burney and the clerk, with Harper's agreement and support, established a regime similar to the one put in place by former prime minister Mulroney. Central to the Cabinet and the effective functioning of the Cabinet committee system were the Priorities and Planning Committee and the Operations Committee. Under Prime Minister Harper, the Priorities and Planning Committee is, in reality, the Cabinet. It is comprised of approximately twelve ministers, presumably holding the key portfolios of Cabinet, with their advice to the prime minister and each other being crucial to the efficient functioning of government. The initial Harper Priorities and Planning Committee brought together the ministers responsible for the five priorities, the chairs of Cabinet policy committees, the chair of the Operations Committee, and ministers whose views the prime minister valued. Harper is the chair of Priorities and Planning, and it meets regularly every Tuesday morning from 9:30 a.m. till approximately noon.

The other central Cabinet committee is the Operations Committee. For the first two mandates, it was chaired by Jim Prentice and was comprised of ministers whose background knowledge and skills the prime minister thought would serve well in resolving thorny issues facing the government. It was the transactional committee of government, whose mandate was to address communications plans for controversial issues, but in reality also reviewed the strategy. Ministers representing Canada abroad, especially in trade negotiations or on missions where agreements might result, also had to report to the committee regularly on their progress on the negotiating mandate, given by Priorities and Planning, especially if the situation was getting critical or a change was needed to such a mandate.

Other committees of Cabinet were policy, social policy, finance, defence, and security. As the government began to experience difficulties in the environment area, an ad hoc Cabinet committee was established to deal with energy and the environment; in the fall of 2006, it became a permanent committee. A Committee on Afghanistan, ably chaired by David Emerson, was established as a result of the Manley Report on the continuing conduct of the Afghan war. The idea behind the composition of these committees was that it was important that all ministers who had departmental responsibilities or mandates related to a particular subject meet on a regular basis to discuss issues, problems, or proposals for action.

While not committees of Cabinet, other committees were established to ensure that House and Senate business moved as best it could. There was a daily House business meeting, chaired by the House leader, which included the parliamentary secretary to the House leader, the whip, the Senate leader, and staff. I attended as regularly as I could, and especially if there was a message to be passed on from the prime minister. Once a week, the caucus chair, the House leader, the whip, the Senate House leader or a representative (usually Senator David Tkachuk), and their staff met with the prime minister, his chief of staff, me, and other PMO staff as necessary, usually the issues manager, to discuss the weekly business in the House and the agenda for the caucus meeting. Finally, there was a regular weekly bill review meeting. That was chaired by the House leader and his parliamentary secretary. The purpose of the meeting was to give ministers the opportunity to present their proposed legislation to caucus colleagues before presenting it to caucus. This committee was especially helpful as it also dealt with private members' bills both from the Conservative MPs and from the opposition. All of these committees, except the weekly caucus planning and House business committee, were supported by representatives from the PCO. Later, in the third mandate, each minister had a committee of Conservative MPs to which he would submit bill proposals for discussion before they were discussed with the whole caucus.

It is important to say that without the support of the PCO, the government would not have been successful. Both Alex Himelfarb in the beginning and then Kevin Lynch, and the people who worked for them, performed their tasks professionally and competently. It is trite to say that all ministers want to move their policy issues or draft legislation through the Cabinet process to the implementation stage as quickly as possible. The PCO function – and believe me, it is not always appreciated or understood – is to perform a challenge function for the minister and minister's staff, and for PMO staff as well. It forces rigor of thought and action in the system. With few exceptions would matters appear on the Priorities and Planning Committee agenda without prior serious consideration by a Cabinet committee, or if it was a new item, without the approval or support of the PCO. Walk-on or tabled items without background comments from the PCO as to their rationale were rare and discouraged. Ministers tried to get around this, but it usually did not work in their favour. Of the two who tried most often, John Baird as minister of environment was a lot more successful in getting policies approved than Gary Lunn as minister of natural resources.

On 5 February, with the addition of Monte Solberg, we were ready for the swearing-in of Cabinet the next morning at Rideau Hall. The transition team gathered in the office boardroom to watch that evening's late-night news. We had all been afraid of leaks throughout our two-week process, but surprisingly, none had occurred. For example, former long-time Mulroney Cabinet minister Michael Wilson had spent considerable time in Ottawa during this period, relatively unnoticed. If the media had staked out the airport to seek interviews with arriving Cabinet prospects, nothing had come of it. So here we were, literally at the eleventh hour, wondering if someone unknown to us had stumbled on the list. CBC, Global, RDI, and Radio-Canada were far off the mark. Then we watched Robert Fife on CTV. He had his first five or six absolutely correct – we all were turning white – but when he went on to others, we knew nothing had been leaked his way. So we were set for 6 February 2006.

The swearing-in was in the morning with a reception to follow, and then the first Cabinet meeting would take place at 2 p.m. There was no question that it was an exciting time. Things to remember: don't drink your usual gallon of coffee before you attend one of these things, because you can't get up and leave halfway through the ceremony to go to the washroom. The most interesting part of being at the 6 February swearing-in was the media reaction to David Emerson's presence. Shortly after election day, what started as a casual conversation with Mike Coates, who runs the Hill + Knowlton firm, moved on to a more serious conversation with John Reynolds and then a meeting with Prime Minister Harper, Derek Burney, and Ian Brodie. No one guessed or speculated that Emerson would be joining the Harper Cabinet. But there had to be a reason why he was there. Eventually, the media hit upon the solution that a member of the previous administration was required to be present to pass on the Great Seal of Canada to the incoming government. As Martin's former minister of industry, it was only appropriate that Emerson be there. Every void or vacuum has to be filled, and this reasoning was as good as any.

Never did we anticipate the media and public protests that would arise over this appointment. Only the passage of time would quell the outcry, and while it did not affect Emerson's effectiveness in Cabinet and the House of Commons, it meant that he would serve only one term as a Conservative MP and minister. Whether or not he would have run in 2008, perhaps in a more Conservative-friendly riding in Vancouver, is just speculation since Emerson was not willing to put his family through the election gauntlet one more time.

The other major surprise related to Michael Fortier. If, in the opinion of pundits, the Emerson appointment had bent, or broken, most of the known political rules, the appointment of Fortier as a Conservative senator from Quebec and directly into Cabinet threw away what remained of the parliamentary/political rule book. Harper stood for Senate reform, not appointing his campaign co-chair to the Senate and Cabinet. He also stood for an elected Senate, so no one anticipated that one of his first acts as prime minister would be to appoint someone to the Senate. But the prime minister wanted to round out his Cabinet with representatives from Canada's major cities, and Fortier, who was so involved in the campaign, was deemed to be the one who would represent Montreal. In reality, no explanation would satisfy the media; but as with Emerson, the controversy did die down. Fortier did run in the 2008 election in a Montreal riding, but fell victim to the misguided Quebec campaign.

At the reception following the swearing-in, the new Cabinet ministers met their deputy ministers for the first time. After the "team picture" was taken, the ministers left to go to their departments for the first time, and to be greeted by the mountains of briefing books that had been compiled by the public service.

The ministers reassembled in the main Cabinet room in the Centre Block at 2 p.m. for their first meeting as a Cabinet. Immediately prior to the start of the meeting, I found myself alone in the prime minister's office with the newly sworn-in prime minister. I looked at him with all the admiration and joy in the world, and said, "Stephen, we really did it." "Yes, Bruce, we really did," he responded. "Now you have to go and chair your first Cabinet meeting." "Yes, I do. Where do I do that?" he said. I replied, "Follow me," and took him down the hall of the third floor of Centre Block that connects his office and the Cabinet room. As we entered the room together, he leaned over and asked, "Where do I sit?" "The vacant chair with the high back," I replied, then took my place beside Derek Burney, and the meeting began.

It was not lost on anybody in that room that this was the culmination of years of work, of ups and downs, and complete dedication by a few to reaching the dream of giving conservatives the opportunity to experience for the first time in more than a decade a Conservative government. While the meeting didn't last much more than an hour, it was important symbolically to assemble the group as quickly as possible and instill in them the idea that this was a winning team with an agenda to implement – while running against the clock. In his opening remarks, the prime minister referenced the message in the mandate letters they would receive after the meeting. These would be their primary marching orders as Cabinet ministers. They were to spend time with their deputies and senior members of their department, but they were not to become captive to the briefing process. It is always looked upon as a great way to tie up the minister, while the bureaucrats get on with running the department. The importance of honesty and integrity was stressed, and there was reference to the upcoming parliamentary session. The Federal Accountability Act would be the first substantive piece of legislation tabled by the government. Emphasis in the near term would be on the five priorities, with one of these taken care of by the Federal Accountability Act, and two more – GST and Child Benefit – in the budget. Getting tough on violent crime would be a series of bills brought in by the justice minister, and the health minister would address the wait-time guarantee in negotiations with the provinces. This gave Vic Toews, as justice minister, the opportunity to talk, and he went on and on. At one point, Burney turned to me and asked, "Who the hell is he?" I told him it was Vic Toews, the person he wanted so badly to be the justice minister.

Looking around the room, I believe I knew everyone there fairly well, except Fortier, Emerson, and Bernier. It occurred to me that while a lot of work had to be done getting them up to speed on departmental matters, they also had to get up to speed in relation to their duties as ministers in the House of Commons and the Senate, in a minority Parliament. Only one person sitting at the table – Emerson – had faced questions in the House of Commons as a minister. Some, of course, had been in Cabinet in provincial legislatures, but this was "the show," and they would be facing questions from opposition Liberals who knew everything about the government departments, where the skeletons were, and how to question Conservative ministers who had just taken over.

I shared my concerns with Keith Beardsley, the issues manager, with Ian Brodie, and with Sandra Buckler, who took over as director of communications. At that point we just had a problem, and no solution – not a good way to start. Then the four of us hit on a practical solution that would at least identify how serious the problem really was. We would hold a rehearsal, with Cabinet ministers on one side and parliamentary secretaries on the other asking each other questions, all of it run by someone in the role of Speaker of the House. So, before the House began sitting, we brought bleachers into Room 200 in the West Block: on one side would sit the Cabinet – first as government, and then taking a turn as opposition; and on the other side, the parliamentary secretaries – first as opposition, and then as government. We had put together questions for them, and one of Buckler's staff, a fluently bilingual communications officer, played the role of Speaker quite effectively. Much to our surprise, it worked! Everyone took it seriously and provided both good questions and answers. My fears were somewhat allayed.

But one more part had to be put in place to make sure that this newly minted group of ministers was ready for prime time. While in opposition, everyone who was going to be involved or asking questions in QP was required to attend a practice held daily at 1 p.m. Harper was always there, as was Jason Kenny, the question period coordinator. Why not do the same every day with ministers and parliamentary secretaries? Thus began one of the major innovations that we brought to government: the daily question period practice. Attendance was mandatory, and the prime minister always attended when he was in Ottawa. Chaired by the government House leader, the questions were put to the Cabinet minister by the issues manager, initially Keith Beardsley and then Jenni Byrne. I would substitute when they were unavailable. This was new; the Liberals never did this. It became one of the best hours of each day. Every issue the government faced was hashed out here, with the prime minister and senior staff in attendance. The other good part was that the practice rarely filled the full hour. Somewhere around 1:45 p.m. we would be done, and the PM would stay and be available to any minister who wanted to talk through a specific problem or needed a quick answer, without tying up the rest of the PM's daily agenda.

The final part of preparing this group of Cabinet ministers came in a series of initiatives to ensure the government got its message out and stayed on message. We had the benefit of having watched the Martin government operate, and it seemed that on most days, the media not the government controlled the government's message. We would watch scrums with ministers after Cabinet meetings on the third floor of the Centre Block when it seemed that ministers were unprepared, and perhaps should have been left alone to go back to their offices uninterrupted by the media, and to prepare for question period. We saw what we perceived to be a government plagued by leaks, which had lost control of its message to the media. By trying to befriend and be constantly available to the media, the Liberals had accomplished very little except to seem confused and unprepared.

If we were going to change this approach, we had to do it immediately. It was made clear to ministers and to their directors of communications that the ministers were not to talk to media unless they had something to say, and that that "something to say" would be vetted by the PMO communications staff. The same message discipline that brought the Conservatives to government was going to keep them there. Learning all of this in the early days of government was tough, since the natural instinct of most politicians is to engage with anyone on any particular subject. Well, not anymore! Protocols for engaging the media were developed as well as talking points on particular subject matters. There was to be no freelancing!

This Conservative approach probably would have received less criticism from the media if it had not been such a stark contrast to the way Martin and his Cabinet operated. The media went from having stories handed to it on a platter to none, or very little, news at all from a government communications shop that believed less is better and much less is best! Better to have no story than a wrong or bad story. New Cabinet ministers who had spent years in opposition developing relationships with certain reporters were now being told they could not speak to them without prior approval. Why? Ministers were important now; people wanted to know what Mr or Ms Cabinet Minister thought. No, actually, for the most part, people don't care. They elected you to do a job, not to keep shooting your mouth off. The message was given loud and clear to Cabinet ministers and caucus: the media are not there to help you or be your friend. The symbiotic relationship that you had with them in opposition is over!

Two other things happened to the media almost simultaneously: they were banned from the third floor of the Centre Block where the PM's suite of offices as well as the Cabinet meeting room are located; and in scrums with the prime minister, Harper would only take questions from reporters who were on a list kept by Dimitri Soudas, the PM's deputy press secretary. Both moves caused a great deal of friction and angst with the media. However, it was the PM's view that media types complaining among themselves in print or on television about lack of access would be ignored by Canadians, and it was.

This view of the media and not "feeding the beast" or ignoring it entirely may have started with Harper prior to the 2004 election, but it was reinforced through that period, and especially when the "Martin supports pornography" story broke just beyond the halfway mark of the 2004 campaign. One can argue that strict message discipline was necessary in the first term and maybe into the second term, but control over the message has now moved to control over the messengers and has struck at caucus discipline, alienating both ministers and backbench MPs. The tone of communications has affected the government negatively as much as the message. The idea that the media is against the government is not unique to this government, but this government seems to have grabbed it and communicates as if it is still in opposition. With a majority, I would have thought that the communications rules could have been relaxed, but if anything, they have been tightened. If the second half of the majority mandate is approached in this same fashion, it will not auger well for getting out whatever the government's message happens to be, since more and more, the government will be haunted by its own record.

Message discipline also came via the process for making government announcements. In order for a minister to make an announcement, an event plan and message had to be submitted to the PM's communications group for approval. The view was that the government could not afford to have ministers trampling on each other's stories. So there was a government message event rollout plan, with all of its contents approved by the PMO. The branding and staging of message events came under the purview of Patrick Muttart.

The brand "Canada's New Government" was to be everywhere, and all announcements and supporting materials had to have the same look and feel. This comprehensive rollout plan was reviewed with Prime Minister Harper on a daily basis at the morning issues meeting. Being prepared and being disciplined was the only way we were going to survive and succeed.

Governing, Part 1:
Implementing the Platform
and Tackling Unexpected Issues

I have been involved with three governments – two federal and one provincial – and have spent almost a decade with the Parliamentary Research Branch of the Library of Parliament in the federal Law and Government Division. Over those years I have seen a number of different methods of governing, but in reality, especially in a minority situation, it distills down to what happens on five different yet parallel tracks.

The first track, easier in a majority than a minority situation, is perhaps the simplest to follow is implementing the government's platform or program. Through either the annual budget or important pieces of legislation, the government establishes a positive track record of implementation. The second track, and the most problematic, is when the train on the track is coming right at the government, with issues or matters that those around the Cabinet table never contemplated having to deal with. Issues management, problem solving, and communications support become of paramount importance. The next track is created when the matters on tracks one and two meet, and sometimes collide. There can be a positive or proactive way in which challenges facing the government actually become opportunities, such as the government establishing a positive plan to deal with the issue into the future. The fourth track is a sometimes-difficult one since it is concerned with personnel. It usually focuses on either caucus management or Cabinet management, and occasionally with the PMO or a minister's staff. It may also affect the senior ranks of the public service under the direction of the Clerk of the Privy Council. The fifth and last track is most important in a minority

The Cabinet. Despite a rocky start, David Emerson (left, with Stephen Harper) was one of the stalwarts of the first Harper Cabinet. (Courtesy of Julie Oliver/*Ottawa Citizen*. Reprinted by permission)

situation: election readiness. There is no question that in a minority situation, one never knows when the opposition is going to determine it is time to bring the government down. Presumably, if the opposition combines to defeat the government, at least one, if not all, of the parties are ready for an election. In these circumstances, there is no excuse for a government not to be on perpetual election alert. In a majority situation with a fixed election date, the greatest gift for an opposition party is knowing the timing of the next election. In a minority, all parties should be ready at all times; that means everything is prepared, from the platform through to equipping the war room, scripting the writ period, and pre-planning the leader's tour as well as secondary tours.

PLATFORM IMPLEMENTATION TRACK

Looking at the this track, it was of prime importance that the new Harper Cabinet spend a day in a "retreat" format, with the prime minister as chair receiving briefings on the upcoming parliamentary agenda, staffing, and generally how the system works from staff, public servants, former Cabinet ministers, and a former leader in the Senate. This occurred prior to Parliament meeting. While the caucus group had worked well together in opposition, this would be different, with little room for unforced errors. The main upcoming matters were on the agenda and discussed at this Meech Lake retreat: the Speech from the Throne, the budget, and the legislative agenda. The importance of co-operating with parliamentary committees was stressed, especially ministers appearing to discuss and defend their departmental estimates. As the Liberals became more and more comfortable in government, they paid less and less attention to matters like this. The role and mandate of Cabinet committees were explained, and especially how they would relate to each other.

The highlight of the day came in the afternoon as former Mulroney Cabinet minister Benoit Bouchard and former senator John Lynch-Staunton gave practical, real-life examples of the role of ministers, the challenges encountered, and how they were resolved. Lynch-Staunton spoke of the importance of linking the Senate into the day-to-day operations in the House of Commons. The message was "no surprises," and the discussion stressed the importance of communication between the House of Commons and the Senate. This was especially important now that there would be two Cabinet ministers in the Senate, Government Leader Marjory LeBreton and Minister of Public Works Michael Fortier. It should be noted that the Conservatives did not have a majority in the Senate. There was not to be any freelancing in the Senate during Senate question period; answers there could come back to haunt Cabinet in the House of Commons.

Two interventions near the end of the day were personal and important. One was Stock Day talking about the importance of balance. As everyone knows, his life in service of the public has been anything but smooth, but his main message was not to get too caught up in the importance of the role you are playing – because that is what it is, a role. At the end of the piece, when the role is gone, all else surrounding it will also be gone – except your family. For Stock, who had been through the worst of times and was now looking forward to some of the best of times, remembering the role of family was paramount.

Because the Federal Accountability Act was to be the first piece of legislation tabled by the government, and due to the role that ethics had played in the campaign, Harper addressed this issue in his concluding remarks. He recognized that as we went along, issues would arise involving matters of judgment by ministers. Sometimes ethical issues would arise. He said what he could handle and work with were honest mistakes, as they will happen. What he could not abide would be ministers cutting ethical corners, and trotting out complicated legal arguments to support a lack of ethical judgment. Being too cute by half in relation to ethics, or any other matter, would not cut it with this prime minister.

This was Harper's view in 2006. It is valid to ask whether this view prevailed through 2013. Events surrounding the Senate expense scandal and the PM's explanation as well as denial of involvement have stretched credulity to the point where one wonders whether his admonition of 2006 applies to his own actions in 2013? As always happens, facts will emerge, but I know that in the Brodie PMO that I was a part of, the PM would have known almost immediately of any untoward actions or activities by a senator – or anyone else involved in the government.

Back at the office, the first order of business was the drafting of the Speech from the Throne. It was a collaborative effort between the PMO and PCO. The prime minister believed it was essential right from the beginning to differentiate ourselves from the previous government. It would be a speech that would brand the government as "new" and contain specifics that were attainable. There would be no laundry list of platitudes or grand schemes, most of which would be unattainable. It would be a practical, workmanlike speech, with set goals. Given that this was the first Conservative government in more than a decade, there were certain entities that had to be highlighted, like the armed forces. We were also conscious of the fact that it had to be passed by the House, so specific promises were made to the province of Quebec, addressing the open federalism part of the platform.

In fact, the speech read like a recitation of the platform that began with accountability and the promise to introduce the Federal Accountability Act and continued on to: reducing the GST; fighting crime; supporting families with children; implementing health care wait time guarantees with the provinces and territories; Senate reform; addressing of the fiscal imbalance; open federalism, especially with regard to Quebec; and building a stronger military.

A number of legislative initiatives were being developed at the same time as the Speech from the Throne. The two most important were the Federal Accountability Act (FAA)[1] and a suite of "tough on crime" measures. The FAA was to be the leading piece of legislation, and we had set out pretty clear guidelines in the platform. Minister Baird was ably assisted by Susan Cartwright in the drafting of this Bill. Her work on the matter resulted in her moving to the PCO as foreign and defence policy advisor to the prime minister and deputy secretary to Cabinet.

The FAA contained a number of significant measures and was seen as an improvement on the existing regime. For example, it addressed reform of financing for political parties, banning secret donations. The role of the ethics commissioner was expanded to administer a new Conflict of Interest Act, and the new position of commissioner of lobbying, reporting directly to Parliament, was established with investigative and compliance powers. The parliamentary budget officer's position within the Library of Parliament was set up to provide independent financial advice to parliamentarians and parliamentary committees. A public appointments commissioner was to be established to oversee and report on the process for selection of appointees. Whistleblowers were to be given added protection, and the powers of the auditor general were increased. The Act also created the office of director of public prosecutions.

On the criminal justice front, Vic Toews as minister of justice and attorney general, was presiding over a shift of emphasis in the Department of Justice, which has continued and, one could argue, has even been ramped up by his successor Rob Nicholson. The approach taken in the first session of the new mandate was to introduce a number of criminal justice bills to show the intent of the government in this area and see which ones actually passed. It has always been the Conservatives' contention that the opposition parties only talk tough about crime during campaigns, but when it comes to legislation, they back off. So bills dealing with topics as diverse as criminalizing the unauthorized recording of movies, reverse onus on bail hearings for firearms-related offences, impaired driving, dangerous offenders, sentencing, raising the age of protection from fourteen to sixteen, street racing, and minimum mandatory sentences were all introduced.

The FAA received a relatively easy ride through the House of Commons both in committee and the chamber. There were amendments desired by the opposition, and John Baird was able to accommodate most of their wishes since fewer than a dozen amendments were actually voted on. In the Senate, the Bill caught a pretty rough ride from the Liberal opposition. This surprised us. We did not think the Liberals would want to shine a bright light on ethics or accountability, having just lost an election where these were seen to be areas in which the Grits were either lacking or challenged. In the Senate, 150 amendments were presented; 90 of them were eventually passed in two sessions where we went back and forth between the Senate and the House.

On reflection, while the FAA was great politics and helped win the election, especially after the RCMP announcement of the income trust investigation, it had all the hallmarks of opposition mentality, with little thought as to how it would affect the practicality of governing. On one side, there was the whistleblower component, which could have been strengthened. As we know, during the second mandate, Richard Colvin came forward, at least as a quasi whistleblower, and rightly or wrongly was severely criticized by the government. Whether he was or was not a credible committee witness on the detainee issue may be debatable, but his intervention and testimony made it easy to see how one government's whistleblower is another government's meddling, know-it-all, glory-seeking bureaucrat.

Another example, perhaps of going too far, deals with the Lobbying Act amendments. The evil that was to be addressed focused on those who changed sides while remaining on the same file: for example, someone working on a procurement matter in a minister's office who left and joined a lobbying firm to work on the same matter to help a client land a contract. This was addressed in changes brought to the Lobbying Act. The free movement of personnel back and forth between the government and the private sector to work on similar matters is now prohibited for at least five years.

Where we may have gone a bit overboard was in prohibiting folks working in the PMO or a minister's office from lobbying or dealing with the government on any matter for five years after leaving government. The natural progression of staff leaving government to find a government-relations position in the private sector was severely restricted. While it is all right to say that people working in government should not unduly profit from what they are doing when they leave government, it is another thing to prohibit them from finding a similar private-sector position for five years. It has had a chilling effect on the recruitment of qualified senior staff to work in the PMO or ministers' offices. The five-year ban is of little consequence if the staffer's main goal is to go back to university, to study or earn another degree, after finishing the stint in government. However, it is a major deterrent for recruitment of senior, experienced staff, the people most needed to work in ministers' offices, especially in a new minority government. Flexibility in their new career path is limited.

The interpretation of the Lobbying Act and Code of Conduct has also given pause to people already involved in government-relations work as volunteers or part-time help during election campaigns. There is a fear of being inadvertently caught by the provisions of the Act, with the volunteer or part-time role prohibiting pursuit of one's main livelihood. The lobbying commissioner's refusal to give advisory opinions in matters such as this has been particular unhelpful. Again, it has had a discouraging effect on participation by experienced and knowledgeable people and on the cross-fertilization of ideas.

One regret is that the Public Appointments Commission was never functional and has since been terminated. The purpose of the commission was not to vet individual appointees or appointments, but to ensure that the appropriate criteria were in place so that those involved in the appointments process would have fulsome guidelines and standards to follow. Gwyn Morgan, a very successful entrepreneur, had agreed to head up the commission and, as part of the process, was to appear before a House of Commons committee to be questioned on his qualifications. Prior to his encounter with the committee, both Keith Beardsley and I met with him to go over possible questions. Unfortunately, the questions from the opposition took a completely different route, and Morgan withdrew his name. The opposition, by scoring its cheap political points, lost big time on this one, since the commission was never established and has since been repealed.

With these caveats, there is no question that the Federal Accountability Act achieved the desired result as the signature piece of legislation by Canada's New Government. It clearly established the Conservatives in the public mind as the party of accountability, ethics, and transparency. The issue for the government has been living up to this high standard on a day-by-day, case-by-case basis.

The next inside pressure was the budget.[2] Given the fact that this was a new government sworn in at the beginning of February, the budget was going to be later in coming than usual in the government's financial cycle. That being said, we had a better idea of the government's financial position going forward than would otherwise have been the case: the contents of the 2006 budget, and indeed the following two spring budgets, came directly from the election platform. It was important for the government's credibility to put both the GST reduction by 1 per cent and the childcare $100 per month in the budget. With those two priorities a must, the issue was how many other platform promises would fit into the budget.

The lowest income tax rate was reduced, and the basic exemption increased on a reduced scale from the November 2005 Liberal Fall Economic Update. The general corporate rate was reduced by two percentage points, and the capital income surtax was removed. Elimination of the capital tax was accelerated. A number of measures were included to help workers, especially tradespeople. Students were also treated generously. And as expected with a Conservative government, spending on the military increased.

With respect to the fiscal imbalance issue, the Department of Finance produced a working and discussion paper entitled "Restoring Fiscal Balance in Canada: Turning a New Leaf." This paper joined two other papers on fiscal arrangements, one by the Council of the Federation and the other on equalization presented by the expert panel on equalization and territorial formula financing created by the Martin government.[3] In the federal fiscal imbalance paper, the suggested reforms dealt with enhancing the economic union through more effective recognition of professional and technical qualifications across provinces, common security regulation, and sales tax harmonization. The equalization paper provided a focus on equity, in that no province receiving equalization payments should have a higher fiscal capacity than a non-receiving province. There would also be a cap on these payments. The Council of the Federation paper on fiscal imbalance recommended an increase in the per capita amount transferred in the Canada Health Transfer and the Canada Social Transfer, as well as a tax point adjustment program. Equalization was to be a ten-province standard, including all revenues, including natural resources. There would be a three-year moving average.

This was all fodder for Budget 2007, which would address the fiscal imbalance and deal with certain aspects of the equalization formula. The federal paper stated all of this was designed to develop "predictable, long term fiscal arrangements" and "build a competitive and efficient economic union." As early as Budget 2006, one could see the Harper view of federalism coming forward – the disentangling of federal and provincial responsibilities. This would grow with each year, but certainly made its presence most felt in Budget 2012, the first majority budget, where the so-called hidden agenda had a bright light shone on it, as Canadian federalism began to be rebalanced back to sections 91 and 92 of the Constitution Act, 1867, with the possibility of the federal spending power falling into disuse.

The next two minority budgets completed the implementation of the fiscal part of the 2005–06 platform. Fiscal imbalance was addressed, as was equalization, with an alternative formula for the offshore accord, which created great consternation and is discussed further on in this narrative.

In addition to drafting the budget and ensuring it contained what the government wanted – worded clearly so there could be no mistakes regarding implementation – we also had to keep an eye on the mood of the opposition to determine whether the budget was actually going to pass. With the 2006 budget, there seemed to be support in the House: to a great extent, the opposition parties believed we should be able to use the budget to implement the fiscal parts of the platform that had just been presented to and voted on by Canadians. It actually passed third reading on a procedural mix-up when no one rose to speak at third reading. It was a different issue in the Liberal-dominated Senate. In order for the budget bill to pass, a number of Liberal senators would have to absent themselves and/or vote for the Conservative budget. The rumblings we received via Conservative senators were that this was no sure thing. On the Tuesday before summer recess, when it was to come up for the final vote, I left the priorities and planning meeting in the Cabinet room, next to my office, to listen to the vote in the Senate. The budget passed and received Royal Assent on 22 June 2006. I returned to the meeting, went over to the PM, and whispered that the budget had passed in the Senate and that the group could keep on meeting. We felt we had dodged what might have been a fatal bullet.

As for Budget 2007, since it addressed the fiscal imbalance, we knew that Duceppe and the Bloc would be reluctant to vote against it. Duceppe is an easy guy to read in some ways and one of the more enjoyable people around the political scene (except, of course, for his obvious desire to break up the country) because most of the time you can work with him – and if you can't, he will tell you up front. The Bloc was going to support Budget 2007. The problem with both the 2007 and 2008 budgets was our east-coast Conservative members and our Saskatchewan MPs; they each wanted their own version of the

Atlantic Accord dealing with offshore oil and gas resource management and revenue sharing, even though Saskatchewan did not have
offshore resources. Again, more on this in chapter 11.

With Budget 2008, I was not sure it was going to pass through the
House of Commons. Instead of going to the budget lockup with Ian
Brodie and Sandra Buckler, I thought the most productive use of my
time would be watching the opposition leader's scrum after the budget was presented and continuing to update our rolling platform.
However, it did not take long before the Liberals announced they
would not cause the defeat of the government over the budget.

One of the better parts of the first few months in office came as a
complete surprise. When in opposition, the Conservatives had gone
after the Liberals on many aspects of Canada–US relations, but one of
the most consistent themes was softwood lumber. The trade dispute
had lasted for years, with the United States collecting duties that trade
tribunals had consistently held that they were not entitled to. On a
morning in the middle of March, Ian Brodie assembled a group of
senior PMO staff, including Sandra Buckler and me, as well as David
Emerson, minister of international trade; Max Bernier, minister of industry; and the clerk, Kevin Lynch. We met in the small Cabinet room.
As we all settled in, not knowing why we were there, the prime minister walked in and sat down. He told us that he had received a call from
President Bush earlier in the morning and that the president felt the
time was right to settle the softwood lumber dispute. The president
had had discussions with a number of his officials as well as Susan
Schwab, his commerce secretary, and he believed that if we acted now,
most of the duties collected by the United States would be repaid with
some adjustments. We could now end this long-running dispute.

Emerson explained that this was something he had been working
on with the US when he was minister of industry in the Martin government and explained the reasons why no agreement had been
reached. According to Harper, these conditions would now not stand
in the way of a settlement. So Emerson and Bernier and assorted staff
were dispatched to Washington, D.C. I went down to the Pearson
building to meet with officials who would brief me on the details, but
all of this was to be done in secrecy.

As we understood it, the deal would mean that Canada received $4
billion of the $5.5 billion in penalties that the US had imposed and
that there would be no further tariffs. There was the obvious realization that to effect a settlement, we were leaving a lot of money on the

table – over a billion dollars. This new agreement also allowed Canada to collect an export tax on softwood lumber exported to the US if the price dropped below $355 per thousand board feet. On 1 July 2006, the final legal text for this seven-year deal was signed. The deal was supported by a bill introduced into the House of Commons, which the prime minister declared to be a vote of confidence. Eventually the Bloc decided to support the bill. While there have been skirmishes since, this settlement was an unexpected bonus in Canada–US relations early in the mandate.

Continuing with the governing track during the 2005–06 campaign, the government had to address a number of First Nations issues, including the residential schools settlement. The national chief of the Assembly of First Nations was Phil Fontaine, and he would be the main Aboriginal leader we would be meeting with on these matters. Given the recent Kelowna Accord and our position that we would not proceed with it, we knew that Fontaine, whom we had always looked upon as a Liberal, might be difficult to deal with. As mentioned earlier, Fontaine and some of his staff had met with Jim Prentice, then the critic for Indian and Northern Affairs, and me at the Ottawa airport about a week before election day. Now Prentice was the minister, and we had these challenging issues to contend with. We had to establish an agenda for action that fit within our platform from both a philosophical and fiscal perspective. The way we looked at the Kelowna Accord was that Martin had thirteen years, one and a half as prime minister, to address the issues of First Nations. An agreement came only as his government faced imminent defeat in the House of Commons, and as usual with Martin, it was a list of big promises with big numbers attached. This time it was $5 billion – I suppose this was the First Nations "fix for a generation," much like health care in 2004. The financial cost of the Kelowna Accord had never been addressed, booked, or set aside. Regardless of Liberal protestations to the contrary, there was no money earmarked to pay for those promises.

The other situation we were unaware of was that the proposal to settle the Residential Schools Class Action lawsuit had not been finalized by the Martin Cabinet. And that there were a number of outstanding issues that had to be addressed before it could be finalized. Again, this matter involved close to $5 billion, which at least in this case had been set aside to address the issue. Minister Prentice, the clerk, the PM, and I met to discuss how we should proceed. We needed to know if the new government was still legally committed to the settlement. As Prime Minister Harper said at the time, "If I had $5 billion to give away, I would give it to the farmers." In order to determine the liability of the government, former Supreme Court Justice Frank Iacobucci was engaged. He did a thorough review of all the documents and came to the conclusion that, while in the strict sense of the law, the government was not bound, a good arguable case could be made that the government had gone so far down the road to settling the matter, any reneging would be considered extremely bad faith, which could form the basis for a lawsuit against the government. The decision was made that we would proceed. However, the PM was clear that this was a matter that Prentice would have to take to caucus for approval. Prentice came from the PC side of the legacy parties – the party of Mulroney and the Charlottetown Accord, which recognized Canada's Aboriginal peoples as a third order of government. Caucus was predominately composed of Reform Party members, and we remembered how, just a few years ago, they had voted against the Nisga'a Final Agreement regarding land claim settlement and self-government. This was to be Prentice's first presentation to caucus. Talk about blowing whatever political capital one has in the first few months of the mandate.

Prentice made his presentation to caucus, giving caucus the complete story as to the history of the settlement and Mr Justice Iacobucci's opinion. The discussion at caucus was for the most part positive, the prime minister gave his view that there was no point in going backwards, and caucus unanimously supported Prentice's position that we proceed. It was an early indication that this disparate group, who only two years before had turned their swords into ploughshares regarding their respective legacy parties, was ready to accept the task that voters had entrusted them with: governing the country.

While there have been challenges along the way in implementing the settlement and in establishing the Truth and Reconciliation Commission and its operation this was a positive beginning to working with First Nations and all the Aboriginal groups and their leaders. In the months that followed the swearing-in of the government, Minister of Indian and Northern Affairs Jim Prentice, National Chief Phil Fontaine, their staff, and me, as really the only person interested in First Nations in the PMO, met numerous times because we knew that issues would arise unexpectedly, which could derail other aspects of the government's agenda. During these meetings, it became clear to

Fontaine that this was not the kind of government he was used to dealing with – not a government of grand vision or grand gestures, but a government dedicated to getting specific work done. Most meetings would begin with Phil telling Jim and me how his people were "the poorest of the poor." We acknowledged that fact and wanted to establish a framework for action that would get concrete results for First Nations, and for all Canadians.

The legitimate desires and needs of all members of the Aboriginal community in Canada are enormous. While some bands have put in place governance models that work to the benefit of their people, from an economic, educational, and security point of view, many bands or groups suffer terrible hardships. It is trite to say there are no easy answers; if there were, they would have been implemented by now. Senate and House committees have studied the challenges, virtually to death, in attempts to arrive at solutions to one or more of them: the remoteness of many of the communities; the passage, for many, of their traditional way of life; social and health issues that exacerbate the foregoing. The government has responded to the issues in a piecemeal fashion rather than holistically, as it should. Then of course, while a holistic approach sounds good, it is so difficult because among the over 630 First Nations bands, the Inuit, the Métis, and the off-reserve Indians, the challenges vary widely and are not given to a one-size-fits-all solution.

So we did the best we could. I would like to think that in the early years of the Harper government, conditions began to improve with the implementation of concrete measures, as this practical incremental approach seemed to work best. Infrastructure in the form of housing, roads, clean drinking water, schools, and community buildings became the priorities.

Our attempts to work together with First Nations leadership did not stop Fontaine from using Canada's National Aboriginal Day as a "Day of Action." This was new territory for all of us, so the Cabinet Operations Committee became the hub for the government's response and defensive actions. Risks were identified by police forces, and a response plan was put in place. A major disruption occurred as the Quinte Mohawks attempted to close Highway 401 between Kingston and Belleville, Canada's major link between Toronto and all parts east. The Ontario Provincial Police put their plan into action and minimal disruption occurred. The whole exercise disrupted the flow of operation of the government more than anything else. Cabinet ministers, bureaucrats, police forces and many hundreds of staff hours were consumed with this matter. The same threat arose in 2007, but less so in 2008 since the spring of that year was focused on a positive matter, the government's apology for abuses in residential schools.

The fact that the national chief designated Days of Action during that time came as a disappointment to the government, whose ministers believed it was taking First Nations issues seriously and was in the process of dealing with the settling of the residential schools class action lawsuit. It was a lesson in First Nations politics for the new government. The government came to realize that the national chief has his own internal political issues to deal with, and from time to time, and whether or not warranted in our judgment, he has to be seen as standing up to the federal government, regardless of political stripe or what it is doing. Perhaps there were lessons to be learned from these actions by the current national chief, Shawn Atleo, whose second term in office has been plagued by internal dissent led by those who claim they would have adopted a more confrontational approach with government.

All of this did not deter the prime minister from proceeding with an apology on behalf of the Government of Canada to all of those Aboriginal peoples who had attended residential schools. At the time, I believed this action and the words spoken by the PM, most of which he penned himself, would be recognized in years to come as the seminal moment of Harper's years in office. Unfortunately, this positive step forward and Canada's Aboriginal leadership involvement in the discussions formulating the 2009 stimulus budget now stand as the high points of this relationship. Events in 2012 and 2013 have clouded the relationship, and the opportunities presented in 2008 and 2009 may now be lost. Nevertheless, the apology that moved the Government of Canada off its position of looking at residential school students only through the lens of litigation rather than of compassion and healing, was for me Stephen Harper's greatest moment in office.

It is said that doing this was not Harper's idea, but Jack Layton's, building off of the apology that Harper gave for the imposition of the Chinese head tax. Regardless of whose idea it was, it became that of the man who delivered it: Stephen Harper. This was to be no half-measure. When he sat down in his seat in the House of Commons after delivering the apology, he did not want any room for criticism of his words, their meaning and intent, or his motives for the action. It was an evolutionary process, both with regard to the words and the ceremony itself. As we approached 11 June 2008, each day would bring a new suggestion as to the nature of the ceremony. There would be initial resistance by the PM, overnight rumination, and the next day discussion and approval.

I do not think we ever realized how big and important what we were doing was for Canada's Aboriginal peoples. In their culture, steeped as it is in tradition, the words were important, but the ceremony around the saying of the words was also important. It was not enough for the prime minister to utter the words; they had to be put in the context of the ancient history and traditions of Canada's indigenous peoples. It was to be a solemn ceremony, in which the Aboriginal leaders took part, and after the ceremony, a celebration.

All of this moved along, and as we closed in on a final text, Harper took control of the wording, ignoring the advice of the Justice Department and the PCO that the apology, worded in a certain way, could expose the government to more litigation. The PM wanted full agreement from the major Aboriginal organizations on the wording, and he did not want any quarrel with semantics when he was done. It was important that the apology recognize that the residential schools system resulted in "killing the Indian in the child." So, for the most part, helpful advice was received from the PCO, Indian Affairs, and Justice, and if the PM liked it, it was incorporated, and if not, it was ignored. He dealt the same way with the advice he received from the Aboriginal leadership. Because the PM wanted to ensure secrecy as well as their approval, we convened a meeting of the Aboriginal leaders for a group read in his office immediately prior to delivering the apology. The apology as presented received their approval.

One logistical issue remained outstanding right up to the day of the apology. Because of his help in resolving this issue and his general support throughout this process, the prime minister thanked Jack Layton at the beginning of the apology speech. The Aboriginal leaders wanted to be seated on the floor of the House of Commons during the ceremony. Initially, the PM had rejected this request, as it was his view that the floor of the chamber was only for Members of Parliament. Layton was of the view that the Aboriginal leaders should be seated on the floor but was not going to embarrass the government over it. The apology was the most important part of all of this, and Layton supported the PM's wording. Late in the morning of the day of the apology, Layton tried unsuccessfully to speak to the PM, and then called me. He wanted to alert us that Stéphane Dion, in a blatant attempt to embarrass the government and hog some of the day for himself, would move a motion when the House began sitting that the Aboriginal leaders be allowed to take seats on the floor of the chamber. The PM did not want to engage Dion in a pissing contest immediately prior to giving the apology, so he agreed to allow the leaders to sit on the floor of the chamber. The PM avoided a confrontation with Dion and, for this, gave Jack Layton specific mention in the preamble to the apology.[4]

As stated above, the First Nations agenda is long and large. The government and the AFN, working together through a joint task force, found a new and efficient method for resolving specific claims. It could be a model for further joint action. The first-ever federal Cabinet Priorities and Planning Committee meeting held north of the 60th parallel occurred in the summer of 2008. Harper also met with the indigenous leaders of the North on their own territory to listen to and discuss their challenges. These types of one-on-one meetings away, from the glare of the spotlight, are amazingly useful, as the setting is informal and the comments candid. For example, one of the main issues raised by Mary Simon, then Inuit leader, was the lack of mental health facilities in the North for indigenous peoples. They are mainly flown to Vancouver for treatment, far away from their family support network in the North.

In the post-apology world, the government and the Aboriginal leaders faced the task of building on what was expressed and, through working together, actually having a positive impact on the lives of all of Canada's Aboriginal peoples. Unfortunately, with few exceptions, this has not occurred.

Governing is a lot like a featured act on *The Ed Sullivan Show*, which aired on TV every Sunday night in the 1950s and 1960s. Sullivan had this one performer on repeatedly: his entire act featured plates spinning on top of poles. He would start with one plate on one pole, adding poles and plates until eventually there would be twenty or so spinning simultaneously all across the front of the stage. The trick was to keep all of the plates spinning with none falling on the floor and breaking. The analogy to governing should be obvious. The government is trying to keep all the policy plates spinning (its agenda); the opposition sees its role as distracting the government so that a plate falls or adding a new pole and plate to see if the government can get it spinning, and then keep that plate and all the others from falling.

In the fall of 2006, prior to the Liberal leadership selection meeting in Montreal, we got very reliable intelligence through Deputy Press

Secretary Dimitri Soudas that the Bloc was preparing a motion to recognize Quebec as a nation.[5] This would have been similar to the bilingual issue in Manitoba that the Liberals tried to confront Mulroney with, when he became PC leader in 1983; it was designed to divide the Conservative caucus. This was a pole and a plate designed by the Bloc to fall and crash, for no other reason than to embarrass all other parties but help the Bloc. The prime minister took this one and upped the ante. The political pole and plate firmly planted by the PM stated: "This House recognizes that the Québécois form a nation within a united Canada."[6] Harper also performed a pre-emptive strike: recognizing that Dion was the former Chrétien Cabinet minister on the national unity file, he got Dion's approval for the resolution prior to tabling. The resolution eventually passed the House of Commons on a 266 to 16 vote. This motion, plus implementing the "open federalism" parts of the 2006 platform, plus restoring fiscal balance were to lay the foundation for the Conservative Party's continued growth in Quebec. Harper's instincts on these matters were trusted by his caucus. After all, he was the one who had established the caucus committee on bilingualism and the Official Languages Act after the 2004 election loss, and its work had not only been productive, but quite helpful in contributing to the 2006 platform.

The one person who either did not trust the PM's instincts on the "Nation Resolution" or felt his own views were better was Intergovernmental Affairs Minister Michael Chong. I suppose at the root of Chong's issue with this tactic and subsequent House of Common resolution was lack of consultation. His opposition to the resolution was completely unexpected, and one could say that his resignation from Cabinet was the first casualty of Harper's style of governing. In the fast-paced world of one-upmanship politics, there is little time to consult, little time to assemble the team to canvass opinions. In this case, the PM saw an opportunity to further the Conservative Party's Quebec agenda, jumped on it, cleared it with Dion, told his caucus what he was about to do at the weekly meeting, and then hit a wall when Chong believed the resolution supported something he did not believe in.

Those of us from the PC legacy party were shocked by Chong's reaction, since to us, the resolution seemed a logical extension of the Meech Lake and Charlottetown accords (which ironically, were both opposed by Harper and the other legacy party, Reform). It was hard to understand or digest Chong's objections. This was not recognition of Quebec as a nation; it was moving "distinct" status to another level.

Chong made up his mind to leave Cabinet; he was not pushed. In fact, Senator Marjory LeBreton, former prime minister Brian Mulroney, numerous PMO senior staff, and many others spoke with him. But he was adamant, and there ended what might have been a prominent career in Cabinet.

The resolution received overwhelming support in the House of Commons, and proved to be somewhat of an embarrassment for the Grits as two of their leadership contenders voted against it. It also solidified the new Conservative Party as the federalist option (at the time) in Quebec, building on what the government had done and would be doing with the fiscal imbalance in the next federal budget.

The loss of Michael Chong as a Cabinet minister over this issue was viewed almost as a curiosity. The government always expects to lose ministers, through scandal; bad, wrong, or improper decisions; or, now a rarity, taking the fall for major administrative errors at the bureaucratic level. A government does not expect to lose a minister in this way. Sure, Turner resigned from Trudeau's Cabinet and Martin was relieved of Finance by Prime Minister Chrétien, but there were back stories concerning leadership ambitions in both cases. Not the case here.

Because it was so odd, it did not lead to a change in Harper's management style. No one ever said, "We don't want to have any more bright young ministers resign in disagreement over policy issues, so we better change how we make the decisions around here." So how were (and are) decisions made in the Harper PMO or by the Harper government in general? It really depended on the type of decision. Administrative decisions that needed the involvement of the prime minister, such as issues with senior bureaucratic personnel, changes in machinery of government, advice on which national or international meetings to attend, trips abroad and the invitations of foreign governments, and agenda for Priorities and Planning Committee meetings would be discussed at the almost-daily PM-clerk-Brodie-Carson meetings, what came to be called the Clerk meetings. Others have commented on these meetings, sometimes in a negative fashion, but I felt privileged to be included. My role was to take notes and to offer comments from the perspective of *not* being the "smartest one in the room." And when Brodie was travelling, as he had to from time to time, I would fill in for him and brief him after. From my perspective, it was similar to attending a master's or Ph.D. seminar on Canadian and international politics. Virtually all imaginable subjects were discussed, with strongly or not so strongly held views expressed, and

Harper making the ultimate decision. This was no "Yes, Prime Minister" meeting. No one in the room got there because he was a shrinking violet afraid to speak his mind, devoid of views, opinions, or knowledge. The nature of these meetings changed as governing continued into the second and third mandates, and perhaps that is understandable. As time went on, most of the matters that consumed early Clerk meetings had been resolved, and some measure of confidence grew in the job of governing. In the Brodie PMO, there was a more trusting relationship with the senior bureaucracy than in the PMOs that followed. We could not have survived in government or accomplished as much as we did in those early days without the help and guidance of the clerk, the senior people in PCO, and the senior members of the public service that we interacted with. This does not mean that the first mandate was run by PCO, but there was a close working relationship, with each group respecting the judgment and role of the other. Yes, there were disagreements, but they were addressed maturely and we moved on to other matters. The bureaucracy was not viewed as the enemy plotting the downfall of the government.

The Clerk meeting was not confined to administrative issues. Especially when discussing the Priorities and Planning Committee meeting agendas, there were significant discussions about policy as well as approaches to various subjects. As time went on, and the PM became more settled in his role, he made it clear that the Priorities and Planning Committee presentations should be brief and focused, leaving plenty of time for discussion. The agenda-setting discussions were useful for what Lynch had to convey to deputy ministers and what I had to convey to ministers and their staff.

Decisions were made at the daily morning meeting with the prime minister and his senior staff. It was preceded by two staff meetings, the first to settle on the issues of the day, and the second, immediately preceding the senior staff meeting with the PM, chaired by either Brodie or me, to go over matters to be discussed when the PM arrived between 8:30 a.m. and 8:45 a.m. This third meeting of the morning, now with the PM, was more of a media review and issues management meeting. But it was a decision-making meeting with regard to how overnight issues were to be addressed, how question period was to be handled, and responses that had to be ready for the QP practice at 1 p.m., or at noon if the prime minister would be handling the issue.

Brodie would start the morning meeting with the PM with a general overview of the previous day and a look ahead at the current day and the challenges it presented, such as opposition motions or bills and how they should be handled. The issues manager, Beardsley and later Jenni Byrne, would give an overview of the issues raised in the print media, and someone from Patrick Muttart's shop would deal with electronic media. I would then set out how I believed question period would look, trying to anticipate which opposition party would raise particular issues. Dimitri Soudas would review the French media and how he thought the Bloc would deal with it in QP.

Decisions regarding pending party advertising were discussed here since Muttart, who was in charge of that segment of the operation, including branding, regularly attended. As the daily and weekly schedule of announcements for the PM and Cabinet ministers were also discussed, decisions would be made as to following through with or amending the schedule depending on what other issues had arisen.

This tight schedule would get thrown off if we noticed Harper carrying a sheet of paper as he walked into the room. These would be issues from home. Whether raised by Laureen or by the PM himself, they were of the highest priority. Usually, these would be stories appearing in the media that had been leaked or government announcements that had been commented upon before their release. The PM needed to have answers before heading home to 24 Sussex.

The main decision-making body of the government was the weekly Priorities and Planning Committee meeting. This Cabinet committee received and dealt with the reports from all of the other Cabinet policy committees as well as from the Operations Committee. In addition to policy issues, discussions could take place on various political situations facing the government. These would be wide-ranging discussions, with Harper seriously canvassing the views of ministers. He also appreciated receiving a regional political perspective. While all ministers have a "bubble-like" existence from the time they are appointed, they do have a group of people they contact on a regular basis, hoping to receive honest and straightforward advice. There is no point in *not* speaking truth to power, especially when one has the opportunity to speak to power. Sycophants and cheerleaders are useless – yes, they will make their bosses, ministers, or the PM feel good for the moment, but cheering on a minister as he or she walks over a precipice is not usually the measure of good advice or success.

At the Priorities and Planning Committee meetings, usually on policy matters, reports and decision items were presented by either the chair of the Cabinet policy committee or by a non–Priorities and Planning Committee minister appearing to advance his or her own matter. The group came to decisions through consensus. Sometimes, on a contentious matter, Harper would call for a show of hands to determine how strong the feelings of members were one way or the other. On occasion, when no decision was arrived at, a matter would be adjourned to get more information or to canvass other alternatives, or the matter would simply be left ad referendum to the prime minister.

As with the Clerk meetings, no one in these Priorities and Planning Committee meetings could be characterized as a shrinking violet, nor did it seem to me that Harper wanted that. A matter would be presented by the sponsoring minister; the minister's deputy or other senior departmental officials would be in attendance to respond to technical questions or to give advice to the minister. After the presentation, inevitably on a slide deck, discussion would ensue, with the prime minister keeping the speaking-order list and a close eye on the clock. He did not try to direct the discussion and would only show impatience with long-winded, irrelevant interventions. He was always looking for a certain level of crispness in the discussions. Inevitably, these followed a pattern: identify the problem; challenge an issue; set out (hopefully all) alternative solutions, usually three; and then thoughtfully discuss which alternative made the most practical and political sense to adopt. The PM would intervene to challenge points being made or to delve further into the discussion, but not to belittle. On a number of occasions, it was helpful to have the clerk and senior bureaucrats in the room as they had deeper background or technical knowledge than the minister. As discussion wound up, sometimes the presenting minister would speak and then the PM. Usually though, the prime minister would be the last to speak, summing up the discussion pros and cons, and then turning it back to the presenting minister for comments before a decision would be made.

While the Priorities and Planning Committee was the main decision-making body, the Operations Committee could also render decisions on matters that had a short time frame for implementation. The Operations Committee met regularly on Mondays, late in the day or early in the evening, so that in most instances, its decisions could be ratified or reported the next morning at the Priorities and Planning Committee meeting. Because of the nature of the matters it dealt with – urgent and pressing, and usually to do with issues management – the Operations Committee would, in addition to regularly scheduled meetings, meet any time at the call of the chair. On occasions when no consensus could be reached, the chair, Jim Prentice, would present the varying views to the PM or to the Priorities and Planning Committee and decisions would be made. In other words, it wasn't necessary that the Operations Committee reach a unanimous conclusion; sometimes, just the airing of various points of view was sufficient.

However, there were some matters, like income trusts, which were so important and so volatile that the decision-making group was kept very tight.[7] But that was more the exception than the rule. At some point, caucus and Cabinet have to place their trust in the leader to make the right decision and to involve and rely on the right people while doing so. It should be noted that in the Harper government, full Cabinet rarely meets, and when it does, it is usually to deal with the discussion and ratification of federal appointments.

While this decision-making process seemed to work without protest in the early years, it has run into opposition lately, with the caucus wanting some measure of relief from top-down decision-making and more input into the day-to-day operation of the government. Is this a matter of lack of trust in the decision-making abilities of Harper and his office or is it a natural evolution after eight years in power? Perhaps some of both.

One curious feature of decision-making in the Harper government is that, unlike most other political leaders, the prime minister does not have an informal group of trusted, independent advisors across the country that he consults on a regular basis – to see how he or the party is doing on various aspects of its agenda. One could argue that this leaves Harper isolated and dependent on a very small group in his employ for advice.

There was no one-size-fits-all method of decision-making, which I believe befits a minority government trying to be agile and accommodate situations as they arose. For instance, in the fall of 2006, the government cancelled the Court Challenges Program. Any government with this prime minister and Brodie as chief of staff was eventually going to do this. It was a program that had outlived its usefulness. Perhaps there was a need to protect and advance rights when the Charter of Rights and Freedoms was in its initial stages of developing a track record of case law, but surely these causes or cases no longer needed to be funded or backed by government. While there were the usual protests when government funding to any program is cut, one element of the protest resonated with caucus members: funding that went to protect the rights of linguistic minorities. The protection of minority language rights both in Quebec and in the rest of Canada, especially in the Maritimes and Manitoba as well as Alberta, struck a chord with government members. This occurred around the same time that the government was dealing with strengthening of the Official Languages Act and moving forward with a new official languages program.

Graham Fraser, the official languages commissioner, along with Graham Fox, who was involved with the Federation of Francophone and Acadian communities of Canada and now heads the Institute for Research on Public Policy, approached me to see if we could put the right people in a room, and perhaps we could settle the lawsuit brought against that government by the Federation of Francophone and Acadian communities of Canada and rethink the Court Challenges Program as it affected official language minorities.

One representative from each of the affected groups, as well as Fraser and Fox, met with me in the small Cabinet room, next to my office and just down the hall from the PM's office. After an hour or so of discussion, it was obvious that the group wanted to bring an end to the litigation and launch a new part of the Court Challenge Program, which could be fashioned as part of the government's recommitment to official languages and bilingualism. We were able to arrive at an appropriate amount of money that the government would provide for the protection of linguistic minorities, with most of the money designated for promotion of minority languages or for mediation. When we had the agreement roughed out, I went down the hall and interrupted the PM-clerk-Brodie meeting; they knew we were meeting on this matter. I brought the PM, Lynch, and Brodie up to speed, set out the main features of the new arrangement, and after a few minutes of discussion, got their agreement. I went back down the hall and reported that the PM, Lynch, and Brodie had agreed and that the follow-up would take place through Lynch and Fraser. One other matter arose and was quickly dealt with by another sortie down the hall. And that is how the new Court Challenges Program dealing with linguistic minorities and mediation was developed. Not that this was easy, but it does illustrate the many, varied ways decisions can be arrived at in a government that wants to make decisions and move on to other subjects.

UNEXPECTED ISSUES TRACK

The second track involved in governing related to those matters that just happen and have to be addressed by the government regardless of political stripe. For the most part, these are what could be called the unforced errors of governing. Sometimes in addressing issues and challenges, errors are committed or even compounded, but in reality there is little that could have been done to avoid them. Sometimes things just go off the rails. Some of these carried over beyond the first mandate, while others arose and were dealt with in the first mandate, and the government moved on with its agenda. The most important thing is to ensure that in addressing matters on this track, the government doesn't become entirely consumed by them and thrown off its own governing track, with its hopefully positive agenda.

When these matters arise, no matter their nature, there is almost a formula into which the challenges and their solutions fall. There is the abject apology. When a videotape of Brad Wall and Tom Lukiwski making inappropriate comments about gay men was unearthed, the prime minister, who was travelling in Europe, told me in graphic terms to find Lukiwski and have him apologize. Lukiwski apologized outside the Commons chamber, to the NDP member who raised the matter, as the House began sitting the next day (Friday), and, quite frankly, anywhere else it was felt necessary. There could be no justification for the comments, and any attempt to justify them would make the story worse than it was, give it legs, and accomplish nothing. The same approach was taken during the 2008 election campaign when it was revealed that the minister of agriculture, Gerry Ritz, on a conference call dealing with Listeriosis, which had been found in processed meat at the main Maple Leaf Foods plant and had led directly to the death of seventeen Canadians, had joked about "death by a thousand cold cuts" and had responded to the report of a new death in Prince Edward Island by saying, "Please tell me its Wayne Easter [Liberal MP]." The Conservative campaign was in a town in northern Quebec, when this was made public. As soon as we were informed, I told the prime minister and was told to speak to Ritz and have him apologize, which he did on a number of occasions for a remark he should never have made. His apology, and the fact that it was understood that in order to relieve stress, people do engage in macabre forms of humour, helped end this matter. While there were the usual calls to replace Lukiwski and Ritz, the PM was firm: they made a mistake, apologized, and that was to be the end of it. And it was. It is unfortunate that the custom of apologizing when necessary and appropriate did not seem to survive much beyond the first mandate. If it had, some of the negative views of the government as arrogant and uncompromising could have been avoided.

Other parts of this second track required more than an apology; they required detailed analysis, strategic decisions, and action, either in the form of push back and/or pragmatic solutions. Initially one has to ascertain whether or not the government faces a significant problem or challenge, obtain the facts (never an easy task), and then determine what has to be done to resolve the situation or, in some instances, kill the story completely. What one doesn't want to do in these situations is make the situation worse. As the old saying goes, when you find yourself in a hole, the first thing to do is stop digging.

One such issue, which has plagued the government almost from the time it assumed office, was the allegations of torture of Afghan prisoners or detainees. Initially, I believe we thought this was a repeat of the situation in Somalia some years before, but that was not the case. The human rights and civil liberties people who were raising the issue did it in the context of Canadian military turning over Afghan/Taliban prisoners taken "in theatre" to the Afghan government authorities to be placed in prisons run by the Afghan government, allegedly knowing that these prisoners would be tortured or could go missing, presumably murdered. Originally, Taliban prisoners captured by the Canadian military were turned over to the United States military, which was running a prison system in Afghanistan. Subsequent to the allegations of abuse of prisoners in Iraq at the hands of the US military, this practice was stopped, with Taliban prisoners handed over to Afghan authorities under an agreement with the government of Afghanistan.

The first allegation of torture appeared in a US State Department memo made public in the late winter of 2006. There was no direct link to Canadian troops handing over Taliban prisoners to Afghan authorities knowing they were going to be tortured. However, it did not take the opposition in Parliament long to make this link. The first item of business in this type of situation is to get the facts. This was made difficult, if not impossible, because of the split jurisdiction between the Department of National Defence (DND) and the Department of Foreign Affairs and International Trade (DFAIT). DND was responsible for the Canadian troops and DFAIT for the drafting and implementation of the agreement dealing with prisoner transfers. And we were fighting a war halfway around the world in a country where living conditions would at best be described as primitive, and the prison even more so.

In the second mandate of the government from 2008 to 2011, this matter took on a whole new aspect. Richard Colvin from DFAIT, who was stationed in Afghanistan throughout that earlier period, surfaced, saying that as early as May 2006, he was writing memos on the subject of alleged abuses of Taliban prisoners handed over by Canadians to Afghan authorities.

However, in the first mandate, no memos, nothing from Richard Colvin was ever brought to the attention of the Harper PMO or, as far as I know, to the attention of any minister involved. I was as surprised as anyone to learn of those memos and hear Colvin's testimony during the committee hearings that took place in the second mandate. From Arif Lalani, Canada's ambassador to Afghanistan during this period, through to the senior public servants, the clerk, the deputy minister on the file – no one ever mentioned this person, his allegations, or his memos. And while I doubt they saw his memos, I believe that if they had, they would have discounted their veracity.

From the very beginning of the controversy through to what I would consider its end – the decision of the Military Police Complaints Commission in 2012 – there has been no proven case of the Canadian military handing over a Taliban prisoner knowing that the prisoner would be abused or tortured.

What surprised us most in 2007 was the vehemence with which this matter was pursued by the media, the opposition, and Canadian civil liberties groups. The prime minister and members of his Cabinet found it incomprehensible that the only questions, the only issues that were consistently raised regarding the war in Afghanistan concentrated on the general well-being or welfare of Taliban prisoners – as Stock Day would say many times in the QP practices, when referring to the Taliban prisoners: "these are the guys who are trying to kill our guys."

Realizing this was a serious issue that would not disappear as long as we were fighting a war in Afghanistan, the solution became one of issue management. We needed to know, in as close to real time as possible, what was going on in Afghanistan. To do that, we instituted daily calls that involved Sandra Buckler and me from the PMO and were chaired by David Mulroney or his designate from DFAIT. This way we would know what was going on in Afghanistan, what our allies were up to, and any new allegations of torture. As time went on, the calls were less frequent, but in managing a long-term issue – and that was what this was – up-to-date information is everything.

Also, there were the constant calls from the opposition for ministers to appear in committee on this matter. I thought a joint meeting of the House of Commons Defence and Foreign Affairs committees for two hours, with every minister who was involved in this matter appearing on a panel of ministers, would shut this down, at least for a while. And it did.

Eventually, however, the misinformation from the field as to the status of agreements and their roles and the constant haranguing by the opposition led Defence Minister Gordon O'Connor to make the claim in the spring of 2007 that all transfers of Taliban prisoners in Afghanistan were supervised by the Red Cross. We, he, honestly believed that to be the case. And if it wasn't, what was the Red Cross doing there?

In the summer of 2007, the controversy having raged for too long, the prime minister made a change in Cabinet at Defence. That same summer, he did one other remarkable thing. I was to call him on a Saturday afternoon to discuss his latest ideas on Afghanistan. It was after one of the many great games the Ottawa Senators played in their Stanley Cup run that year. As always, the beginning of our conversation dealt with hockey, and I believe, the Senators win that day over Buffalo in the Eastern Conference finals. Then the PM said that he had come up with an idea on Afghanistan, which he didn't think I would like. He wanted to put in place a "blue ribbon" or "wise persons" committee to deal with all aspects of our involvement with Afghanistan. Contrary to his expectations – I have never liked hiving things off to be dealt with by committee – my reaction was extremely positive, especially when he said he would try to get John Manley, Chrétien's former minister of foreign affairs and of finance to chair it. This was a good idea since it would take the focus off the government, obtain independent and real solutions, and, if we worked with the group, mean our not being surprised by their recommendations and thus probably being able to implement them. Its report on Afghanistan and Canada's involvement was incredibly helpful in dealing with the war and Canada's ongoing involvement.

Continuing with the second track, in November 2007, the government faced another unexpected issue: the possible worldwide shortage of medical isotopes caused by the closure of the Chalk River nuclear power plant for routine maintenance and the refusal by Linda Keen, the head of the Canadian Nuclear Safety Commission (CNSC), to allow its reopening. This matter, which lasted only about a couple of weeks, started innocently enough with a junior member in the office of Minister of Natural Resources Lunn taking a message on a

Friday afternoon that due to safety concerns, the Chalk River nuclear power plant would not reopen as scheduled. This meant little or nothing to the person receiving the call, and it was not until question period practice the following week, when Health Minister Tony Clement raised the isotope shortage possibility, that anyone realized what was actually going on, and what the consequences were. As it was explained, there was a long-standing dispute between the folks who ran Chalk River and the head of the CNSC with regard to certain repairs that the latter wanted carried out at the facility. When it closed for a few days for routine maintenance, Keen ordered that it not reopen until such time as the repairs she wanted carried out were completed. This would mean that the reactor would not be functioning for some time. We also learned that, since the plant expected to reopen in a few days, there was no buildup or stockpile of medical isotopes when it shut down. Although the effective life of a medical isotope is not long, a stockpile in reserve would have been helpful. We further learned that this fifty-year-old reactor in Chalk River manufactured over half of the world supply of isotopes and that isotopes were used in diagnosing and treating serious diseases such as cancer. Another factor was that, if Keen got her way, the plant would be shut down for a considerable period, thus ensuring a worldwide shortage. As luck would have it, the other major isotope manufacturing plant, in South Africa, was shut down as well, leaving only some smaller European suppliers who were hard pressed to keep up with the existing demands on them. The last fact to be considered was that there was a dispute as to whether the repairs were actually necessary; there was considerable opinion that the plant could operate safely without the repairs being carried out.

Just that suddenly, something we previously knew nothing about had the potential to become a life-and-death matter unless action was taken. Whether we knew anything about medical isotopes or what they did or how necessary they were to medical diagnosis and treatment, the lives of those relying on those isotopes as part of their medical care were now effectively in the government's hands. What to do?

Obviously, sit down with Linda Keen and reach some accommodation, as perhaps she did not appreciate the severity of the situation that was unfolding. Surely, we could reach an agreement to do the repairs she felt were necessary in stages over the next while, but the facility could continue to operate in order to deal with the medical isotope shortage. This track was left to officials, but the clerk report-

ed back that Keen was not going to move off her position. She finally had the folks at Chalk River where she wanted them, and she was
not going to relent until everything she wanted done at the facility
was completed. This would take weeks, if not months – time we
believed we did not have.

The next steps were ones that we never thought we would have to
consider: introduce legislation to order the reopening of the plant,
and subsequently consider and then replace Keen as chair of the
Nuclear Safety Commission. Kevin Lynch brought in a lawyer from
Toronto to help us with this. It was a rare treat for me since it was John
Laskin, who had been my LL.M. thesis supervisor at the University of
Toronto back in 1980–81. Believing we had no other choice, and given
that we had expert opinion that the plant could operate safely without the repairs, we proceeded: the legislation was prepared.

On the legislative front, we caught a break. Liberal leader Dion was
on a trip to the Far East and Ignatieff was acting in his stead. The situation was explained to him, and he agreed not to unnecessarily delay
the bill. He did say that he would pull no punches in debate, as he
would attempt to make the point that the government had completely mishandled the situation. I thought that was quite fair since at this
point only the result mattered.

The next hurdle was expediting the bill. In the Senate, it is not
uncommon to hear witnesses on a bill in Committee of the Whole,
rather than sending the bill off to a specific committee. As a rule, it is
only done when time is short, as in back-to-work legislation, or sometimes when an important issue arises and all senators wish to question
a witness, such as former prime minister Trudeau's appearance as a
witness in Committee of the Whole in the Senate on the Meech Lake
Accord. I met with our House leader, Peter Van Loan, and tried the
idea out on him: the bill could be dealt with in Committee of the
Whole in the House of Commons. He liked it and shopped it around
to the other House leaders, who also agreed, as did the Speaker's
office. We would deal with the Chalk River plant legislation in Committee of the Whole in the House of Commons in the evening so as
not to disrupt the normal flow of business in the House.

The next issue was the availability of witnesses. Predictably – it was
December – there was a huge snowstorm, but the call went out for
witnesses, and they arrived pretty much on time. By evening's end, the
bill had passed. Bill Blaikie who chaired the session, felt that this was
the way the House of Commons should always operate. It was the first

time since the late 1940s that the House of Commons met in Committee of the Whole to hear witnesses and deal with legislation.[8]

While we believed the reopening of the Chalk River nuclear power plant in a timely fashion saved lives, it came at a cost to the government. The firing of Linda Keen as head of the Canadian Nuclear Safety Commission gave commentators the evidence they thought they needed to show that the PM and his government were anti–public service. This was definitely not the case in this instance. However, through the years, the Harper government has attracted this view, and as recently as the "enemies list" published on the day of the summer 2013 Cabinet shuffle, it demonstrated that there may be some truth to this impression.

In the fall of 2007, two incidents occurred that affected Harper personally, but fortunately, for him and the party, did not seem to affect him politically. One arose out of the book written by Tom Zytaruk, *Like a Rock: The Chuck Cadman Story*,[9] and the other arose from the sworn affidavit of Karlheinz Schreiber as part of his attempt to stave off deportation to Germany to face justice and prison time (both of which were subsequently meted out by German courts).

In his book, Zytaruk made the case that certain favours had been promised to Chuck Cadman to secure his vote in the May 2005 non-confidence motion. He alleged that a million-dollar insurance policy had been promised to Cadman, and perhaps more. He included a quotation in his book that made it sound like Harper, then leader of the opposition, upon leaving Cadman's house after a courtesy call, knew something about such an offer, then added that Harper did not want to be quoted on anything. The Liberals jumped on the quotation and alleged on their website that the prime minister had been complicit in a bribery attempt of a sitting member of the House of Commons.

Remembering back to May 2005, Harper and I knew there were meetings between Cadman and Doug Finley and Tom Flanagan. This is all set out in Flanagan's book, *Harper's Team*, but we did not know the exact nature of the discussions. We simply assumed they were about all the reasons for Cadman to vote with his former party and against the government. Neither Finley nor Flanagan were authorized to offer anything at all to either put Cadman in a secure economic position or reimburse him for anything lost financially because of an election. The morning after news of Zytaruk's book and the quote broke in Ottawa – I believe it was a Friday – Ian Brodie got Sandra

Buckler and me, and we drove to 24 Sussex in Ian's car. I will never forget entering the living room and seeing Harper sitting on one of the couches. He was talking about the possibility of an RCMP investigation into what might be allegations of criminal activity and the real possibility that he would have to step aside while the investigation was taking place. Two thought-lines occurred to me simultaneously. One, did this mean I was out of a job? Perhaps not. The PM would probably be replaced by Cannon, MacKay, or Prentice. I had a good working relationship with all of them. I was probably okay. Two, I remembered Chrétien. During the Shawinigan affair, which did actually involve an RCMP investigation, he stayed in office. He probably never gave a thought to stepping aside. So, why would this prime minister even think about it?

The PM was quickly disabused of any thoughts of stepping aside. Next, it was important to respond to the allegations made by the Liberals on their website. These comments did not have the protection of parliamentary privilege. In order to fight back, Richard Dearden and Wendy Wagner of Gowlings law firm were retained. They came down to 24 Sussex later that afternoon to meet with Harper, Brodie, Buckler, Jenni Byrne, and me in order to plot a course of action. The prime minister and Ray Novak then went off to Toronto to fulfill the PM's scheduled commitments.

Upon Harper's return, we met late into the evening to go through what he remembered of the day he met Zytaruk in Vancouver. We had obtained the full transcript of the taped interview with Harper, but as we read it, it made no sense. It was as if paragraphs had been moved around and answers were purposely repositioned to go with a question other than the one that had been asked. Doug Finley was also contacted, to find out what exactly had taken place in the meeting or meetings with Cadman. Furthermore, it made no sense that the Conservative Party would be able to take out a million-dollar insurance policy on a man so near death.

The team met again on Sunday evening at 24 Sussex to discuss and settle on a go-forward strategy. Finley had confirmed that no such offer had ever been made, and this was actually corroborated by Cadman himself before his death. But we could not let the allegations stand; we had to get to the bottom of what was actually on the tapes and in what order the statements attributed to Harper were actually made. His recollection was that he was leaving the Cadman home and had not thought he was going to be pursued by anybody for an interview, let alone Zytaruk. Whatever he said, was said on the laneway leaving the house, and he had been more interested in getting to the next event than answering Zytaruk's questions. The plan we put in place was, first, to obtain the tape or tapes and submit them to an expert for authentication; second, to serve Dion and the Liberal party with notice to withdraw their allegations; and third, to prepare a statement of claim.

Although this issue percolated to the surface from time to time, to a large extent this initial strategy worked to kill it. The tapes were acquired and then began the long process of authentication. Eventually, in the 2008 election campaign, the matter of the authenticity of the tapes came back to haunt us. However, the case was eventually dropped in February 2009. It had served its purpose – neutralizing the Liberals – and there was no point in prolonging the dispute over the authenticity of the tapes and what Harper meant by the words Zytarek quoted. Dion was gone as leader, and there was a country to run.

The whole Cadman episode demonstrated to me how allegations can be developed that appeal to people's baser instincts. Also, how quick others can be to jump to the worst possible conclusion to score political points. The prime minister had to push back the way he did. If he had not, and had allowed the allegations to stand without contradiction, his moral authority, if not his legal authority, to govern would have been severely compromised. Purists will say that a sitting prime minister should not sue the leader of the opposition for libel, seeking damages, and for the most part they would be right. Allegations are made in the heat of the moment and, on sober second thought, are subject to apology or simply withdrawal. But this was not a run-of-the-mill case. The official opposition was accusing a sitting prime minister of a serious breach of the Criminal Code. That called into question the ethics of those at the head of our parliamentary system of government. Yes, countering with legal action was an extraordinary measure, but a necessary measure, and it allowed the prime minister to rise above these allegations and continue in office.

While this whole affair shook Stephen and Laureen, they were able to put it behind them and carry on. As Laureen said at the time, we always expected to be attacked when we formed a government, but on our policies, which is fair game, not on this type of thing. A second matter, which arose about the same time, also affected the prime minister personally. From the time Stephen Harper re-entered politics as leader of the Alliance Party, there were overtures back and forth between him and former prime minister Mulroney. At the PC Convention that selected Peter MacKay as leader, Mulroney spoke of working with the Alliance Party. He would not have said that if Preston Manning had still been the leader; he blamed Manning for attempting to destroy the PC Party. Mulroney was also a supporter of the merger discussions and their ultimate result. He spent hours convincing PC colleagues to support the merger. So as time went on, relations between the two men continued to grow, and Mulroney was of great help in the 2006 campaign. He had also been Prime Minister Harper's guest at Harrington Lake.

The revelations late in 2007 on CBC's *Fifth Estate* about the relationship between Schreiber and Mulroney caused Harper some angst, but were not actually worrisome at that point. Mulroney working for Schreiber for cash was not wise, but could be overlooked, given it had subsequently been reported by Mulroney to Revenue Canada. People are quick to judge and criticize what they cannot comprehend or don't want to understand. I believe Mulroney's actions with regard to the cash from Schreiber are understandable, given the working-class family Mulroney came from and the fact that he had gone to university and attained high office, always with the thought of never wanting to be poor again. Facing an unknown future in 1993, Mulroney agreed to take the envelopes of cash. His relationship with Schreiber has cost him dearly, but relationships like that are formed not to do anything illegal or wrong, but to ensure that your family continues to live in the style to which they have become accustomed. And sometimes, inadvertently, untoward things occur, but that was never the intent.

Initially, the Schreiber revelations did not cause a problem, but an affidavit sworn by Schreiber, implicating Harper, created huge problems. Schreiber alleged in the affidavit that he knew the former prime minister would be seeing Harper at Harrington Lake and that Mulroney would bring correspondence supportive of Schreiber's fight against extradition to the attention of Prime Minister Harper. Harper felt betrayed, since Mulroney had told him that he had had no contact with Schreiber for at least seven years – but that was seemingly now not true if one believed the affidavit, which Harper chose to do. Harper distanced himself from Mulroney and said he would convene a public inquiry. He believed he should do no less, as Mulroney had initially asked for one himself.

Harper also believed that while Mulroney was under suspicion, the government and those working within it should have no contact with Mulroney or those supporting or working for him. I had to cancel a meeting that I had scheduled with Robin Sears, who was helping with communications for Mulroney.

During this period, I attended a meeting on this subject in Kevin Lynch's office. I made it clear that Mulroney had faults, like all of us, but he had done great things for Canada and had been a great leader of one of the legacy parties. He did not deserve to be treated as a pariah.

After I left the PMO, in 2009, I spoke frequently with Mulroney. We talked on the morning after the Oliphant decision, and I told him, "You may not like the decision, but it is over. You can put it behind you and move on."[10] Time has passed and feelings have died down. Hopefully, in the next election and in the time between now and then, the relationship between Harper and Mulroney will move closer to where it was pre-Schreiber. This would be good not only for both of them but also for the Conservative Party and for the country. Mulroney is a veritable fountain of knowledge about Quebec and its place within Canada. That knowledge should not go to waste. Arguably, lack of intimate knowledge of Quebec cost Harper a majority in 2008, and since that time Harper has been unable to recover the ground in Quebec that seemed to be his in 2006.

Until the Senate expense issue of 2013, these two matters, Cadman and Schreiber, more than any other events since 2006 directly affected Harper himself. What do his reactions tell us about him as a person, a politician, and a leader? With Cadman, Harper was on the receiving end of an attack on his personal credibility – that he countenanced some form of deal making or outright offer to bribe a sitting MP to vote against the Martin government. He did everything he legally could to protect his reputation, to keep it as pristine as it could possibly be. I believe he also felt personally hurt that such allegations would surface and hoped, believed, and expected that his Cabinet and caucus would support him through what was undoubtedly going to be a rough patch in the mandate. He expected those who knew him to discount these allegations.

With the Mulroney–Schreiber incident, Harper again moved quickly to protect his own reputation. In believing Schreiber, not Mulroney, and in not giving Mulroney the benefit of the doubt, Harper cut Mulroney adrift and then convened an inquiry. But isn't Harper being inconsistent in light of how he wanted to be viewed and treated in the

Cadman affair? To use the Cadman model, Harper should have reached out to Mulroney, given him the benefit of the doubt, and stood by the former prime minister while the truth was ascertained. Instead he shunned him and instructed everyone else to do likewise.

One can draw one's own conclusions about Harper's character from these two incidents. However, I believe we see a man who will move heaven and earth to save his own reputation, even if it means not treating others as he himself wants, or believes he deserves to be treated. One can see this behaviour repeating itself in 2013 in the Senate expense matter.

In addition to the above matters, the first mandate was replete with other unplanned and unexpected track two issues. We tried our best to address them and learn from them. They ranged from evacuation of Lebanese Canadians from Lebanon when that country was involved in war. Who knew there were that many Canadian citizens concentrated in a foreign country? Arranging ships and flights was a nightmare, not something in the course of a usual day's work for Canada's Minister of Foreign Affairs Peter MacKay. But it was done successfully. It also forced DFAIT to look at other countries involved in conflict that might have a significant Canadian population, and how an evacuation, if deemed necessary, would be conducted.

The reversal of the taxation status of income trusts was a financial decision we did not anticipate we would have to make. Given the evidence of companies with major financial holdings converting to non-taxable income trusts, it was a relatively easy decision. The evidence indicated that if the trend continued, Canada's tax revenue situation would be in severe difficulty. At the same time, it was a difficult decision, because it meant reneging on a campaign promise, and a great number of the trusts were located in Alberta. Having determined what needed to be done, it had to be kept secret until the announcement, and then caucus had to be sold on how it was the right and only choice.

Two issues we dealt with required a change from the approach of the previous government. One involved the Canadian on death row in Montana for committing a double murder, and the other was Omar Khadr's imminent return to Canada from US custody at Guantanamo Bay.

In November–December 2007, it came to our attention that Ronald Smith faced execution in Montana. Under the previous government,

Canada would automatically seek clemency and request that the prisoner be transferred back to Canada to serve the remainder of his sentence. This was exactly what we did not want to do. We did not want to argue for commuting his sentence, and we certainly did not want to bring him back to Canada, as he had been in prison in the United States for twenty-five years. If we brought him back, we would have to figure out how to deal with him, as he would have served his full sentence under Canadian law.

The public service pointed out to the government that if we made any change from how the government had previously dealt with these types of cases, the decision would be subject to a court challenge. Therefore, reasons had to be developed that Cabinet could articulate. This was made all the more difficult because most of the decisions on this issue were worked through during the daily question period preparation meetings, where no formal or informal minutes are kept. The view was that if one commits murder in a jurisdiction that is free and democratic and that has the death penalty, then one is subject to the penalty. Just because Canada doesn't have the death penalty does not preclude other countries from adopting the death penalty. So, at that time, the government decided not to intervene to seek commutation of his sentence.

Similarly with Omar Khadr, the Conservative government viewed him as an enemy combatant who should suffer the full effect of American law for killing US soldiers. Why would Canada do anything to make it possible for him to leave Guantanamo? And similar to Smith, upon his return, we might have little control since he would have virtually served out his sentence and would have to be released with no restrictions on his movements.

In 2012, Khadr was transferred back to Canada to serve the balance of his sentence. This occurred when all avenues to keep him out of the country had been exhausted. The issue now is how long will he remain in prison and what conditions will be placed on him when he is ultimately released.

While focus on these first two tracks, especially the governing track, consumed a lot of time and energy, three other tracks still needed to be addressed.

Governing, Part 2:
Solving Issues – Policy Clashes, Managing People, and Staying Election Ready

The previous chapter began with a description of the five governing tracks in play during the first mandate, and then went on to look at the first (what the government wants to do as it implements its agenda) and the second (unexpected things coming at the government that may derail track one efforts). This chapter carries on with the last three tracks: where a problematic issue can combine with a policy initiative and turn what might have been a negative into something quite positive; personnel; and the omnipresent, election readiness.

PROBLEMATIC ISSUE –
POLICY INITIATIVE COLLISION TRACK

A track three issue doesn't happen often, but it does happen. An example would be Canada's role in the war in Afghanistan. Begun by the Liberals when Canada joined the United States, other NATO nations, and other countries after 9/11, it was now the Conservatives' war, and the government was committed to it. Legally it became our war when we won the election and took office formally on 6 February 2006, but after engineering the first extension of Canada's commitment in the spring of 2006, it really became Stephen Harper's war. Enduring and responding to the allegations of Taliban prisoner detainee torture and realizing we would have to deal yet again with a possible extension in 2008, it was important that such action have a solid policy base. Rather than divide Canadians, which an election over a continuing commitment to Afghanistan might do, Harper, in what can only be described as a stroke of genius, established an independent panel on Canada's future involvement in Afghanistan – and he recruited Chré-

The Advisors. The panel on Canada's future role in
Afghanistan, chaired by John Manley, provided sound
advice for a government looking for a path forward on
the war in that country. (Courtesy of Bruno Schlum-
berger/*Ottawa Citizen*. Reprinted by permission)

tien's former foreign affairs and finance minister, John Manley, to
chair it. Manley realized that his acceptance of the request from the
prime minister would not sit well with former colleagues in the Liberal Party, but responding to the call of service to his country was of
paramount importance to him. Manley was joined on this by task
force by equally dedicated people: Derek Burney, Pamela Wallin, Paul
Tellier, and Jake Epp. During its short existence – appointed in October 2007 and reporting in January 2008 – it worked hard; heard a lot
of witnesses; travelled to Afghanistan as well as New York, Brussels,
and Washington D.C.; and formulated a report that addressed numerous issues, giving the government a clear path to follow if it wanted
to continue to pursue this war.

The recommendations of the Independent Panel on Canada's Future Role in Afghanistan were prefaced by the chair's comments on the importance of Canada's commitment in Afghanistan as it relates to global and Canadian security, Canada's national reputation, and the "well being of some of the world's most impoverished and vulnerable people." Manley also outlined the importance of this commitment "because it had already involved the sacrifice of Canadian lives."[1]

The panel made five recommendations.[2] The first dealt with Canada's diplomatic position as it relates to Afghanistan and other regional players. Canada should take a more disciplined position, pressing for a high-level civilian representative of the UN secretary-general to ensure better coherence in the civilian and military activity. The next three recommendations relate to operations in Afghanistan. More troops to bolster security and training, deal with neighbours such as Pakistan, and end corruption in the Afghan government so that focus turns to helping deliver basic services to Afghan people. Canada's combat role should continue beyond February 2009, but increasingly concentrate on training the Afghan National Security Forces so they can take the lead. An additional battle group as well as medium-lift helicopter capacity is needed if Canada is to continue in this mission. Finally, Canada should give higher priority to reconstruction and project development, and the government should do better in its communications with Canadians about progress in Afghanistan, including diplomatic and reconstruction efforts. The recommendations within the control of the Canadian government were implemented, and a special Cabinet committee on Afghanistan, chaired by David Emerson, was created.

Another area in need of creative solutions was federal–provincial relations. As has already been set out, Harper's view of the theory and practice of the Constitution's division of powers is very different from his Liberal predecessor's. He made it clear early in his political career that his view, as a Conservative, respected the power given to the provinces and did not see all knowledge as residing at the centre. He also committed to a very limited use of the so-called federal spending power, to be used only when provinces with more than 50 per cent of the population agree. Provinces that decided not to participate in the main initiative would be compensated by the federal government for their costs should they determine to run a similar program.

The regular federal–provincial bun fights known as executive federalism would become a relic of Canada's Liberal past. Discounting the dinner reception with the premiers held shortly after the election, there have been only two federal–provincial meetings since February 2006: a reception and dinner in January 2008 and a gathering in mid-January 2009 to deal with Canada's economic situation and to seek input into the stimulus federal budget to be presented later that month. The evening before the 2009 First Ministers' Meeting, attendees met with the leaders of Canada's national Aboriginal organizations.

The January 2008 reception and dinner for premiers at 24 Sussex had a very fluid agenda. The country and most provinces were still in fairly good shape economically, so the major concerns of the premiers were the usual – health care, environment, and economy. In order to soften the discussion on the environment, prior to the meeting, the prime minister had established a $1 billion ecotrust fund, with the money spread among the provinces and territories to fund green energy projects. The terms of the trust were fairly vague so that the money could be accessed easily. However, for the few months after, getting this money into the hands of the provinces and territories for relevant projects became the bane of our existence for Mark Cameron, PMO director of policy, and me.

The discussion around the dinner table that evening was predictable, except for the intrusion of the Harper cat into the mix. Louis Lévesque, deputy minister for intergovernmental affairs, and I were seated at the table in the dining room alcove directly behind the prime minister. Halfway through the meal, the cat entered the room along with Roger, who was in charge of serving the meal. With the unerring instinct of going where it was least wanted, the cat headed toward Louis, who is not only allergic to cats but also afraid of them. As the cat approached Louis, Roger sprang into action and grabbed the cat, who being no dummy, dug claws deep into the carpet. The PM and the premiers on his side of the table had no idea what the premiers on the other side of the table – with a clear view of the unfolding drama – were laughing about. It was the highlight of my night as Roger eventually detached the cat from the rug and headed out the dining room door with it firmly in his grasp.

As I said, the discussion was predictable to a certain extent, with the usual complaints about revenue sharing and never enough money to do what the provinces felt needed to be done. I was quite surprised by

Premier Danny Williams of Newfoundland and Labrador. At these gatherings, the premiers speak in the order that their provinces joined Confederation, so inevitably our eastern-most province goes last.

I expected Premier Williams to be his usual bombastic self, but he wasn't. His intervention dealt mainly with Aboriginal issues and the need for premiers and the PM to collectively deal with the poverty and joblessness of Canada's Aboriginal people. He felt this was the most pressing issue of the day and, if it weren't addressed, conditions would simply spiral downward out of control and a real crisis would be the result. The approach was meaningful and heartfelt, quite out of keeping with the public persona we had witnessed in the fights over the Atlantic Accord and options brought to it by the federal government. It was one of those moments when you expect a fight, it doesn't happen – indeed, it's quite the opposite – and you're left wondering, what just happened here?

The next morning Harper and I met with Premier Paul Okalik of Nunavut since he had some specific concerns he wanted to address. Nunavut is the sprawling eastern Arctic territory with too many square kilometres and too few people. His concerns dealt mainly with the financial health of Nunavut, ports, and fishing – and seeking federal help for these and other issues. The prime minister, since assuming office, had fallen in love with the North. He went there every summer and planned to hold a first-ever Priorities and Planning Committee meeting in Inuvik later in 2008. Harper questioned Okalik as to what it was like to live in the Arctic in mid-winter in January, a time of virtually total twenty-four-hour darkness. Okalik was quite forthcoming as he said that it was very difficult and something one did not ever become accustomed to. He said that the total darkness makes one lethargic with a "heavy" feeling, making movement around the community difficult. It was like a weight on one's shoulders that is always present.

From the beginning of the 2006 mandate, the major federal–provincial issues have predictably focused on economic matters. For the most part, the provinces believe they are being shortchanged by Ottawa. As mentioned above, the 2006 federal budget contained a discussion paper dealing with the fiscal imbalance between the federal and provincial governments, and it contained typical Harper solutions. If the federal government were going to give up tax revenue to the provinces or tax points to solve this imbalance, something would have to come back in return. The "something" was eliminating inter-provincial trade barriers and strengthening the economic union. Around the time of the budget, two other papers emerged: one on equalization, which was a study started under the Martin Liberals, and one on fiscal balance, from the Council of the Federation.

All three papers[3] were put into the mix during preparation of the 2007 budget, which would address two items: fiscal imbalance as well as equalization and the Atlantic Accord. Settling the former was of prime importance to Premier Charest, who was fighting a provincial election in Quebec. We also knew it was key to having Bloc support for the 2007 budget. Up until this time, while the relationship with Charest was always a challenge, it was proceeding fairly well. As with Bourassa before him, Charest had to walk a fine line between being a federalist and a nationalist, and sometimes had to sound like a sovereigntist. Bourassa drove Mulroney crazy; he never knew which side of an issue Bourassa would land on, because there was no coherence or consistency to his thinking. Bourassa's views evolved to address the current situation and evolved again to face new situations – sometimes being internally consistent and sometimes not, again depending on the circumstances.

So when Charest needed the fiscal imbalance addressed, Harper accommodated him, and then saw Charest use the transfer as an election ploy to fund lowering of taxes, which of course would create yet another fiscal imbalance. I believe Harper looked at this as a blatant misuse of the money, since he had worked long and hard to achieve general agreement that a fiscal imbalance existed, and that it should be addressed. From that time forward relations cooled considerably between Harper and Charest.

The other major fiscal issue that affected federal–provincial relations in both 2007 and 2008 was equalization and the Atlantic Accord dispute. Changes to the Atlantic Accord in the form of adding an option that Danny Williams eventually accepted to his benefit and its effect in Nova Scotia bedevilled federal–provincial fiscal relations with the 2007 and 2008 budgets. In 2009, it was made worse as changes had to be made to accommodate Ontario becoming a have-not province.

The 2007 and 2008 dust-up with Newfoundland, and incidentally Nova Scotia, was completely uncalled for. The Atlantic Accord had not been changed, but an option had been added that, if acted upon, could result in more generous payments. While Premier Williams implemented his scorched-earth policy against Stephen Harper, the federal Conservative Party, and the three sitting members for New-foundland, he also opted for the proposal that he was severely criti-cizing. All of this made no sense in Ottawa, but made for great politics in Newfoundland. In the end, Williams was quite successful on all fronts: he opted for the deal that he had criticized, received more money for his province, and succeeded in shutting out the Con-servative party in 2008. Only in 2011 were the Conservatives able to elect one member from the province of Newfoundland and Labrador, a seat that they later lost in a by-election caused by the MP's resigna-tion due to overspending on election expenses.

In Nova Scotia, we survived 2007 with a one-off grant, but 2008 was different. As PC premier Rodney MacDonald, in a minority govern-ment, faced re-election, it was important that he be seen to extract a win from Ottawa. That win was evaluation and payment by the fed-eral government for what was known as the "Crown Share" in Nova Scotia. This was the resolution of a twenty-two-year-old obligation of the federal government to Nova Scotia for oil and gas projects in the Nova Scotia offshore. The independent panel established in the fall of 2007 reported in July 2008 that the evaluation of this obligation was $234.4 million for past payments up to 31 March 2008.[4] The value in future years was established to be close to $633 million for the Sable Island and Deep Panuke offshore projects. While the settling of the Crown Share payments resolved a long-standing federal–provincial dispute, it did not save the government of Rodney MacDonald.

In addition to the MacDonald PC government in Nova Scotia, the other casualty was Bill Casey, the Conservative MP for the Nova Scotia riding of Cumberland–Colchester. He believed the 2007 bud-get changed the Atlantic Accord as it related to Nova Scotia, and on 5 June 2007, he voted against it. That afternoon Jay Hill, then whip, moved Casey out of the Conservative benches and across the aisle to the opposite side of the House. The action was swift and without regret. It also showed what the word discipline meant in the Conser-vative caucus.

The only traditional First Ministers' Conference convened to date during the Harper years occurred in January 2009, when the federal government was putting the finishing touches on what has become known as the "stimulus budget." This day-and-a-half event com-menced the first evening with a meeting of first ministers with Cana-da's national Aboriginal leaders. The precursor to this meeting was an informal meeting held in the prime minister's Langevin Block office with these same leaders, Chuck Strahl, the minister of Indian and northern affairs, and me. Harper let the leaders know that the budget being presented later that month would create a deficit since the government had determined that a significant economic stimulus package was needed to keep the Canadian economy going through what was clearly a worldwide recession. We had determined that this influx of money could address some of the critical infrastructure issues facing Canadian Aboriginal communities, so the prime minister and Minister Strahl were looking for ideas from the assembled leaders. As with the major package itself, Harper did not want to put money into program spending since that would not achieve the results he was after. The financial resources to be made available from the government would be better placed in infrastructure projects – housing, roads, clean water systems, health care facilities, and the like.

The suggestions from this meeting and subsequent proposals to Indian and Northern Affairs formed the basis of the Aboriginal component of the 2009 stimulus budget. The purpose of convening Aboriginal leaders and first ministers prior to the federal budget was to provide a forum for the exchange of ideas among all the leaders as well as to give Aboriginal leaders some sense of what the premiers and the federal government would be doing. Aboriginal leaders could then plan for the work that could be done with available stimulus funding.

At the end of the evening meeting with the premiers, each Aboriginal leader met with the media. There seemed to be genuine appreciation for the time spent, promises made, and the inclusion of Aboriginal leaders in the dialogue to arrive at mutual solutions.

The next day's First Ministers' Conference was structured to give premiers as much of a heads-up as possible on federal proposals to deal with the recession. For example, Finance Minister Flaherty gave an update on the country's finances, and Minister of Human Resource Development Diane Finley gave a preview of intended changes to Employment Insurance to enable the system to respond more effectively to the immediate needs of the unemployed. First ministers exchanged ideas, but the mood in the room was positive, as it should be when premiers are convened to find out how much federal cash will be available for carving up amongst them.

Federal–provincial issues now fit within the new paradigm of a Conservative majority government. If anything, the 2012 federal budget and the health care block funding announced by Minister Flaherty demonstrated the Harper version of federalism in full flight. This view of the way Canada should work was in Stephen Harper's mind even before he became prime minister. It was evident in the Firewall Letter, his reaction to Chrétien almost losing the country in the 1995 referendum, his support of the Clarity Act, his refusal to budge on industry handouts in the 2004 platform, his containment of the use of the spending power as set out in the 2006 platform. After he became prime minister, it can be seen in the conditions addressing the fiscal imbalance, and the 2012 budget where it is clear that the federal government will operate within section 91 of the Constitution Act, 1867 and that the provinces will deal with "local works and undertakings" and "property and civil rights" as set out in section 92. If the Harper majority years continue, will there ever be another First Ministers' Conference?

PERSONNEL TRACK

This track is about managing the human resources given to the prime minister by the voters – the elected MPs – in a manner to most effectively govern the country. It touches on three areas: Cabinet, the PMO, and caucus. With Cabinet, overarching issues include who is in or out, what each minister should be assigned to do, and when to make changes. The PMO is really the operational arm; it is important that those involved are loyal to the PM, but also not afraid to give frank advice. Caucus management underpins all of this. Without caucus support, the PM cannot function.

What Sir John A. Macdonald is reputed to have said is still true today: "If I had better wood, I would make a better cabinet." Governing in a Westminster-style democratic parliament – the British parliamentary system – provides the prime minister with limited choice as to who will be on his executive team. If he wants to go outside the team provided by the voters, he has two routes: appoint a person to the Senate and then put that person into Cabinet, as Harper did in 2006 with Fortier; or name someone to Cabinet, who then runs in a by-election. Sometimes this second method works; other times, it backfires, as when former prime minister Trudeau wanted Pierre Juneau in his Cabinet but Juneau could not win a by-election in Quebec. This same situation arose when Trudeau wanted Jim Coutts in the House of Commons in order to subsequently put him in Cabinet.

A vacancy was created in Toronto, but the voters of Spadina rejected Coutts and Trudeau's plan. Such attempts to populate the Cabinet can raise internal caucus management problems, especially when fragile egos are passed over in favour of newcomers.

A crucial part of personnel management in government deals with the Cabinet. There are four aspects: how the minister performs in his or her Cabinet role, the relationship of the minister to other Cabinet colleagues, the relationship of the minister to non-Cabinet, caucus colleagues, and the relationship between the minister and the prime minister. In the Harper government, it was crucial that a Cabinet minister fully grasp and run with the assigned portfolio. It was also important that the minister know what was going on in the department and that the mandate letter be fully implemented. Regular meetings with the deputy minister and senior bureaucrats were encouraged, if not mandatory. Harper was very skeptical of a minister who complained that his or her job couldn't get done because the deputy was not providing the necessary support. Changes had to be made, and were made in a few instances, but, by and large, the deputy minister was not moved to satisfy the whim of a minister who was having difficulty mastering the assigned portfolio. On the other hand, Harper was quick, especially in question period practice, to ensure that the minister distanced himself or herself from decisions made and implemented by the bureaucracy that caused grief for the government. As always, it was a fine line to walk.

For the most part, ministers got along with each other. The turf wars of the Chrétien–Martin years were either gone or better managed. The QP practice meeting had a lot to do with building the feeling of a team. One time, after a particularly good session, I described it like being in a winning team's locker room, where everyone tried to help and encourage everyone else. It would be naive to think that all was sweetness and light, and certainly, there were rivalries among ministers in their respective provinces. The provincial or regional minister has an important role to play, and trying to circumvent the regional minister was never a good idea.

At the beginning, and throughout the mandate, it was made clear to ministers that they had to pay attention to their caucus colleagues. As far as Harper was concerned, there was no hierarchy in the Conservative caucus: they were all MPs, with different roles and tasks to fulfill. Letters from caucus members to ministers had to be answered and dealt with properly, not blown off. When a minister made an announcement, all Conservative MPs from local ridings were to be invited. MPs being left off the invitation list or announcements being made and no MP in the area being notified always seemed to be a problem. This was not tolerated by the prime minister. Cabinet ministers who really got it, formed caucus committees of MPs interested in the subject matter and held dinners at regular intervals to discuss relevant matters. This respect for caucus colleagues was also insisted upon in respect of House of Commons and Senate committee work. Ministers were to make themselves available to be questioned by parliamentary committees. It is difficult to understand how this view of equality among all members of caucus has morphed into a situation where, in the last year, there has been a palpable feeling of discontent and exclusion emanating from the government's backbenches. The mid-2013 Cabinet shuffle was to help address this, especially with the appointment of John Duncan as whip. But the situation that presents itself now demonstrates how far the Conservatives have moved from where they started in 2006.

The relationship between the prime minister and his ministers was more problematic. Stephen Harper is no Brian Mulroney. Mulroney's relationship with his caucus, even at the darkest times during the period between 1988–93, was excellent. He had their loyal support 110 per cent of the time, achieved by his constantly reaching out, especially on a personal level. While Harper is capable of reaching out, it is more an exception than the rule. It was not by design, but on many occasions ministers were left wondering if they were on the right track or had pissed off the PM, or if their opinion just didn't count for anything.

Ministers like Prentice and Baird were called on regularly for one-on-one political discussions with the PM since their opinions were frank and honest, and they did not hold back if they believed the government was off track. The same rapport existed with Senator LeBreton, government leader in the Senate. And Harper's relationship between Minister Flaherty was a decided improvement over the Chrétien–Martin relationship. The PM believed Flaherty knew what he was doing at Finance; except for Flaherty's constant desire to establish a national securities regulator, which caused the PM grief with certain premiers every time it popped up, they saw eye to eye – despite their significant height difference.

Harper, I believe, is typical of most leaders: when he spots a weakness or if there is a fall from grace, it is a long climb back. Early on, the PM decided that Rona Ambrose was spending too much time doing other things than looking after her portfolio. He couldn't understand the media's interest in the fitness regime of this Cabinet minister and why she would take time away from work to discuss such "trivial" matters with the media. He also believed she did not listen to advice. This was a hard one even for me to deal with, especially in the summer of 2006 when I was shuttling between the PMO and the minister of environment's office; I didn't think the situation was as bad as Harper believed it was. On one occasion after the morning meeting, I was sitting with the PM and Brodie, with the PM expressing his view that I really wasn't accomplishing much in my summer job as acting chief of staff to the minister of the environment. I tried to explain everything we were doing and was simply met with the rebuff that nothing was being accomplished – because she wouldn't listen. Another example was Gary Lunn, after the isotope incident when Chalk River closed down and Linda Keen would not allow it to re-open. As pointed out earlier, the matter of the Chalk River closure was first raised by Tony Clement as a medical-supply issue. It seemed to catch Lunn by surprise, and while he recovered and was helpful in solving the problem, his credibility at Natural Resources, especially on the nuclear file, was always in question. In the end, after the 2008 election, he was the only minister demoted, to the minister of state for sport portfolio.

There were two major Cabinet shuffles in the first mandate, both in 2007. The January 2007 shuffle was mainly directed at getting Minister Ambrose out of Environment and Minister Toews out of Justice.

Many things came together to militate against Rona Ambrose ever having a fair chance in the Environment portfolio. Samy Watson, the deputy minister, should have been moved from Environment before the Cabinet was put in place. We completely underestimated the groundswell in the country of Canadians calling for action on the environment since Canada was experiencing economic growth. We thought the focus of Canadians would be on that economic growth, making the most of it. When we went looking for the previous government's environment policy, the cupboard was bare: the Liberals were always going to do something, they just never did, especially with regard to the implementation of the Kyoto agreement and the reduction of GHGs. We had no idea of how to deal with the international United Nations Conference of the Parties on climate change and GHG reduction. And we did not have a good handle on how to push back on environmental groups and their constant criticism. These groups became even more shrill since the Conservative Party was looked upon as comprised of climate-change deniers, and that included the prime minister.

So, we attempted to play catch up. The Clean Air Act was developed and tabled in the fall of 2006[5] and was promptly dismissed by the media and the opposition as not tough enough. The Liberals had elected a new leader, and Dion was the face of environment for the Liberals. It was time to move John Baird, the most shameless communicator in the government, into position at Environment.

The other necessary change was at Justice. Vic Toews couldn't help himself when it came to *not* carrying the government message. Canadians knew the government was tough on crime; they saw that during the campaign in Harper's response to the Jane Creba Boxing Day murder. What they didn't need to hear were scary messages from the justice minister about locking up twelve- and thirteen-year-olds. Whether or not Toews thought it was a good idea, that was not this government's message. The prime minister was quite tired of morning meetings where the main topic was Toews going off message. So the ever-accommodating, moderate, but effective Rob Nicholson moved from the House leader's job into Justice. The rest of the moves were basically the domino effect of accomplishing these two changes.

The other shuffle, in August 2007, was again primarily to move select ministers – this time, three. But as it turned out, one of the three never moved and the rest became window dressing. It was imperative that Gordon O'Connor be moved out of Defence. In many ways, this was a shame, as certainly – in the last few decades – no one has been more qualified to hold that position than O'Connor. The defence/armed forces part of the platform was his creation; he knew the job Canada's armed forces had to do; he was familiar with the war in Afghanistan, he could not be bullshitted by anyone about Canada's armed forces, needs, or capabilities. However, he had become a lightning rod for the entire Taliban prisoner/detainee allegations of the torture issue. He was a casualty of the political wars, and he knew it was coming.

The other two moves that Harper wanted to make were to transfer Max Bernier out of Industry and Flaherty out of Finance. Bernier had become fixated on a couple of files at Industry, one dealing with Bell Canada, and had accomplished little. The prime minister viewed Industry as a key economic portfolio and wanted to make a change.

He also believed that Flaherty had done a good job with two budgets and could handle the Industry portfolio. Jim Prentice, who with Emerson and perhaps a couple of others was proving to be among the most solid of ministers, would take over from Flaherty at Finance. These changes would give this government bench strength on economic issues, and with MacKay at Defence, we would be better able to push back on the detainee and other issues instead of constantly wearing them.

But a funny thing happened on the way to do the shuffle. Flaherty refused to move. He told the PMHarper that he was owed one more budget, and if he was not going to be finance minister, he did not want any other portfolio. He then walked out of 24 Sussex, got into his car, and began the drive to Whitby.

Fortunately, he was the first minister Harper and Brodie met with on that August afternoon. After Flaherty left, I came in, and the three of us sat down and discussed what to do. The PM softened his view about moving Flaherty. He did not want to create a crisis of confidence within his own government, it being a minority. He also did not want to lose Flaherty from the Cabinet table. He and Brodie both believed this was not an idle threat from Flaherty. So we regrouped, took a look at the list, and made some quick decisions. Going back to first principles, the idea was to get Bernier out of Industry and get Prentice into an economic portfolio. So if the Flaherty domino was not in play, then we could move Prentice to Industry and keep the rest of the shuffle intact. I suggested that Lawrence Cannon was having such a helluva time with infrastructure – it had been a major subject of debate at the summer caucus in Charlottetown – that we take infrastructure out of Transport and put it with Prentice in Industry. The PM did not think that was a good idea. Displaying his not-often-seen compassionate side, he did not want to hurt Cannon's feelings, and removing infrastructure, the PM believed, would certainly hurt Cannon.

So, with those minor adjustments we carried on. Brodie and the PM would meet the ministers in question in the alcove off the living room, and I would be in the dining room with Jenni Byrne to then discuss staffing in the new portfolio that the minister would be receiving. On that day, pretty much everybody was happy – except Chuck Strahl. He really liked the Agriculture portfolio and was not entirely happy about being moved, but unlike a couple of shuffled ministers after the 2008 election, he was quite willing to take it on and give it his best effort. Among the general happiness that afternoon, no one man in Canada was happier than Gerry Ritz. He looked upon being named minister of agriculture as receiving the best job in the world. It was an area he knew and loved, and it was an ideal appointment for a hard-working member of our Saskatchewan caucus.

With regard to Prentice, he was happy as well. First he was out of Indian and Northern Affairs, and second, since he didn't know he might have been finance minister, he was very glad to be in the Industry portfolio. It's not like Prentice didn't like Indian and Northern Affairs, but there are so many unsolvable issues, and one never knows when the next one will arise; it was a heavy weight lifted off his shoulders. He saw the Industry portfolio as something he could really get his teeth into, and the way the organization chart worked, he was responsible for landing the Mackenzie Valley pipeline proposal that had been hanging over the head of many governments since the early 1970s.[6]

Gordon O'Connor took his move to Revenue as he takes everything. He really is the ultimate loyal soldier and team player, willing to be used wherever the leader sees best. He knew this was coming since the PM had spoken with him previously – he just seemed happy to still be part of the team.

We had no fears about putting Peter MacKay into Defence. He had done a good job at Foreign Affairs, despite unwarranted criticism over the Lebanon evacuation and delays in the issuance of passports. It was a natural fit for MacKay.

The wild card – and it would certainly turn out that way – was Bernier's appointment to the position of minister of foreign affairs. The PM was conscious that he could not take one of his main Quebec stars out of a major economic portfolio and put him into something minor. So Foreign Affairs, which is in reality run by the PM, seemed a safe bet at the time. When I met with Bernier after his meeting with Brodie and Harper, I stressed to him the huge learning curve he was about to embark on. I told him that Sandra Buckler and I would be glad to help him with briefings from a political viewpoint, as he certainly would receive briefings from the public service from their perspective. Initially, all went well.

Everyone knows the story, has consumed the pictures of Bernier and Julie Couillard at the swearing in of the ministers at Rideau Hall that August. At the reception afterwards, I gave Max a briefing binder, which he promised to start working on that evening. Well, he didn't

– and it was maybe a first sign of things to come. His time at Foreign
Affairs was fraught with difficulty. In this portfolio, every misstep
along the way reflects badly on Canada, and especially on the prime
minister, who everyone believes is actually directing Canada's foreign
policy. Eventually all of this began to add up and take its toll. As nice
a person as Bernier is, this is an area where surefootedness is essential.
The last straw was not the secret documents left behind or misplaced
or whatever at Julie Couillard's house; it was actually Bernier going
off message in relation to activities in Afghanistan. He mused openly
that the governor of Kandahar province needed to be replaced
because of alleged corruption. He should never have publicly insult-
ed the governor of the province where Canada has deployed its
troops, and the revelation undermined months of quiet diplomacy to
have the governor removed. Shortly after that, the document issue
arose, and Bernier tendered his resignation.

The issue of Julie Couillard's questionable past had been raised
with Harper, and he had received assurances from Bernier that the
two of them were no longer involved. I agreed with the PM that if
Bernier, once learning of the issues, had withdrawn from the relationship, he should be allowed to continue in his ministerial role.
However, when the document issue arose, and it was obvious they
were still together, the PM's patience had been reached its limit. To his
credit, Bernier co-operated in every way to minimize the embarrassment of losing a minister. He tendered his resignation, and David
Emerson added Foreign Affairs to his International Trade portfolio.
As the minister of foreign affairs was to appear in Committee of the
Whole the next evening to defend his estimates, the briefing of Emerson began in earnest the next day, but it did not take long for him to
get up to speed. He did his usual remarkable job in Committee of the
Whole.

One final note to show that there is some humour in all of this.
When we became aware of the missing document issue, Dimitri
Soudas raised the question with Harper and the rest of us assembled
in the PM's office: if Julie had read the documents and was now in possession of secret information, what do we do? The PM replied that he
didn't think either one of them would be reading anything, let alone
those documents.

Management of staff in the PMO, particularly senior staff, is left to
the prime minister's chief of staff. The PMO with its chief of staff is
really the orchestra leader for the government symphony. A tightly

knit group answers directly to the chief of staff. In the first mandate, that was Ian Brodie and the group included: the director of communications, then Sandra Buckler; the issues manager, Keith Beardsley and then Jenni Byrne; the deputy chief of staff, Patrick Muttart; the director of policy, Mark Cameron; Carolyn Stewart-Olson and Dimitri Soudas on the press secretary side; Harper's executive assistant, Ray Novak; and me. These are all-consuming jobs that start early, before the sun is up, and end late, long after it has gone down. Rarely is there a free weekend or holidays without interruption. Each of the people named above had a group to manage and for which they were responsible. I was the lucky one with no staff, undefined and unlimited territory, and immediate access to everyone. As we moved through the transition from opposition to government and settled in, as well as one can, to governing in a minority, I assumed responsibility for the legislative agenda – what went on in the House and Senate – and for working with others when things went off the rails – trying to put them back where they were supposed to be. I worked most closely with what became the three *B*s in my life: Brodie, Beardsley, and Buckler.

I am not sure how it came to be that Brodie and I worked so well together, but we did. We came from opposite sides of the Party, but we trusted each other's instincts and judgment on all matters. The two of us also worked closely with the clerk, Kevin Lynch. We trusted his judgment on how government worked or should work. Being new to government, Lynch's advice was invaluable in the early days. Neither of us viewed the public service as our enemy, and I believe the best working relationship between the Harper government and the public service came during the Brodie PMO.

Keith Beardsley, supported by his staff, did a great job in identifying issues and helping craft the government's response. He was never shy about speaking his mind in the morning meetings with the prime minister, or at any other time.

The hardest job in the Harper PMO (other than being the chief of staff) belonged – and still belongs – to the director of communications. Buckler had to implement and deal with the change of communication practices from the Martin regime. And once the new system was established, she could not relent. She also had to manage Cabinet ministers and MPs who wanted to share their views with the media. In addition, there was the communication challenge of getting the message out when the government's chief messenger, Prime Minister Harper, saw little or no value in communication with the media. As I said earlier, less was best in his mind. Moreover, she had to do the job knowing that her strong-arm tactics with the media and caucus were subject to constant criticism. But no one could have done a better job of implementing the prime minister's approach to communications than Buckler.

And then there is caucus management. Unlike previous prime ministers, Harper did not have a caucus liaison or relations group in his PMO. I played that role as much as possible, informally, during the first mandate. When I came back in January 2009, I was officially assigned that role by Guy Giorno and Harper. There are really three aspects to caucus management: dealing with individual MPs, addressing issues raised through meetings, and then caucus retreats.

With regard to dealing with individual MPs, I have already touched on the issues surrounding Michael Chong's resignation from Cabinet and Bill Casey's removal from caucus for voting against the budget. As I have said, as much as this was a surprise to Casey, there was no other choice. From a practical point of view, it did not have to happen. The changes Casey thought we had made to the Atlantic Accord were, in fact, for the benefit of Nova Scotians. Furthermore, Nova Scotians received a benefit when we settled the value of the Crown Share and payment was made by the federal government to Nova Scotia. Casey presumed the worst, wanted to make a point – which he did – and from that time until he retired from federal politics, remained outside the Conservative caucus.

In the first mandate, the other problem child was Garth Turner. Turner had run for the leadership of the PC Party in 1993. He had served in Cabinet for the brief period of the Campbell government. He fancied himself an expert on economic issues and the use of high-tech methods of communication. He was not put in Harper's Cabinet. This created the perfect storm for caucus turmoil. All of this peaked with Emerson's appointment as minister of international trade. Turner could not contain himself. Perhaps it would have been different if Turner had been placed in Cabinet, or maybe not. Beyond the deliberations of caucus, those of Cabinet might also have appeared on his blog and the webcast usually run out of his parliamentary office. It was an intolerable situation that could not be allowed to continue. His criticism of the Emerson appointment combined with the continual second-guessing of government actions and policy on his blog brought him into conflict with a number of senior Conservatives and then the prime minister. I am not sure why Ian Brodie rather than me dealt with Turner, but Brodie's scolding was no more effective that Harper's. Eventually, too many leaks and too big an ego meant Turner had to go. After being dumped by the Conservative caucus, he joined the Liberals and was, for the most part, never heard from again. As has been reported, and reported accurately, on election night 2008, the group assembled in the prime minister's suite at the Hyatt Regency in Calgary let out the biggest cheer and applauded as Lisa Raitt's victory over the troublesome and quarrelsome Turner was announced.

Personnel management also means dealing with the weekly caucus meetings that give members an opportunity to raise issues in what is a surprisingly frank manner. However, they are limited in time, and there is a built-in structure and agenda dealing with current and projected House and Senate business as well as discussing proposals yet to be put before the House of Commons. There are no punches pulled in these weekly meetings as MPs and senators line up at the microphone to comment on anything and everything that is bothering them or, on the rare occasion, to say something nice about a particular achievement. On most, if not all, of these interventions, the PM will respond.

There are also caucus retreats, outside of Ottawa, every summer. I attended the three held during the first mandate: 2006 in Cornwall, Ontario; 2007 in Charlottetown, Prince Edward Island; and 2008 in Levis, Quebec. Usually planned over three days, these retreats give MPs and senators time to socialize – some bring their partners – and to explore certain issues in more depth and, given the extended time, actually reach solutions. Each of the three retreats I attended was memorable for specific discussions.

The 2006 Cornwall caucus occurred after the evacuation of Canadians from Lebanon. There were anti-Israel marches in the streets of Montreal, which some Liberal MPs had joined. Since members of caucus can count, they knew there were many more people in Canada of Arab origin than of Jewish. So why was the Conservative Party taking such a pro-Israel stance? The previous Liberal government was sufficiently nuanced, or some might say disingenuous, on this subject that no one knew where it stood on most of the Middle East issues.

This gave Harper his opportunity to address the criticism from caucus and respond in a fulsome, meaningful way to the concerns expressed. He started by saying that Israel is the only democratic country on the face of the earth that some countries, mainly its neighbours, do not believe has a right to exist. If it doesn't have a right to exist, and the situation presented itself in an advantageous way, most of its neighbours would go to whatever length it took to wipe it off the face of the planet. He likened Israel's enemies to Hitler and the genocide of the Second World War. He then went on to say that if we stand by and let Israel disappear, if we take no action, then what other targets will these countries decide need to be obliterated? Which democratic country would next fall victim to the same hatred and loathing that was visited upon the Jewish people in Israel? So it was up to us and other like-minded countries to take a stand against genocide and the destruction of Israel. Quite frankly, I don't believe Harper cared whether or not caucus members supported his view. This was the way it was going to be, and if you didn't like it, shut up or leave.

The Charlottetown caucus in the summer of 2007 occurred approximately halfway through the first mandate and before the second Cabinet shuffle. One of the main issues raised there was the lack of progress in getting the "Build Canada" funds out and into projects across the country. Lawrence Cannon was in charge of the program to rebuild crumbling infrastructure or to move new plans forward. He described the process for approval and dissemination of funds to his caucus colleagues. Poor Lawrence – by the time he finished, everyone was completely confused as to how the process was supposed to work. Pierre Poilievre summed it up best: "Lawrence, this is a bureaucrat's wet dream."

The good thing about this type of discussion being held outside of Ottawa is that there is opportunity and time not only to present the problem but also to discuss possible solutions. It was obvious that this was way too much for Cannon to deal with on his own. During the lunch break, we convened a meeting with Cannon, as lead minister, and all the regional and provincial ministers, whose involvement seemed to be key in liaising with provincial and territorial governments, identifying projects, and moving forward. The best example of how bad the situation had become? We were actually fighting with the Stelmach government over whether infrastructure proposals previously identified for funding by the Alberta government would qualify under this federal program or whether the government had to develop a new list with the same projects on it and then submit it for funding. I believe that post-Charlottetown, the system worked more efficiently and effectively. Nice to get one win in Charlottetown.

The 2008 summer caucus retreat was held in Levis, across the river from Quebec City, with a huge rally/dinner in Jacques Gourde's riding. Not many knew it at the time, but most of the retreat was spent with the PM meeting only with select people, ensuring that all was ready for an early-September election call. The rally/dinner was especially heartening. Close to a thousand people from all walks of life – seniors, women, men, children – assembled in the middle of rural Quebec to hear the prime minister. It was a sight to behold, and one could not help but think back to the days in opposition and the Belgium-federalism speech in the fall of 2004. How far we had come. And with a little luck, how far would we go?

ELECTION READINESS TRACK

When the House of Commons rose for the summer in 2008, it was evident that when it reconvened in the fall, it would be no picnic. Economic storm clouds were gathering and Harper became concerned about how productive the fall and winter sessions would be. He talked openly about a dysfunctional Parliament. The issue was what to do about it. One option would be to try to work with opposition parties to get through what would be a difficult year: that is, find out what their views were and see if we could agree on a common path forward. The other option was to ignore the fixed-date election legislation that had passed in this Parliament and to go to the people seeking a renewed mandate to deal with what would be a tough economic time.

If we needed an issue upon which to force an election, Dion had presented us with one: his "Greenshift"[7] or carbon tax proposal – or as we described it, "Dion's tax on everything." From the moment he announced it, Dion had been touting what he believed to be its benefit, but the sales job wasn't working outside of his own party and the environment movement that loves a carbon tax. We had done a pretty good job of defining Dion as weak, and his inability to articulate the benefits of the Greenshift only fed into that narrative. He was unable to specify how much carbon would be reduced through the imposition of the tax. There was no easy way to explain the Greenshift plan, except to say that it amounted to a complete overhaul of the Canadian tax system. What might have been a good plan in 2006, when the economy was rolling along and environment was top of mind with many Canadians, was in mid-2008, a complicated plan to tax Canadians so that their carbon emissions would fall – but the proponent of the plan had no idea how effective it might be. We believed that we could galvanize Canadians against the issue, and obviously then, against the Liberal Party as well.

Pursuing the first option, the PM held meetings with the opposition leaders throughout the summer months. It was unlikely that anything positive would come out of them, and the low expectations were met. One can always wonder what would have happened if one of the leaders had said to Harper: "I will put party differences aside and support you through the economic turmoil till the next election." But looking back, it was fortunate for the prime minister and the Party that did not happen.

We were now well launched into the fifth track of governing: election preparedness.

Preparing for an election as government is quite different from preparing as opposition. The platform becomes a catalogue of achievements coupled with promises of future action. Loose ends have to be tied up. As many projects or proposals or funding announcements as possible have to be completed. It really is an exercise in "clearing the decks." Guy Giorno, who had taken over from Ian Brodie as chief of staff for the PM, established a small PMO committee to get as much done on this as possible in as short a time as possible.

The target date for the drop of the writ was established for early September, perhaps 7 September, for an election on the Tuesday after the Thanksgiving weekend. But since we believed we had some element of surprise working in our favour, governing as usual still had to take place. So Priority and Planning Committee meetings continued, especially the one in Inuvik, and issues such as Listeriosis had to be dealt with.

We had kept a rolling platform almost since the beginning, so the challenge was to determine what had been done, what was left to do, and what new things could we offer knowing that finances would be tight.

Throughout this period, the platform was being worked on primarily by Director of Policy Mark Cameron, especially on long plane rides with Harper. I must admit that the meetings on the platform conducted at Harrington Lake were much more pleasant than the countless meetings on the fourth floor of the Centre Block when we were in opposition.

One issue that we created for ourselves and were never able to solve was the reallocation of funding for the arts, especially as it related to Quebec. Perhaps we were fools or naive, thinking that we could make changes in the funding, cancel programs, and actually add money to the pot elsewhere, and explain it all. The arts community in Quebec, whose funding had been cut or changed, was complaining to every media outlet in the province. While it may have been the right thing to do – to cancel or change programs that seemed to have outlived their usefulness or that could be done by the private sector without government subsidies – it was incredibly bad politics. Trying to figure out what we had done and what were the right messages for Quebec hung around our necks throughout the lead-up to the election.

As hard as it may be to believe, sometimes the most difficult thing to find out is what you, as government, have actually done, especially when things start to go bad. What I mean is that, in broad strokes, you know what has occurred, but breaking it down into chewable chunks so that you can deal with and react to it on a micro basis is almost impossible. With regard to the arts: what did we actually cut, who was affected, which program did we increase funding for and why? These all seemed to be simple questions, but when ministers, staff, and public servants are running for cover, it is often tough to discern what the actual effects of the announcement were, especially when those directly affected have unlimited and direct access to the media. Regardless, we had no idea that this issue in Quebec would hit us like an oncoming train.

The issue of the fixed-date election, in my opinion, could be easily dealt with. The statute creating the fixed date still gave discretion to the governor general to issue the election writ on the advice of the prime minister. I reminded the PM and staff about Chrétien calling the 1997 election in the middle of some of the worst flooding in Manitoba history and calling the 2000 election because the new leader of the Alliance Party, Stockwell Day, dared him to. In both situations, the PC leader, Charest in 1997 and Clark in 2000, was outraged and tried to make the calling of the election an issue. While it is interesting for the first week, after that no one cares –an election is happening whether the opposition likes it or not. In addition, we believed that we could sell the idea that Parliament had indeed become dysfunctional. One could argue that we wouldn't know this until the House met in September, but opposition leaders, by ramping up their demands all summer, did little to persuade Canadians that fall would yield a productive Parliament.

As we moved through the summer of 2008, preparations were put in place piece by piece for a fall election.

Financial Crisis, 2008:
House Manoeuvres
and a Stimulus Budget

The autumn of 2008 and winter of 2009 saw the beginnings of the worst worldwide financial collapse since the Great Depression of the 1930s. In Canada, the governing Conservatives forced a September general election in spite of fixed-date election legislation, and the newly elected Conservative government, after a near-death experience in late November–early December 2008, delivered a planned deficit, stimulus budget in late January 2009, which was approved by the House of Commons in February 2009. In the relatively short period of five months, both the Canadian political scene and the economic, budgeting situation had gone through enormous upheaval. But after presenting the stimulus budget, the Conservatives settled in for another term of governing, albeit still as a minority government, but with increased numbers over the 2006 results. That term would end in March 2011 with the passage of a non-confidence motion in the House of Commons supported by all three opposition parties. While the September 2008 to February 2009 period was a time of great change and turmoil after February, the Conservatives began the long run of governing in uncertain economic times.

In preparation for the election call, which the prime minister had decided in the early summer of 2008 would take place in September, the scene had to be set: perfunctory meetings with opposition leaders to justify the call; finalization of the platform; laying the groundwork with the electorate to ensure its support for an election, which would produce a stable majority government. As I said earlier, I am not sure what would have happened if either Dion or Layton had taken the position that political stability was more important than short-term gain and had offered to support the legislative program of the gov-

The Financial Crisis. Lawrence Cannon, Peter Van Loan, Jim Prentice,
and Stephen Harper (left to right) met with the Obama
administration in Washington, DC, on matters of mutual interest.
(Courtesy of Jim Prentice. Reprinted by permission)

ernment, something they ultimately did anyway. It is quite possible,
given Harper's desire for a new mandate and to take on the weakest
of Liberal leaders, that whatever Dion or Layton said would have been
interpreted negatively so that an election would have been the inevitable result.

It is perhaps quite naive to think that, in the winner-takes-all game
of electoral politics, there can be an honest exchange of views or proposals between government and opposition with the end game being
to work together for the common good. This didn't happen in the
lead-up to the election. Even in the election campaign, as economic

storm clouds gathered, there could be no discussion of running a deficit in order to stimulate the economy and keep Canadians working. Is this just too naive a thought, or is it the fault of political leaders who don't want to be hampered by the challenge of working together or sharing power, or is the media coverage of electoral politics such that any sign of compromise becomes a sign of weakness? What would have been so hard about any party leader, including Harper, saying: we will do whatever it takes to keep the economy going, and if that means running a deficit, so be it. Is the honesty worth the possible backlash, and possible defeat? Obviously not.

Harper decided that he did not want to experience a fall and winter of economic turmoil in the face of constant questioning and threats from the Liberal leader Dion. It was just that simple. For the good of the country's economy and navigating through the recession, a new mandate was sought.

The fixed-date election legislation amendment to the Canada Elections Act had the usual escape clause in it, leaving the governor general's prerogative intact to use discretion in times of a minority government or at any other time. In the British parliamentary system, all acts such as this are worded to ensure there is no interference with the royal prerogative of dissolution. The opposition parties were reluctant to support this bill, but then realized that it restricted the government as to what it could do regarding an election but that the opposition could force an election whenever it wanted to. Seemed like a good arrangement. They didn't count on Harper deciding to sweep it aside and visit the governor general seeking dissolution. Governor General Michaëlle Jean really had no option but to grant it, since the opposition parties were in no position to form an alternative government. And once the election was on, while the opposition and media might cry foul for the initial period, the opposition parties had to move off their positions of what was right and engage. In other words, they had to get out of the stands and onto the field or risk being spectators at their own execution.

On 7 September, the prime minister visited Rideau Hall and Canada's 39th Parliament was history. The ballot question was fairly simple: strong leadership for difficult times or the alternative, weak or no leadership in difficult times. The 2008 campaign was a new adventure for me. I had never travelled during a campaign, other than to the debate prep sessions whenever the debates were taking place. I had always stayed in Ottawa, either working on the policy part of the campaign or writing speeches. This time I was on the road with Harper for the entire campaign.

The leader's tour began with a trip from Ottawa to Quebec City for a late afternoon rally. The mood was buoyant, we were comfortably ahead in the polls, and it looked like Harper's Quebec-centric focus since the fall of 2004 would reap sizable dividends. On the tour bus heading into downtown Quebec City, we saw the Bloc signs and its campaign slogan, "Present pour le Québec." We ridiculed the slogan because even it admitted the Bloc weren't going to do anything for Quebecers except show up. The Bloc had, in its own slogan, admitted how ineffective it really was. Contrast that with a Harper-led government that had addressed the fiscal imbalance; the participation of Quebec in UNESCO as part of the Canadian delegation; and, at least to some extent, the concerns of Quebecers through co-operation with the government of Quebec. Open federalism under the leadership of Prime Minister Harper was working, or so we thought.

The Quebec City event was followed by a short western swing, then back to Ottawa, and off to Montreal. The week went well, despite gaffes such as the video of a puffin, a bird idolized by Ignatieff at the Liberal summer caucus held in Newfoundland, pooping on Dion and intemperate remarks by Conservative communications about the political affiliation of a father whose son had been killed in Afghanistan and who disagreed with the PM's announcement that Canadians would be out of Afghanistan in 2011 – both instances eliciting an uncharacteristic apology from Harper. There was a brief discussion on the tour about making changes in the war room, but that was soon forgotten.

During the second visit to Quebec in less than ten days, a Léger poll had the Conservatives with a slight lead over the Bloc. I spoke with L. Ian MacDonald, a long-time friend, former Mulroney speechwriter, and editor of *Policy Options*, who had spoken with former prime minister Mulroney and friends: opinion held that, if all went well, the road to a majority ran right through Quebec. Predictions of winning as many as thirty-five seats were being tossed around during this visit. These predictions and the feeling of a real breakthrough were, of course, dependent on nothing going wrong – a smooth campaign, building on the accomplishments in Quebec since the Belgium-federalism speech. In the rest of Canada, success would be based on leadership – strong versus weak. Polls started inching toward majority territory. Then two matters combined to pull the rug out from under the Quebec strategy, and when combined with the growing unease presented by the economic crisis, put the election strategy and its predicted results in jeopardy.

The economic part of the 2006 platform required reductions in government spending, which resulted in strategic review of expenditures. This strategic review,[1] required by Cabinet and supervised by the Treasury Board, was to affect all departments. It is a difficult project in a minority government since the review inevitably visits itself on program spending. Any cuts or reductions in program spending will inevitably touch stakeholders, who count on receiving their portion of program spending to supplement income for ongoing projects. The Department of Canadian Heritage was the last department to report its reductions or changes in spending, and they were accepted with little, if any, scrutiny, since we were in the full throes of election preparedness.

Even in August, when ministers, especially Fortier and Verner, became aware of the impact of the cuts, the electoral liability occasioned by the cuts was not fully appreciated by all. Both Fortier and Verner wanted the cuts cancelled. However, from a purely philosophical, or even practical, point of view, why would the government of Canada be pouring money into a program that enabled Canadian artists to travel abroad to perform? Surely, this was something the marketplace could address. The Heritage department funding reductions were never analyzed properly through a Quebec-centric lens in either the PMO or Cabinet. Discussion at an Operations or Priorities and Planning committee meeting, with Quebec ministers present, would have been an opportunity to highlight what was proposed and its potential political fallout. Instead, we had, on one hand, the PMO chief of staff telling an Issues Management Committee meeting that these cuts made him "proud to be a Conservative," and on the other hand, some Quebec Cabinet ministers saying that this had to be reviewed or all that we had worked for in Quebec would be for naught. These ministers at least understood the strength and vehemence of the opposition that would come, given that those opposed had immediate access to the airwaves.

We lost touch with what was important in the Heritage discussion. If it was important that Canadians have a strong majority government to manage through the economic crisis, and if that majority could be found through support in Quebec, then to hell with the cuts. The ends were the most important part of the discussion, not the means.

One only forces an election because one believes a particular favourable result is achievable. And in order to achieve that result, if one has to eat a bit of humble pie and reverse $10 million to $50 million in spending reductions – just do it. But we didn't. And then, in Saskatoon, Harper threw some good fuel on the Heritage fire with his disparaging reference to people who attend fancy galas supported by government handouts as opposed to hard-working Canadians. If the arts community was not energized before, it certainly was now!

Another challenge on the arts and culture front came in trying to understand what we had actually done in Quebec. Money had been designated for the celebration of the 400th anniversary of the founding of Quebec City. Also, arts funding had been reallocated and added to a tax credit for parents enrolling their children in arts activities, such as ballet, music lessons, or painting classes. In total, we had actually added money to the arts in Canada and Quebec. But it really didn't matter. We had poked the arts community with a conservative, anti-French cultural stick held by the PM from the West, once again demonstrating, in the minds of Quebecers, that we did not understand Quebec, regardless of the work we had done in previous years.

Perhaps the arts funding issue alone might not have been enough to derail the momentum in Quebec. However, as that debate was raging, we made what was supposed to be a safe, good-news announcement in Ottawa on our signature item, "being tough on crime." Among the measures announced this time were ones that would see young offenders where they were convicted of serious crimes being named and having to serve adult sentences. Finally, we had a get-tough approach on young offenders. While this was throwing red meat at the law-and-order folks outside Quebec, it threw a huge policy bone straight at Gilles Duceppe. There are few better communicators than Duceppe, and few better with a turn of phrase to suit their own cause.

The announcement was made in the morning in Ottawa. By the time evening rolled around, Duceppe had reworked and characterized our announcement as throwing fresh young flesh into penitentiaries to service the needs of hardened criminals. He did such a good

job, that by mid-week, Harper and I were not sure what we had announced. We were out west, and during some downtime waiting for
an event to start, we got the war room on the phone to find out what
we had been trying to do. We spent about an hour on the phone with
Ottawa, and finally it was clear: while young offenders convicted of
serious crimes could be named and given adult sentences by a judge,
they would not be serving their sentences in penitentiaries; they
would serve them in youth facilities until eligible to be transferred to
an adult facility. We thought about calling for an apology from
Duceppe – but that would have only given the story more legs, more
credibility, and by then the damage was done.

Reflecting back on that period, it is amazing that we could be
involved in two policy challenges, at virtually the same time, negatively affecting our standing in Quebec – and with both, not really
being sure what we had done. L. Ian MacDonald would later refer to
both of these as "unforced errors" that cost us dearly. In retrospect,
both could have been prevented.

Three things that were Quebec-centric lay at the source of this confusion, aided and abetted, quite frankly, by lack of judgment on our
part. First, as a result of the controversy created by the Schreiber affair,
we lost Brian Mulroney and his network in Quebec as a sounding
board and a source of sage advice. Prior to the Schreiber allegations,
there had developed an easy relationship between Harper and Mulroney. Senator Marjory LeBreton contributed to this in her almost-daily
conversations with Mulroney; advice would be received and passed on.
All of that ceased with the publication of Schreiber's affidavit in which
he claimed that Mulroney had promised to raise his case with Harper
at Harrington Lake, along with some documentation.

A second difference between 2006 and 2008 was the fact that
Lawrence Cannon did not have his hand in the platform, looking at
it through a Quebec lens.

And third, the falling-out between Charest and Harper meant a loss
of intelligence as to how announcements would be received in Quebec. Two things happened in 2007 to help this along. One was
Charest's use of much of the fiscal imbalance money received by
Quebec to fund his election-campaign promise to lower taxes in
Quebec; Harper looked on this as a betrayal of all the work he had
done on fiscal imbalance. The second was Harper establishing a close
relationship with Mario Dumont, leader of the l'Action démocra-

tique du Québec (ADQ). After his rise in the 2007 provincial election, it looked like he could replace the Liberals as the federalist and more or less the conservative option in Quebec. You can't ride two political horses at the same time without serious injury, and you surely can't ride two political horses in Quebec at the same time. So, any help from Charest on these issues was not forthcoming. In fact, he had his own list of demands, which he put to Harper during the 2008 campaign.

The lack of Quebec political intelligence from reliable sources, internal disputes in the Conservative Party, and lack of attention to detail really hurt the Conservative cause in Quebec. To this day, it has not recovered.

These two issues, plus the economic downturn, gave Quebecers the answer as to why they needed the Bloc "Present pour le Québec." Duceppe could now argue that a vote for the Bloc was a vote against a Harper majority, and Harper with a minority meant the Bloc could protect and advance the cause of Quebec.

Outside of Quebec, prior to the debates, we were still holding a lead, still sticking to the original messaging. Neither the arts and culture cuts, nor the young offenders announcement hurt our standing outside of Quebec – hard to tell if it helped, but it certainly didn't hurt. Harper stuck to his vision of Canada as a country where "ordinary, hard-working, law-abiding Canadians can get ahead" and where only the Conservative Party cared about this group, would protect it, and had policies that would benefit and make life easier for "hard-working, law-abiding, ordinary Canadians."

In mid-September 2008, Lehman Brothers collapsed in the United States, and in the days immediately prior to the debates, the economic downturn started to be more than just images seen on the nightly American news. Having called the election in order to deal with the economy with a stronger hand, we couldn't seem to come to grips with how to reassure Canadians that they had a strong leader, schooled in economics, and that when he said Canada's banking and financial fundamentals were strong, he knew what he was talking about. As the debates approached at the beginning of October, the message began to get muddled when the campaign team asked Harper to demonstrate empathy, in his announcements and in his answers to questions, for those who might be suffering from job losses or losses in income.

This period was marked with uncertainty. We were being told that in the "hotly contested, battleground seats," where we were doing overnight tracking, we were losing ground to the Liberals. Prior to, during, and immediately after the debates, we couldn't seem to get our message out. There was actually concern that Canadians might just say, "Let's give the other guy a chance." If that message caught on, and we fell behind in the polls, we might never recover. Having forced an election that we felt sure of winning, there was now real apprehension that it might go the other way.

This was the backdrop against which we did debate prep for the 2008 election. As we broke from the tour and remained in Ottawa for a few days, we received up-to-date polling statistics from Patrick Muttart, none of which looked promising at this stage. The great thing about checking with Muttart on polling information is that you get an honest, straightforward opinion. Unlike many people who will try to put a happy face on polling information, Muttart will always give the upside and the downside, and what he believes are the problems and solutions. This is incredibly helpful, especially if you are on the road while trying to guide the messaging that inevitably will come after the prime minister's morning announcement and the media availability. The great thing was that, now, we were getting it in Ottawa, and we could have a general round-table discussion about where we had been, where we were now, and where we seemed to be going, where we needed to go, and what we needed to do to get there.

Prior to the election, Harper and Layton had agreed that Elizabeth May should not be part of the debates for very valid reasons: the Green Party that she led had no seats in the House of Commons, and quite rightly, there would be a general outcry from all the registered parties running in the election who had no seats in the House of Commons that they should be represented in the debates as well. Also, because of her close ties to the Liberals, May was looked upon by both Harper and Layton as a shill for the Liberal Party. Her presence would be like having Dion and his deputy leader participating in the debates. However, in a conversation between Harper and Layton early in the campaign, the latter explained that he was under enormous pressure from his own people to allow May on the podium, or, in this case, around the table. Harper explained to him that a sign of a leader is being able to resist this pressure, to not always do what is easy and popular but to take a tough stand. This was especially true in this case, since May's presence was not going to hurt us on the environment, but it could very well hurt the NDP. It was not in Layton's self-interest to allow May to be present. Harper made it clear that it was Layton's call, since we were not going to be the lone holdout blocking May from appearing. Ultimately May was allowed to participate.

Another conversation occurred between Harper and Layton at the point in this election when the NDP were either tied or slightly ahead of the Liberals and Layton's leadership numbers were significantly better than Dion's. Harper told Layton that this was his opportunity to strike out and bury Dion and to start talking about himself as leader of the opposition. Layton demurred and started talking about forming a coalition with the Grits. Given the change in Layton's performance and attitude from the 2008 to the 2011 election, it would seem he finally did settle on what would be in his and his party's best self-interest.

Knowing that May would participate, we began preparation on two fronts – ensuring that the PM's knowledge was up-to-date on what the other parties were advocating and on our platform promises, particularly in sorting out what we did on arts funding for Quebec and in the young offenders announcement; and determining how best to deal with what could be a very unpredictable May sitting beside him throughout both the French and English debates. We also agreed that because of the uncertain economic times, the time period should be extended for the economic portion of the debates.

The first day of preparation took place in the studio constructed as part of the war room, to hold news conferences, push back by a minister, or message events. A great deal of time in the prep is spent on sample questions. As this was the first time Harper was debating as PM, he had a record to defend, and his attacks would concentrate on the deficiencies in the platforms of the other parties. He was no longer in a position to attack the PM for not doing the right thing or not having the right policies – he was that PM! This may sound trite, but it is a huge mind reset. On the other hand, you don't want the prime minister playing defence all night, so knowledge of what the opposition has been announcing and promising in the campaign, and the weaknesses, is essential.

Line Maheux, who had been doing debate prep with us since 2004, played the part of the Green Party leader as we worked through issues raised by virtue of May sitting next to Harper on the same side of the debate table. The Party had spent significant resources on advertising, both pre-writ and during the writ period, presenting a softer side of the prime minister and developing policies that would appeal to families, in order to close the gender support gap with women. According to our polling, it had been successful. The point here was that one wrong move with May and all of this effort could go down the drain. So Maheux, a touchy-feely person herself, sat next to Harper during debate prep. We dealt with issues such as how he should react if May put her hand on his arm to make a point. It was a new dynamic, and had to be considered as we prepped for the televised debates. The other issue with May was tone. Harper could take a severe tone with the other three leaders, all of whom he knew well and had interacted with in the House of Commons and two of whom he'd debated with before. His tone with May had to be different, more low-key, and in no instance, could he put himself in a position where he could be called a bully.

The next two days of prep took place at Harrington Lake, the prime minister's summer residence. It is a big rambling house in a beautiful setting above the lake. Harper loves it, and it has the advantage of no interruptions. When he was in the war room, there was a natural tendency to involve him in extraneous discussions. Also, there would be those in the war room who wanted to meet the prime minister. All perfectly natural, unless you are preparing for a national leaders' debate in the midst of a federal election. Harrington Lake provided the solitude needed for concentration as we led up to the French debate, which was scheduled first this time, having been second in Montreal in 2006.

While we thought we had prepared sufficiently for the debates, I believe we were not completely prepared for this new format, for discussion around a table. It put all of the leaders on the same level and took away from Harper's size and the leader-like qualities he exhibits when standing and speaking from a podium. The format also allowed all four opposition leaders to attack sequentially and together. We were also not prepared for Dion's performance – and we should have been. The venue was like a university seminar, where Dion felt right at home. He had also come with a sketched-out plan to deal with the economy. It was simply a plan to make up a plan and to hold a bunch of meetings with no real purpose – but again, it was more than we thought he would come with.

To my way of thinking, Harper has never lost a debate, including this one – although many commentators were surprised that Dion could hold himself together for two hours and gave the debate to him. If we failed the PM in the prep, it was by making him too cautious and concerned about tone, facial expression, and body language.

For the English debate, Mike Coates, who had led debate prep since 2004, believed we needed to respond to Dion right off the top. So, most of that debate day was spent dealing with what Harper should say and how he should say it. We also backtracked a little on our early advice, assuring Harper it was all right to be combative, especially when there is a four-on-one pile-on. Coates hit on the idea that Harper should ridicule Dion's initiatives, and go back to our initial messaging about Dion not being a leader because, in the face of adversity, he panicked. "Leaders don't panic and you are not a leader." That statement, delivered forcefully by Harper at the beginning of the debate, shook Dion, and he never recovered. Harper pushed back, so the pile-on in the English debate was not as effective as it was the previous evening. All in all, the feeling was that Harper had held his own against the four attackers and had put Dion back in his place.

We were now about ten days from election day, and as a result of the debates, the Grits were starting to close the gap. The advice being given to Harper was to show empathy with those who were affected by the economic crisis. This was when he decided to start referring to his mother and her concerns over economic issues, which she relayed to him every evening. Well, sure, every evening Stephen would talk to his mother, but in the context of phoning his children before bedtime. Empathy from Harper did not come naturally.

Then there was the 7 October luncheon speech in Toronto where Harper gave a stirring defence of the government's economic record, and made it clear that the tax reductions, its economic program since 2006, and the strength of Canada's financial institutions would ensure that Canada was best placed to survive what was starting to look like a global recession. The speech was well received. We still didn't have a specific plan, but we had sufficiently ridiculed Dion's attempt to develop one that simply recounting what we had done was sufficient. After the speech, talking to the media, Harper said out loud that the decline in stock prices would present Canadians with great buying opportunities. While maybe true, beyond the fact that giving stock market advice to Canadians would not seem to be his job or at all appropriate, was it really the kind of thing a prime minister should be saying? Guy Giorno called me from the war room and told me to tell Harper to disabuse himself of the temptation to give stock market advice – it would hurt us. It was too late, Harper was already sitting in front of Peter Mansbridge repeating his stock market advice to Canadians. Suffice it to say that after that interview, those words were never uttered again.

The morning of the stock market buying-opportunity speech had been given over to the release of the platform. The overall theme was that a Harper government would continue to provide strong leadership on a steady course during a time of global instability. It was a modest, affordable platform that contrasted with risky tax-and-spend experiments that would drive up the cost of living, with no appreciable benefits, at a time when Canadians could least afford it. For once, the release of the platform did not create much controversy; much of it had already been announced, and the spending was modest.[2]

The workmanlike document was divided into five sections that supported the overarching theme of strong Harper leadership and coincided with areas where Conservatives had a legislative track record, but could also promise to do more. Under "Cost of Living and Quality of Life," there would be a reduction in taxes on diesel fuel to help reduce cost of delivery of goods to keep prices low for consumers. For families, it promised income splitting for seniors, tax credit for first-time homebuyers, and education agreements for First Nations. The theme "Jobs for the Future" concentrated on providing EI for self-employed Canadians, reducing tax on small business, new copyright legislation, new trade agreements, and a new regional development agency for Northern Canada and for Southern Ontario, as well as continuation of the municipal infrastructure program. Under "A Strong United, Independent and Free Canada," there were promises protecting Canadian resources and building a clean energy superpower, Arctic sovereignty, and continued support for the mission in Afghanistan. "Ensuring Health and Environmental Well-Being" spoke to developing a cap-and-trade system, tough enforcement of environmental laws, and stronger tobacco laws to protect children. The young offenders programs were contained in the final section, "Protecting the Safety and Security of Canadians."

Within a day or two, it was Dion's turn to speak to the same group that Harper had addressed with his economic message. I talked with Marjory LeBreton about it and told her my advice to Dion would be to go into this speech telling the audience that he was putting his Greenshift plan on hold until the economy turned around, and to then stress the so-called plan that he had unveiled during the leaders' debate and position himself as someone who was worth taking a chance on. Maybe the risk would be worth it. This would take away the Greenshift tax-on-everything stick we were using to beat him like a piñata. LeBreton disagreed. She believed Dion was so stubborn and sure of himself that he would just soldier on. I bet her twenty dollars – which I don't think I ever paid. True to form, Dion shoved his Greenshift – with its tax increases on everything – right down the audience's throats as the main course. In what had been a pretty tough few days, it was the first indication that the Grits, especially Dion, did-n't get it.

Even so, the Grits were too close for comfort, and with only a few days left in the campaign, it was time for a come-to-Jesus meeting with Harper. Empathy wasn't working. What else would work?

We were somewhere in Southern Ontario, and after the morning meeting with Harper broke up, LeBreton and I stayed behind to talk to him. LeBreton's theory, which she had to repeat a number of times, was that the election would be decided when voters sat down over the Thanksgiving weekend and discussed politics. Her fervent view was that the general consensus among Canadians would be that they sure as hell would not want a Prime Minister Stéphane Dion emerging on Tuesday, 14 October 2008. It was time to go back to the original mes-saging of strong leadership for difficult economic times. We told Harper that we had had enough of the empathy gig. It wasn't work-ing. He didn't look comfortable or credible doing it. So, when he went downstairs to do his media availability, he should be the tough SOB Canadians thought he was – a tough SOB who was a leader and could manage Canada's economy through anything. It was time to stress leadership and time to emphasize the stark contrast between him and Dion.

That is what he did, and the campaign had wind in its sails once again.

Now it was time for Harper to catch a couple of breaks. One was the World Economic Forum ranking Canada's financial and banking system as the best in the world. If it was the best in the world under Harper, perhaps he should stay on as prime minister to ensure that it remained the best in the world. Also, Finance Minister Jim Flaherty had given the prime minister something to talk about: he left the campaign trail to make an announcement that our banks would be provided with more liquidity to help out people and businesses during this time of restraint or distress. Flaherty also attended a G7 emergency finance ministers' meeting, again solidifying the view of the Conservative Party as the governing party.

And then on 9 October the Dion do-over interview occurred. When a good part of your campaign, and the ballot question you want, is based on the weakness of your opponent and his inability to deal with or make tough financial decisions, it is a wonderful thing when fate conspires to prove both points out of the mouth and by the actions of that very opponent. As has been well reported, we were in Winnipeg waiting to leave for Ontario, when news of this broke. The campaign team, including Harper, gathered in front of a television set in the hotel to watch. Contrary to what the commentators have said, we did not think the question was difficult or full of tricky verb tenses. Dion had spent most of the interview criticizing the prime minister, either for what he had done that Dion believed was wrong or for doing nothing. Either way, it left the interviewer, CTV's Mike Murphy, the logical question: if you were prime minister, what would you do differently? For whatever reason, at that moment, Dion couldn't grasp the question, or the people advising him had never walked through with him what he would do as prime minister. He would have saved himself by going back to the plan he revealed during the leaders; debate. But he didn't, and whether it was fair or not, CTV played the clip over and over, without giving Dion a heads-up that they would be doing so.

I do not believe any of us hesitated for a second on this one. It was time for Harper to lay down some markers as to what leadership of a major economic country meant. The beauty of having our own plane, and the constant attention of the media travelling on it, meant ready access to the airwaves – and we took advantage of that, I believe not unfairly. Harper made it abundantly clear that leading a G8 country, you don't get a chance for do-overs, and managing a trillion-and-a-half-dollar economy was not a time when you want your leader stuck in do-overs. This incident provided, through Dion's own words and actions, the construct we had been trying to get across to Canadians. Strong versus weak, competent versus incompetent – and finally, for the first time since the debates, all the pieces started to fall back into place.

In the final days, the campaign moved along the north shore of the St Lawrence in Quebec as we tried to reverse the downward slide in Quebec. It was a valiant effort; and while it was too late to achieve gains, Harper was able to get out his message on the economy and review what he had delivered for Quebec since 2006.

On the Friday before the Thanksgiving long weekend, Statistics Canada released employment figures showing the creation of 106,000 new jobs in Canada in September. This, on top of having Canada's banking system ranked number one in the world by the World Economic Forum on the previous day, started to solidify our lead.

Thanksgiving dinner on Sunday in Prince Edward Island was turkey or fish, depending on when you showed up for dinner. The walk back to the hotel included a relaxed prime minister with wife Laureen, all of us now believing in LeBreton's exhortation about Canadians deciding over turkey dinner to vote for Harper to lead Canada through tough economic times. The concern on that Sunday evening was how best to use the final day. Because of the great support across the country, there were a variety of options open. The day would start with a rally in Summerside, and then move to New Brunswick where Senator Kinsella had organized events – but from there we had options. The first concern was how many people in PEI would get up really early on a holiday Monday to send the prime minister off for his last day of campaigning. For a few years it had been the province where we should win at least two or three of the four seats but were continually shut out. We had a good chance this time at two seats, but it still felt like Charlie Brown and Lucy and the football. No matter what we did, the PE Islanders would snatch the football away at the last minute, and once again, there would be no Conservative MPs from the island. We were confident that Kinsella would arrange a good group on the tarmac in New Brunswick, with appropriate media, and we would get a substantial hit. There was no point going back to Quebec – we had just come from there. So where was the last shot from the PM needed most on a Thanksgiving Monday? There was the option of shoring up votes in Saskatchewan, but the Roughriders were playing at home on Monday. The next option was to go straight across the country and do some campaigning for local candidates in the City of Vancouver. It seemed odd to decide to spend most of the day in the air, but it seemed the best option, since stopping anywhere on the way might mean arriving in Vancouver too late to be effective, even with the time zones in our favour.

As we went to bed in PEI on the Sunday evening, we were pretty confident of winning – how big a win was the question. As well as whether anyone would show up for the Thanksgiving Monday rally.

We got our answer the next day as dawn broke over the island: the hall we'd booked was absolutely jammed. The cheering, enthusiastic crowd buoyed everyone's spirits. In New Brunswick, we were greeted by a smaller but equally enthusiastic crowd, that was still bigger than the one Dion had attracted just a few minutes before. We had Kinsella's reassuring words that New Brunswick was for Harper. Then it was time to relax, read, and watch a movie as we spent the next six hours going straight through to Vancouver. We always knew we were having a good day when Harper pulled out his hockey research to work on his hockey book, which he finally finished and which was published in November 2013. He had plenty of time to work on it that Monday. On the bus taking us to downtown Vancouver, Harper remarked on the high cost of gasoline and said it must be the damn carbon tax in BC. The visit was worthwhile as the PM addressed a very supportive crowd. Then it was back to Calgary to await the outcome, to see what Canadians would deliver to us.

As we watched the results come in across the country, it became obvious that, with no breakthrough in Quebec, there would be no majority – but there would be quite a strengthened minority. We won all the ridings we had campaigned in on Monday, including one in PEI for Gail Shea. We cheered the election of Lisa Raitt over Garth Turner in Milton. The result was twelve seats shy of a majority, but it gave us enough to make the exercise worthwhile. On the Tuesday night in Calgary, Harper struck a conciliatory tone as he accepted another minority term as prime minister.

I had already accepted a position at the University of Calgary, to start at campaign's end, but met with Harper the morning after the election to discuss our mutual futures. I was one of those who actually really enjoyed working with Stephen Harper. Oh yes, he has a temper, and he has his good days and bad, but overall he is bright, hard-working, and knowledgeable, and always has the best interests of the country close to his heart. People may not agree with his policies or politics, but they can never disagree with his commitment to making Canada the best country in the world in which to live. His sense of humour and his ability as a mimic may not be well known, but they are endearing qualities to those who have had the privilege to work closely with him.

While there are not many laughs on the campaign trail, there were a few. Marjory LeBreton had us both laughing till we cried when she described events on the Diefenbaker funeral train as it made its way west after the Chief's funeral in Ottawa. She also told the story of Father Sean O'Sullivan, who represented Hamilton–Wentworth riding. He had become quite proficient at writing Dief's signature, such that the order of service booklets used at the funeral in Christ Church Cathedral in Ottawa looked like they'd been autographed by Dief himself.

On another occasion, as we neared Kitchener in the evening for an overnight stay, Harper, who was sitting across the aisle from me, asked me about the next day's announcement and whether we were actually addressing a valid issue. It was about cigarillos or cigarettes that came in flavours that would entice children to smoke – flavours like cotton candy, strawberry, vanilla, etcetera. We had been told that these cigarettes were the rage among teenagers, and the anti-smoking lobby in Canada wanted the sales to minors banned, and perhaps manufacture of these cigarettes banned as well. Harper started the conversation in his usual complimentary way by saying that, since I was familiar with every vice known to man, perhaps I knew about this problem. I told him I didn't. Since he didn't either, the answer was to do research, gather pertinent information. We decided that we needed to buy some of these cigarettes to see what they were like – as neither of us smokes, I am not sure how we thought that was going to work, but, nevertheless, it was worth pursuing. We spotted a COST-CO store, but neither of us had a COSTCO membership and neither of us wanted to buy a membership at that moment. As luck would have it, down the road a little was a small convenience store. We believed it would sell what we wanted, so we ask the driver to stop. The RCMP got out first to go into the store, and then Harper and I walked in. We went up to the clerk, and I asked to see the packages of flavoured cigarettes he was selling. He said no. Then we noticed all the closed shelves behind the clerk – presumably where cigarettes were hiding. After much toing-and-froing with the clerk, we finally got him to tell us that he had vanilla-flavoured cigarettes – so if we specifically asked for them, he would sell them to us. We bought two packs. Harper asked, now that we were here, if there was anything else I wanted. Between the two of us, we decided on a Diet Coke and an Aero chocolate bar. Since the PM had no money, I paid. Carson and Harper's excellent shopping adventure. When we got back on the bus, smokers on board assured us that we had purchased the real thing. To this day, I am still not sure if the clerk knew Canada's prime minister had been in his store that evening. The next day's announcement went off without a hitch, Harper firmly believing we were protecting the health of young Canadians against the evils of big and conniving tobacco.

Those anecdotes, along with reflections of more serious times during the campaign, came to mind as I sat with Harper on the morning of 15 October. He talked about how far we had come in such a short time and the rocky road that lay ahead. He believed that his leadership would be in some jeopardy because he didn't win a majority over Dion, the weakest Liberal leader ever, until the next one. He also did not believe the government would last long. He believed the opposition parties would take advantage of the worsening economic times and, at some point early on, defeat the government, and we would be into another election. We agreed that, even though I would be at the University of Calgary, I would remain as helpful as possible as he moved through the initial period of putting his new government together.

Back in Ottawa, the first item on the agenda, not surprisingly, was to put together the new Cabinet. While ministers such as Emerson, Hearn, and Solberg had decided not to run in 2008, no minister had been defeated. There would be vacancies and plenty of new wood, but for the most part, the faces around the Cabinet would be pretty familiar. That said, there were a couple of guidelines that Harper wanted to follow: first, to move any minister who had spent the entire first mandate in the same portfolio and, second, to promote as many women as possible into Cabinet positions. As always, there is some humour in the possible matchups – like when the prime minister thought it would be fun to put "Stock in Trade" and "Cannon in Defence." But the joke fizzled as we ran out of names to suit portfolios.

There were a couple of appointments that deserve mention. Jim Prentice loved being industry minister. It suited him perfectly as he had business sense and experience and a way of getting things done. Being again in minority status, Harper realized that environment was an area that needed a steady hand, and also a hand that was trusted by the oil and gas folks in Alberta not to do anything stupid. So, as the prime minister said, "Prentice has a lot of political capital in Alberta; it is about time he spent some of it." Environment was not a portfolio that Prentice saw himself in, nor was he happy about it during much of his tenure there. However, he did a great job moving all of it forward, especially on the parks and regulatory side, and basically shutting down much of the criticism of the government in the environment area. Where he wasn't able to shut it down, he certainly had credible answers to whatever happened to be the environmental issues of the day.

The appointment of Lisa Raitt at Natural Resources Canada only became humorous after she left Harrington Lake, where MPs were being told about their appointments. When discussing staffing with her, I kept referring to Natural Resources by its acronym NRCan. She had no clue what NRCan was but was happy to take it over, staff it, and run it. Only on her way back to Ottawa, through a phone call, did she become certain as to what she had agreed to take on.

The only real demotion was Gary Lunn's appointment as minister of state for sport. Lunn was really upset and thought the demotion unwarranted. This dated back to the nuclear file, starting with the Chalk River shutdown and moving through the government's attempt to deal with Atomic Energy Canada Limited through either an outright sale or development of a completely new business plan. Both Brodie and Harper had become dissatisfied with Lunn's performance during this period. Whether they were right or wrong, this is how it was dealt with.

When Lunn came to talk about staffing, he wasn't sure that he would actually take the appointment. But about half an hour later, he called me to say he would accept it, and we would work on staffing issues together. It turned out well, since the 2010 Winter Olympics were to be held in Lunn's home province. What better time to be minister of sport?

The last appointment that was settled was Helena Guergis. She had done an outstanding job as parliamentary secretary for international trade on the softwood lumber issue. She understood the issues and did an excellent job getting the enabling legislation through committee. Since that time, she had received a promotion to minister of state for foreign affairs and international trade, but her performance was uneven, and there were frequent staffing issues that had to be dealt with. Harper was also not pleased that her husband had lost a safe seat in Alberta by simply not mounting a campaign. My advice was to leave her out; Harper believed this would only cause problems. He kept her in as minister of state for the status of women.

With the Cabinet in place, I headed back to Calgary believing that the prime minister was set for easy sailing for at least the next two to three years.

What happened next caught me completely by surprise. It was early evening in Calgary, and I was having dinner at the Kensington Hotel prior to a lecture in a series put on at the University of Calgary. I received a message telling me that the Grits, the NDP, and the Bloc were going to join together to bring down the government and replace it with a coalition led by Stéphane Dion. I said that was nonsense, would never happen, and went back to my dinner. Later that evening, I turned on the TV and discovered what all the fuss was about.

Lawrence Martin, in his book *Harperland*, claims that the final word on putting in the poison pill dealing with the cancellation of political party subsidies came via a BlackBerry message from Harper, who was attending the 22–23 November 2008 Asia-Pacific Economic Cooperation meeting in Lima, Peru. The PM does not carry a BlackBerry, so if it were a direct instruction from him, it would have come via Jeremy Hunt, his executive assistant. This was a surprise but was unanimously endorsed by caucus when the PM returned to Ottawa.

However, during the time when I returned to Ottawa, mid-December to 4 February 2009, there was no trace of how the cancellation of political party subsidies got into the Economic Fall Update (EFU). Putting it in was a gross political miscalculation, and it certainly made no sense for the PM to order it in for presentation on Thursday and revoke it on Friday. It defied logic and certainly my understanding of the way Harper had operated previously.

The suspension of the right of public servants to strike made no sense. The government was in the process of concluding negotiations with the unions, and Vic Toews at Treasury Board was publicly pleased with how negotiations were progressing and with the anticipated outcome, when ratified. The limit on women's access to the courts to deal with pay equity similarly made no sense. We had spent the entire campaign trying to appeal to female voters, and the PM made it clear when considering Cabinet opportunities that we were to include as many women as possible. But whether or not any of it made sense, it was the hand we had dealt ourselves – clearly an unforced error on ourselves. The question now was, what were we going to do about it?

The only part that made sense was that the EFU contained no stimulus package. The decision could be defended, given that the government was still uncertain as to how the economic turmoil would affect Canadians, and if there was to be stimulus, it could wait until the 2009 budget.

While still in Calgary, I received a phone call from Guy Giorno on Friday, 28 November, the day after the EFU was presented. He asked me to check with some of my friends in Ottawa to discover how serious the opposition was about its plans to defeat and displace the government. After calling around, it was evident that this was serious. The opposition parties were ready to take on the government. So on that Friday came the climb down by the government, but it was too late. The Liberals had an opposition day on Monday, 1 December, and it was going to be used to bring down the government. The next move in the chess game was the government's: opposition day got shunted to 8 December.

Then the opposition got too cocky and too smart by half and held a coalition-signing ceremony in the Centre Block. The Grits and the NDP were to form a government with the Bloc, led by Duceppe, signing a political accord to support them for two years. The Bloc was not to be part of the coalition government, just support it. That was enough to re-energize a beaten, down-and-out Harper. No coalition with the Bloc either inside it or supporting it from outside was going to wrest power from him without a fight. As usual, the reasons behind these actions – the fact that the government had caused this crisis – had evaporated. The argument was framed as being all about coalition or no coalition – a coup supported by the separatists and the other two opposition parties. The Bloc was going to get near the levers of power or, worse, get their hands on the levers of power and perhaps get the combination to the financial safe.

The evening of 1 December, Harper addressed the assembled throng at the Christmas Party, and there was no doubt then that regardless of how the fight got started, the PM was going to do what he could to keep this illegal, unconstitutional coup from taking place. He didn't have to wait long for his chance to end it. The TV networks had agreed to play back-to-back video statements on Wednesday evening, 3 December, from Harper and Dion, giving each a chance to argue his case before the Canadian public. Harper's was crisp, professional, and on message, vilifying the Grits, the NDP, and their attempt, after having lost an election, to take over government with the support of the party that wanted to end Canada as we know it. All of this was remarkably similar to what Harper wanted to do in the autumn of 2004 with Layton and Duceppe and a joint letter to Governor General Adrienne Clarkson. But that was quite beside the point.

The argument on behalf of the coalition was to be presented by would-be prime minister Stéphane Dion. Except, instead of taping his remarks early in the day to ensure that both audio and video worked perfectly, he spent the day perfecting a letter to the governor general. The taping of his remarks was completed late and of poor quality, and demonstrated once again why he was not leadership material. It turned the tide against him and the coalition.

The prime minister and Kevin Lynch, the clerk, called on Governor General Jean the following day, 4 December, requesting prorogation until a day in late January. This strategy was decided upon as there was none other that would save the government. Eventually, the opposition day would have to be held as required by the House of Commons Rules, and as things seemed at the time, the opposition would unite and the government would suffer defeat on a non-confidence motion. The only way to avoid this was to seek prorogation. The government believed it was entitled to prorogation since the Speech from the Throne had been approved by the House. Prorogation would give the time necessary to put together an early budget as promised by Finance Minister Flaherty and then to present it to the House of Commons. Let there be no mistake about it: the governor general was going to grant the prorogation. It was just a case of putting sufficient fences around it to make sure this did not become habit-forming. Peter Hogg, the governor general's constitutional advisor, is a cautious, well-respected constitutional scholar. In the history of Canada, a sitting prime minister had never been refused prorogation when it was requested. Hogg was not going to advise breaking new ground. Harper had governed since 2006, won a sizable minority in October 2008, formed a Cabinet, met the House, and had a Speech from the Throne approved. Harper could argue that this was not a situation of requesting dissolution to avoid a confidence vote. He wanted prorogation to give his government time to bring in a budget to respond to the economic crisis. Then there would be a confidence vote.

The question arose afterwards as to why this meeting took two hours. The people around that table took their roles seriously. According to Michael Valpy, who has written on this, they had a good conversation about the state of the country's finances, the mood of parliament, and the coalition possibilities.[3] The governor general and her secretary, Sheila-Marie Cook, left to consult with Peter Hogg, came back, and the prime minister's request was granted. All of this took time. It's worth noting that the group had been meeting together regularly since early 2006. Although they had met a couple of times since 14 October 2008, this was another chance to catch up and discuss the business of the nation before them as well as prorogation. There was also discussion as to the timing and nature of the budget that the government would bring in at the end of January. There is a human element to all of this that seems to be constantly and consistently ignored.

So the stage was set for the battle for the hearts and minds of Canadians. It had begun that previous weekend with rallies staged across the country. I attended the one in Calgary, which, as one would expect, was vehemently pro-Conservative and anti-coalition. This was an episode where no one involved gained any glory. It was a crisis that did not need to occur, and for causing it, no one takes credit. It ended the leadership of Stéphane Dion, who was replaced by Michael Ignatieff, after a short skirmish with Bob Rae, in the middle of the following week on Wednesday, 10 December. The governor general was put in the position of making a decision she should never have had to make. Harper's constant demonizing of the Bloc and separatists sealed his party's fate in Quebec through to the next general election. And finally, the aura of Harper as a master tactician lost its brilliance.

At this point, I discussed with Giorno the possibility of coming back to lend a hand through all of this. I had talked to the board at the Canada School of Energy and Environment and secured a leave of absence. I was meeting with the prime minister in his Centre Block office on the afternoon of 10 December, when Ignatieff ascended to the Liberal throne. Harper was ill, still fighting something he had picked up a while before, at the APEC meeting. He was not optimistic, since at that time he viewed Ignatieff as a formidable foe. He wasn't sure why I wanted to help when we could be done right after the budget was presented. He thought it a distinct possibility that his government would only last another month. To his surprise – I guess it was the first time I had ever said it – I told him I liked working with him and being of whatever help I could be. The experience of working with Ian Brodie and the team he had put together to support the prime minister was one of the best work experiences of my life. Harper and I then had a good discussion about the challenges that lay ahead. I left feeling comfortable that we would get through this and would develop a budget that would be help all Canadians who were now grappling with the economic crisis.

Prior to coming on board full-time in January 2009, I met with Kevin Lynch to discuss the structure of the budget, the amount of deficit we were prepared to own and for how long, and the return to balance. We also discussed what the deficit could be used for. These were useful discussions that we followed up on in January. What surprised us the most was that, having survived a near-death experience we basically had to wait until after the holidays for things to get up and running again.

Over the Christmas holidays, Harper decided to fill the vacancies in the Senate. Senator LeBreton, her office, and I set up a workshop for the new arrivals, and with Senator Terry Stratton, the whip, I worked on assigning office space and staffing for senators' offices.

Harper set out the parameters for the stimulus budget in early January. As hard as it was for a former Reformer, fiscal conservative, and trained economist to run a deficit, he could justify it because of the extraordinary international economic crisis, provided the budget did not create a structural deficit. The phrase "shovel ready" became the watchword, and no money was to be put into programming that would go on forever. Projects had to spend the designated money within two years and employ Canadians. It was also imperative that the provinces and municipalities contribute to these projects. Harper was not going to run the only deficit in the country for the benefit of all of the provinces, territories, and municipalities.

The main point that I stressed with Lynch was that whatever we did, whatever monies were allocated to projects, we had to get the money out the door. This issue came up at the Priorities and Planning Committee meeting, raised by John Baird, who, as usual, was at the hot corner as the go-to guy for whatever the prime minister needed done. This time it was stimulus spending. John went on at length about how he, his staff, and his officials would ensure the legitimacy of the projects so that no money would be wasted, so that the government would not be embarrassed. Harper's view was do your due diligence, but the most important thing was to get the money into circulation creating jobs and getting projects completed. There would be mistakes, but as far as Harper was concerned, the greater good was stimulating the economy. We were not creating another "Build Canada bureaucrat's wet dream." The money was to flow!

So within these parameters, the budget was developed. It was an opportune time for the government to put money into areas that it would not normally have had at the top of its list, such as social housing. Spending on infrastructure for Canada's Aboriginal peoples was increased and the infrastructure deficit, which the Federation of Canadian Municipalities had long spoken of, was to some extent reduced.

Also during this period, I was assigned the task of following up with at least five Canadian constitutional scholars on a project that Guy Giorno and Ray Novak had begun. They were concerned that the coalition would revive itself at the end of January, defeat the budget, and request that it be allowed to form a government. I suppose this was part of Harper's unease when we met in mid-December. The government needed sound, scholarly opinions from recognized experts that if the budget were defeated, the prime minister would be entitled to ask for dissolution and an election. It was not difficult to find those who would support this position; from a former Supreme Court of Canada justice to the dean of a faculty of law, there was unanimity that it would be time to go back to the people. The letters we received in support of the government's position were well thought out and fulsome, sufficient in my opinion to counter any arguments that the coalition should be called on to form a government should the budget be defeated. This, of course, never occurred, and the opinions are safely tucked away, perhaps never to be used by this prime minister.

The preparation of the budget went more smoothly than we had anticipated, and through the convening of a First Ministers' Meeting and one involving Aboriginal leaders, support was enlisted.

The one humorous public policy incident occurred on a Saturday morning meeting as we closed in on finalizing the budget. We had to establish a maximum amount for the Home Renovation Tax Credit.

At a meeting chaired by Harper and attended by Minister Flaherty, his deputy, Kevin Lynch, a few others, and me, it became obvious that none of us had any idea what would be an appropriate limit. I thought of phoning my son Eric, who was finishing his basement, to find out how much he was going to spend on the project. Then we got into the usual home renovation horror stories. Finally, it was agreed that Flaherty would phone the head of Home Depot and find out the cost of finishing the average basement. We believed $10,000 sounded about right for the upside limit, and that was confirmed by Flaherty. Public policy on practical matters such as home renovations should not be left to a bunch of guys in suits.

The budget covered many areas and was generally well received. Layton and Duceppe were not going to vote for it. The Liberals would support it, but required regular updates as to its implementation; Ignatieff sounded tough when he said he was putting the government on probation. We were only too happy to oblige since it gave the bureaucracy deadlines to work towards and a reporting function on progress.

The budget[4] contained $39.9 billion of federal stimulus funding over two years to be supplemented by provincial and territorial spending of $11.7 billion. To Harper's point, it wouldn't be just the federal government running a stimulus deficit; the provinces had to have skin in the game. Infrastructure, including First Nations infrastructure spending, was a priority, but it had to be shovel ready; this was not to be continuous stimulus spending. Employment Insurance was made more generous and would last longer. The budget also improved access to financing for businesses, income tax relief, and support for homeowners through the highly popular Home Renovation Tax Credit and ecoENERGY Retrofit program.

There were glitches during the week of 27 January when the budget was announced, but they were handled quietly, out of the glare of the media. Adjustments were made to the equalization formula to accommodate Ontario entering into the status of a have-not province – that affected every other province's share. It took a couple of attempts to satisfy Premier Campbell of British Columbia that our calculations were correct. On the Friday of budget week, senior Liberals approached our House leader Jay Hill requesting a briefing on the changes created in the Atlantic Accord by the budget and suggesting that the briefing could take place on Monday morning in the

OLO. It seemed a reasonable request for information, made in a non-threatening manner. After Hill phoned me, I went in to see Harper, who was on his way to Quebec City for Carnavale. He agreed that we could do the briefing: what we didn't want was the budget being defeated because of misinformation or misunderstanding. The briefing took place, and the Grits supported the budget.

Minority Second Mandate: Governing like a Majority

In the period immediately after the approval of the 2009 stimulus budget through to the 2011 election, the most important day was 2 May 2011, polling day. It delivered the long sought-after majority government for the Conservative Party. But between these two dates were myriad issues, challenges, and opportunities that, when taken together, helped fashion the result in May 2011. For veteran observers, this approximately twenty-seven-month period had to be one of the most fractious periods in Canadian parliamentary history. However, through the stimulus measures of the 2009 budget, it was also a productive time as Canada persevered through and began its recovery from the worldwide economic downturn. Having survived the near-death experience of December 2008, the Conservatives were buoyed by a new self-confidence that was evident in their approach to governing and, of course, in how they dealt with the opposition. Christopher Dornan, in his introduction to *The Canadian Federal Election of 2011*, termed this Parliament as "toxic in its hyper-partisanship."[1]

My view is that the Conservatives decided to govern as if they had a majority, unlike the period 2006 to 2008, when they were very conscious of their minority status and trying to establish a defendable track record, and get re-elected. From 2009–11, they just dared the opposition to unite and bring them down. The Conservatives had acquired the sole rights to use the picture of the three opposition leaders shaking hands and smiling gleefully on the day they signed the coalition deal. Whenever the opposition threatened to bring down the government, as Ignatieff did in the late summer of 2009, the Conservatives knew that all they had to do was trot out that picture and holler "coalition with the separatists" at the top of their lungs and

The Global Stage. The Canadian contingent (from left) of Jim Prentice; Michael
Wilson, ambassador to the US; Bruce Carson; and Bill Rodgers, director of
communications, met with the American contingent led by Steven Chu (right),
Barack Obama's energy secretary, on the Clean Energy Dialogue. (Courtesy of
Jim Prentice. Reprinted by permission)

the opposition would be dead as dead could be, at least outside of
Quebec.

When the government refused to play ball on Afghanistan by withholding documents; to reveal the costs (provided they actually had
them) of the F-35 jets, the prison build, the corporate tax reductions;
or to explain why a "NOT" had mysteriously appeared in a funding
document, this was, based on my experience, Stephen Harper actually daring the opposition to do what it eventually did – vote down the
government on a non-confidence motion. It was him essentially saying: If you (the opposition) don't like what we are doing and are serious about it, bring us down and let Canadians decide. From past experience dating back to the planning of the non-election of May 2005,
the Conservatives knew that an entire election campaign could not be
run on allegations of corruption or, indeed, on allegations that the
government had somehow hijacked democracy, as Ignatieff would
have Canadians believe. One cannot argue in an election campaign,
the ultimate democratic act, that Canada is not a democracy. Also, all
polling indicated that the most important matter for Canadians was
the economy and jobs. On both of these matters, Harper was way
ahead of the opposition in both trust and competence. During the
minority period, fraught as it was with partisanship on all sides, the

opposition parties – certainly the Liberals and the Bloc – missed the end-game. Harper didn't care if he was defeated in the House on a confidence measure; the economic issues, that wonderful coalition picture, and ultimately Canadians were on his side, and he knew it. It was like running a government with nothing to lose.

However, one can argue that this is no way to run a government. Ignoring orders from committees or the Speaker, wilfully withholding information from Parliament and ultimately from taxpayers: the government was accused of flouting Parliament and stonewalling committees. Believing Canadians cared more about the government's economic record than anything the opposition parties would dredge up, the government gambled that it could brand all of this as simply partisan wrangling.

In dissecting the entrails of the 2011 election, it is interesting to note that both Harper and Layton had basically the same focus: an economic message. The Grits concentrated on scandal, corruption, and, in the midst of an election, that Canada under Harper was no longer a democracy. Canadians were receptive to the economic message, but not to the other messages; the Conservatives had successfully convinced Canadians that the anti-democratic concerns and perceived scandals espoused by the Liberals amounted to the opposition playing partisan politics, trying to embarrass the government. The rise of the NDP can be explained because it had the right campaign message – the economy, its platform appealed to soft nationalists in Quebec, and it was all wrapped up in Layton's heroic, happy-warrior campaign style.

During the Christmas break at the end of 2009, during the second prorogation in this Parliament, I spoke with Harper about the political dynamics of the country. I said that his biggest fear in the next election should be the cry, " time for a change." He had been such an overpowering presence that few Canadians could recall the Martin interregnum, and the Chrétien years were a relic of another distant time. The response since then had always been: yes – but Canadians will not change to Ignatieff. We never thought they might consider a change to Jack Layton!

The months of February 2009 to March 2011 in the second mandate were characterized by a minority government that was not exactly plotting its own demise, but was figuratively saying to the opposition: if you want to bring down the government and face the consequences of a general election – fill your boots! Most commentators, who decried the so-called high-handed actions of the government on matters like the long-form census, Afghan documents, and the costs of various initiatives, missed that backdrop. So too did Ignatieff and Duceppe. Unfortunately, Layton did not live long after the election, and was gravely ill, so his perspective on all of this has been lost. But given the type of campaign he ran and the issues he addressed, I would venture to say that he understood what was going on better than the other opposition leaders, and ran a campaign to win. No one who studies parliamentary government would condone the Conservatives' tactic as a productive way to govern. However, for this government, at this time, it was successful.

So let's take some of the major issues, challenges, and opportunities that presented themselves in this period and consider them against this backdrop. Conducting the economy in a way that shielded Canadians, for the most part, from the economic issues emanating from the worldwide recession was obviously the most significant challenge faced by the government. It was important that the government act quickly with both the stimulus budget of 2009 and the follow-up budget in 2010 since that helped keep Canadians working and money circulating in the economy. While manufacturing suffered – though bolstered to a certain extent by the government's automobile manufacturers' bailout for both General Motors and Chrysler – it was the time for natural resources and specifically energy development to lead the way, to become the most important part of the economy. In many ways, energy and its spinoff effects kept Canadians employed from coast to coast to coast. Studies done by the independent agency Canadian Energy Research Institute, based in Calgary, have shown the widespread economic impact of oil sands development as well as development of conventional oil and gas.[2] The Conference Board of Canada, in a report released in the fall of 2012, reinforced these conclusions.[3]

This was also not a time for the Conservatives, or Harper as the prime minister, to become hidebound by ideology. If some economic measure needed to be adopted to keep Canada ahead of the curve of the economic downturn or recession, regardless of its ideological underpinning, it at least had to be considered – and if found helpful, then done. The most practical example of this thinking came with the automotive bailout. In 2004, we ran a campaign stressing that the Conservative Party would not be involved in supporting private industry through cash grants, loans, loan guarantees, or indeed any

other kind of support. In 2006, the platform found regional development agencies to be useful tools to help the economy. In the 2009
budget, an economic development agency was established for southern Ontario, an area hit hard by manufacturing decline, and was given
$1 billion in seed capital. This represented a real, practical evolution
in the Party's economic thinking. It was Harper's belief that if Canada did not move to help the automotive sector at the same time as the
United States did, at the very least, we would lose the Canadian portion of that North American industry sector. Whether or not he was
right, he did not want to take the gamble, so Canada participated with
the US in propping up both Chrysler and General Motors.

Stimulus was continued in the 2010 budget,[4] but accompanied with
a path to balance, which was reiterated in the 2011, 2012, and 2013
budgets. Once in deficit, the important matter for the government was
to get out of it and get back to balance – so much so that in the 2011
campaign, Harper announced that balance would be achieved a year
earlier than initially projected. This was a rash promise, unsupported
by economic data, and was not kept.

The government held that this was not to be a structural deficit in
need of new taxes or tax increases in order to be eliminated. The
deficit was composed of one-time spending initiatives. The best example demonstrating this position was non-renewal of the popular
Home Renovation Tax Credit. The stimulus measures were to be simply that, stimulus measures, not long-term spending commitments or
program initiatives that would result in a structural deficit.

Sound banking, financial, regulatory, and monetary systems enabled
Canada to respond decisively to economic conditions at home and to
take the lead internationally at the G20 meetings in Pittsburg and
Toronto. Accompanying the 2010 G20 meeting in Toronto was the G8
meeting in Huntsville, Ontario. The G8 had become more of a policy-
making group, addressing significant issues around the globe (until
the 2013 meeting in Great Britain, which dealt with the civil war in
Syria); the centerpiece was maternal and children's health as presented
and led by Canada. At the G20 meeting, the theme was restoring fiscal
balance among the assembled countries. Again, Harper led the way in
establishing a consensus communiqué with a carve-out from balance
requirements for Japan.

It is hard to imagine how focusing the G8 and G20 foreign aid or
assistance on maternal and child health could end up in a controversy, at least within Canada, about contraception and abortion, and how

a G20 consensus agreement led by Harper that would see the wealthy nations of the world half their deficits over the next three years in order to provide international economic market stability could end up being overshadowed by stories about the cost of the summits, fake lakes, and policing and protests. But that is what happened. And the fact that it did is an indictment of the communications role of the government and its issues management.

On the G20 consensus, Prime Minister Harper worked with President Obama and German chancellor Angela Merkel to ensure the deal was made. It was also important to France's president Nicolas Sarkozy, as host of the next G20, that this deal be done so that he would have some concrete economic steps upon which to build. Harper gained a win amongst his colleagues on the world stage. Canada not only looked strong but was strong in the discussions on the worldwide recession and alternative solutions for recovery. Through the prime minister and Minister Flaherty, Canada was able to lead by example from a position of considerable strength.

It is unfortunate that three years after hosting these two successful, landmark international meetings, where no security threats marred the proceedings, the courts are still trying to sort out allegations of police brutality and, until recently, Commons committees were still questioning the costs of hosting these meetings. Again, the government could have been more forthcoming about the latter and saved itself considerable grief. While these are important matters, surely they could be dealt with in a timelier manner and we could move on.

In addition to the economy, another major issue facing the government was the war in Afghanistan. It was a war that Canada joined, and played a significant role in, and it was, for Harper, a war that he inherited from the previous Liberal government. Being part of a war effort halfway around the world in a land so very different from Canada – especially when the enemy is unknown and the tactics employed by that enemy are almost beyond our comprehension – was taxing on Canada's armed forces and on the government. This war continues to be fought in the real time of the twenty-four-hour news cycle, so virtually nothing is secret and bad news travels at the speed of light.

As explained above, Harper had a realistic view of what could be accomplished in Afghanistan, and was committed to Canada doing its part in the war against terrorism. He believed in it to such an extent that his first foreign trip was to visit Canada's troops there. As far as Harper was concerned, we were not going to be able to turn Afghanistan into a functioning western democracy. At best NATO and its allies would be successful if they left behind a stable government, with some sense of equality of women and men, educational opportunities for women, and an economy not based on the drug trade.

The Afghanistan task force chaired by John Manley provided a good road map for the government and also helped educate Canadians as to what Canada was trying to accomplish there, the dangers, the humanitarian efforts, and the likelihood of long-term success. The implementation of the panel's recommendations, with agreement by the Liberals, brought Canada's commitment to an end in 2011. A significant part of the Manley panel report focused on rebuilding the country, the need for humanitarian aid, and the obvious goal of at some point leaving Afghanistan to the Afghans. In order to implement this part of the report, the government, again with support from the Liberals, re-profiled and reconfigured Canada's role in Afghanistan post–mid-2011 to the provision of training in Kabul and extension of humanitarian aid to 2014. While Harper had hoped to be finished in Afghanistan by 2011, he did not want to be in this war longer than ten years – Canada had never been in a war anywhere for that long. However, it was probably unrealistic to believe we could just pull out, leaving nothing behind. This training role will allow Canada to see how the transition takes place as the country moves from being occupied by NATO troops, mostly from the US, under a commission from the UN, to having its defence and security provided, for the most part, by Afghan police and military. This is still a significant role for Canada.

The other part of the Afghan war has been waged far from the IEDs planted on Afghanistan roads and the bullets shot by the Taliban – on battlefields at committee hearings, court proceedings, and the Military Police Complaints Commission.[5] These battles were about the treatment of Taliban prisoners handed over by the Canadian military to Afghan prisons. Civil liberties groups and certain journalists raised numerous allegations, basically stating that the Canadian military was complicit in alleged torture when our troops turned over their Taliban prisoners. In other words, our troops knew the prisoners would be tortured.

All of this came to a head with the testimony of a Canadian foreign service officer, Richard Colvin, who was stationed in Afghanistan in 2006–07 and who claimed he had notified senior military, through memos, that Canadian soldiers were handing over their Taliban captives to be tortured in Afghanistan prisons. He testified before the Special Committee on the Canadian Mission in Afghanistan that the handing over of Taliban prisoners as he described it actually took place and that this practice alienated Canada from the Afghan population. This was all news to General Rick Hillier and Minister MacKay. I'll add that in the two years that I had been monitoring Canada's military activities in Afghanistan through David Mulroney and others, I had never heard of Richard Colvin,[6] and to my knowledge and recollection, neither David Mulroney nor I ever saw such memos. Given that Colvin is the only person to come forward and attempt to corroborate these allegations, it is not surprising that both General Hillier and Minister MacKay would greet his testimony with a stiff rebuke.

Going back to the point made at the beginning of this chapter, it is also not surprising that the government was unwilling to provide secret documents to the opposition so it could try to substantiate claims of complicity in torture against Canadian troops. If the opposition didn't like the fact that the government wouldn't share sensitive documents in relation to a war Canada was trying to prosecute halfway around the world against a group of insurgents – not in uniform and not identifiable – then vote the government down. The prime minister and the minister of national defence's position was: if the opposition wants to fight an election over how we deal with the guys who are trying to kill our guys in Afghanistan, go for it! The government's view, substantiated by polling, was that Canadians did not care about this issue. They cared that our guys were getting killed, and they wanted to know if Canada was making progress. But Canadians did not care about the fate of captured Taliban insurgents. However, that did not deter the media, nor the opposition, and eventually the Speaker. The latter ruled on the production of documents, requiring the government and the opposition to work out a compromise by which documents could be produced and, if national security were involved, it would be protected.

While the issues were not exactly the same, Canada's engagement in the war in Libya also created controversy. In this case, it was not over the way Canada was prosecuting the war, but over whether the minister of national defence had misled the House about the costs of the mission. There was some controversy regarding the length of time Canada stayed in Libya, but the opposition was more interested in scoring political points about the cost and whether the minister knew the full cost at the time he disclosed a cost-to-date of $50 million.

As long as this government is in power, Canada will continue to be involved in operations in support of its allies. We have interests to protect, and now we have the means and the will to protect them. But military operations or wars fought in this era of instantaneous communications are far different from those that took place even as recently as the Gulf War, which saw participation from Canada under Mulroney's leadership and United States under George H.W. Bush's. The government's attitude toward sharing the Afghan documents should never have become an issue needing the Speaker's intervention. The government must find a way to work with the opposition, to share information so that wars are not being fought simultaneously in theatre and in Ottawa, in the Commons committee rooms and in question period. This creates an intolerable situation for those in the field, who may believe their efforts are not being supported, and for the government, which wants to ensure nothing is released that might be of aid or comfort to the enemy. During the First World War, Prime Minister Borden's approach was to create a coalition government. However, this would not work when the war is fought over many years, as with Afghanistan. Also, today's wars are not as all-consuming as the two World Wars were in their time – they seem now to be add-ons to whatever else is on the current national agenda. One thought might be to have certain opposition members sworn in as Privy Council members, with whom secret information could be shared. Some solution must be found or the situation will continue to deteriorate, and the main group that suffers is the one on the battlefield.

Canada–United States relations during the second mandate covered a number of fronts from economic to energy and environment to border security. There was no question about the excitement in Kevin Lynch's voice as he walked into one of our January 2009 budget planning meetings in the prime minister's boardroom to inform us that President Obama would make Ottawa his destination on his first foreign trip after assuming office. I gathered that this had been the subject of some negotiations between the Department of Foreign Affairs and the White House for some time, but it was now confirmed. This news was greeted warmly by Harper and the others in the room. It was my view that we had better draft a budget that would not result in the defeat of the government.

There was lots of idle speculation in the media about the differences between Harper and Obama. Lawrence Martin does his best with not much to work with, trying to draw out differences that put Obama in a positive light and cast the usual dark shadows over Harper.[7] The reality was best expressed by Derek Burney who, prior to the visit, emphasized what the two men had in common and the two things Harper had at that time that Obama would appreciate: experience and an excellent reputation on the world stage. In common, both men are young, have young families, and are bright; and while Obama was new, he was now saddled with a depressed American economy, an issue Harper knew all too well. At the time of the announcement of the visit, Harper was in the midst of planning Canada's stimulus package, which by the time of Obama's visit, in February 2009, would be in the public domain. Harper took former prime minister Mulroney's advice to heart: regardless of the usual Canada–US irritants, make sure you have a good working relationship with the president. One can disagree without being disagreeable. This advice served Harper well when George W. Bush was president, and he would attempt to have a cordial, if not friendly, relationship with President Obama. Sitting now at the end of 2013, one wonders what went wrong. Relations between the two countries, at least over energy and environment matters wrapped up in the Keystone XL Pipeline, are as strained as they ever have been in recent memory.

The Obama visit, while short, was satisfying. Discussions concentrated on energy and environment, Afghanistan, border issues, trade, buy America, and international security. The outcomes of the meeting pointed toward a productive start for Canada–US relations with the new administration: they concentrated on a new border strategy; energy and environment were rolled into the Clean Energy Dialogue; and greater co-operation and exchange of information on economic issues was promised.

Dealing with the border issue has taken some time but, as of late 2013 and although mired in IT problems, seems to be bearing some fruit. Under former president Bush, everything was seen through a security lens – especially trade. At the Security and Prosperity Partnership of North America meeting in New Orleans in 2008, Bush was unaware of the issues surrounding the Windsor–Detroit corridor, and the fact that the bridge was privately owned, with the owner not wanting to lose his monopoly. Solving the Windsor–Detroit border-crossing issue had been a priority for Harper from the time he assumed office. Ian Brodie had mused about appointing a border-crossing czar to try to move ahead with solutions. With President Obama, it was hoped that the importance of the Canadian–American trading relationship would manifest itself in real progress on thinning the border. And near the end of 2013, some progress has been made.

The other major takeaway from the Harper–Obama meeting was the Clean Energy Dialogue. At the beginning of the Obama administration, there was great optimism that he would tackle climate change and promote the development of clean energy. He appointed Nobel Prize–winner Steven Chu as secretary of energy and Todd Stern to look after environment and climate change issues. Unfortunately, like so many things, if they don't start well, they often come to naught. The energy, environment, and climate change hopes of the Obama administration floundered on the shoals of a Congress that couldn't make up its collective mind about how to deal with the new administration's view of energy and environment. Handing the file off to Congress to solve, with little direction, ensured that a lot of noise would be forthcoming, but little action. Canada's concern with what the United States was or wasn't doing was seen primarily through the lens of the oil sands. Were the efforts of California and other states to establish a clean fuel standard, the end of exports from the oil sands to the United States?

The three parts of the Clean Energy Dialogue (CED) were designed to enhance joint collaboration on the development of clean energy, science, and technologies to reduce greenhouse gasses and combat climate change. They were: (1) clean energy research and development and energy efficiency concentrating on carbon capture and storage, (2) development of an efficient electricity grid, and (3) expansion of research and development into clean energy. Secretary of Energy Steven Chu led the US efforts, and Minister of the Environment Jim Prentice led Canada's.

By this point I had left the PMO, but still remained connected to the government as I tried to assist with energy and environmental policy development from my position as executive director of the Canada School of Energy and Environment, located at the University of Calgary.

I think it is fair to say that Prentice and the Canadians participating in the three working groups held out great hope for this initiative. The challenge for Canada – as in all dealings with the United States – is to get their attention, and once we have it, to get them to move on what is Canada's agenda when the US typically has so many agendas. There was also some frustration on Prentice's side in that he was now directly responsible for the successful implementation of the first major bilateral agreement between the president and the prime minister, but all the levers he needed to pull to make a success of this venture were situated at Natural Resources Canada (NRCan) under the direction of rookie Cabinet minister Lisa Raitt.

While the turf wars between NRCan and Environment Canada were legion during the previous Liberal administration, this had not been the case under the Conservatives. While Gary Lunn may have had his faults as minister of natural resources, all ministers whose portfolios touched on energy and environment had good relations with Lunn. Prentice's frustration was that in order to move ahead on the CED, he had to go through his own bureaucracy, which would then interface with the bureaucrats at NRCan. In order to solve what he saw as the problem, Prentice believed that a special Cabinet committee should be established that would include, in addition to the minister of natural resources, three other ministers – foreign affairs, international trade, and industry – and possibly the minister of finance. This would get all the people with an interest in the CED around the same table on a weekly or ad hoc basis, much as we had done in 2006 for energy and environment and, as recommended by the Manley panel, for the conduct of the Afghan war. The prime minister and the clerk disagreed with Prentice. At an early morning meeting at the beginning of June 2009, the clerk, ministers Prentice and Raitt as well as their deputies and chiefs of staff, and I met in the small boardroom on the fourth floor of the Langevin Block. Our aim was to work through how the directive from the prime minister and president could be accomplished in the most effective manner possible, given the tight time constraints. Other than an agreement to make material available and to work closely together, little was accomplished – any issues that Prentice wanted to put before his Cabinet colleagues would be dealt with by the existing Environment and Energy Security Committee of Cabinet.

With the Clean Energy Dialogue as a base for interaction with the US on energy and environment, Canada was then invited to participate in a group originally established by Bush, and revived by Obama: the Major Economies Forum on Energy and Climate. This was a group of seventeen countries plus representatives of the European Union and of Denmark, as host of the Conference of the Parties (COP) scheduled to meet in Copenhagen in December 2009. These countries are the largest GHG emitters. As has often been characterized, the group produced about 90 per cent of the problem and together could develop 100 per cent of the solutions. I attended two of these meetings as an advisor to the environment minister. Seating was alphabetical by country name, so Canada was between Brazil and China, a noisy place to be. These were particularly productive meetings – for what they accomplished, for the discussions, and for the fact that in a small group, differences of opinion could be isolated and dealt with constructively. These meetings took place throughout 2009 as a lead-in to the Copenhagen COP meeting. The good thing about being in the room for these meetings was that Prentice was able to protect Canada's interests, and set the record straight when any country attempted to criticize Canada by singling out the oil sands for censure. It also gave the minister the opportunity, prior to going to Copenhagen, to establish rapport with the Americans who were involved in the climate change issue.

The environment file was changing at home as the economic recession deepened. Only for a few environmental groups was it still the number one priority. The key was to ensure that whatever we did on the environment was not to the detriment of economic recovery. Therefore, plans for a comprehensive policy discussion paper on the environment were scrapped in favour of a sector-by-sector approach. Prentice established working groups on electricity and on oil and gas. These groups were to report to the minister on targets for GHG reduction and the means by which these targets could be achieved. There was also a working group on vehicle emissions, which included the minister of transport, minister of natural resources, minister of finance, and representatives of the Canadian Vehicle Manufacturers' Association, as well as vehicle manufacturers themselves. It was through these working groups that the regulations for vehicles, as well as for the electricity sector, were developed.

The initial proposals for the electricity sector created some concerns in Alberta; they were looked upon as forcing a fuel choice to generate electricity from natural gas, not coal or even clean coal. At a meeting hosted by Minister of Energy Prentice with Alberta's Minister of Environment Rob Renner and Minister of Energy Mel Knight and their deputies, it was agreed, after much discussion, that any new regulations for electricity generation would not leave any stranded assets and would not specify a fuel type, just a clean-burning standard. To a certain extent, the electricity sector, at least in Alberta, was easy

to deal with since most of the coal-fired electricity plants were near-
ing the end of life. If the government didn't achieve 90 per cent GHG-
free electricity production by 2020, it would be reached by 2025.

The oil and gas sector, and especially the oil sands, have become
more difficult since this is a growing industry. Minister Prentice established a federal–provincial–industry working group, which I chaired,
on GHG reduction in this sector. It met on a regular basis in 2009 and
2010. There was a general recognition that the government had to
address this issue. The questions were how and by how much? And we
always had to keep in mind that anything proposed could negatively
affect the economy if not implemented carefully.

The Copenhagen Climate Change COP 15 meeting held in Copenhagen in December 2009 was looked upon by Canada as a success –
with the only drawback being the performances of Premier Charest
and Toronto's Mayor David Miller, who both seemed more intent on
criticizing the federal government than on moving forward in a positive fashion. The meeting accomplished the goals Canada had envisaged going in. Minister Prentice had with him a group of academics
and business people, as well as Shawn Atleo, the Assembly of First
Nations national chief, and Mary Simon, leader of the Inuit, whom he
used as a sounding board, meeting with them on a daily basis. Near
the end of the last week of the COP meeting, Harper arrived, as did 150
leaders from all over the world. The leaders' segment of the meeting
had a rough beginning and a pretty rough middle as the chair was
forced to resign. There was little progress until, as is usually the case,
a small group of experienced leaders met and developed a text. The
text was one that countries could sign on to with their individual levels of ambition for GHG reduction until the end of January 2010. The
main features of the accord were agreeable to Canada since it would
include the large GHG emitting countries, Canada would contribute to
a quick-start fund for countries immediately threatened by climate
change, and it gave Canada the opportunity to work in concert with
the United States on GHG reduction targets as well as on technologi-
cal developments.

It was imperative that Canada's reduction target be similar to that
adopted by the United States because of the interdependence and
integration of the two economies. We were also concerned about
some green protectionist proposals that were being developed by
Congress to restrict goods from countries with lower levels of ambition than those being adopted by the US. Having the same level of

reduction of GHGs as the US would exempt Canada from these measures. Copenhagen allowed Canada to establish what it thought were realistic and achievable targets for GHG reductions.

In January 2010, prior to attending the Olympics in Vancouver, Harper and Prentice convened a meeting in Calgary of Alberta's leaders in the oil and gas and industrial sectors. The prime minister led off the discussion by explaining that, regardless of where he goes in the world, while countries talk about doing something to fight climate change, in reality they are doing very little or nothing at all. However, these same countries point to northern Alberta and criticize Canada for its "tar sands" and "dirty oil." His message was that this has to change, and if the developers don't change it, he – meaning the Government of Canada – will. In other words, the oil sands developers had to up both their environmental game and their communications game. If they didn't, the government would impose a levy on bitumen extracted and do the job for the industry. The message was delivered in Harper's usual forceful way. And in that basement meeting room of the Westin Hotel in downtown Calgary, it put to bed any thoughts on my part that Harper was soft on GHG reduction or willing to give the oil and gas, and particularly the oil sands, developers a free pass. Today, the thought on my part is: what happened to the resolve Harper expressed in January 2010 in relation to the oil and gas sector, especially the oil sands?

The industry spent the rest of 2010 developing and implementing more comprehensive environmental tools as well as developing ways to get this environmental message out to Canadians, Americans, and populations abroad, especially in Great Britain and the European Union.

By the time Prentice had resigned from Cabinet in December 2010, a great deal had been accomplished, albeit quietly, on the environmental front. The concern was, who would be capable of carrying the ball on this issue so that the remaining sectors would be dealt with. In addition to new national parks or park reserves, there were regulations in place on vehicle emissions, harmonized with the United States; the working group on electricity had reported with regulations being developed[8]; and there was general agreement among the oil and gas sector as to GHG reductions for conventional oil and gas. The issue that remained was what to do with the oil sands – whether there should be a carve-out for the oil sands; and if so, how much, taking into consideration that production from the oil sands was to double by 2020. Canada is unique in the world as it has a growing energy sector, a growing population, and a growing economy. The energy and environment challenge is to ensure that all aspects continue to grow, at the same time as Canada acts responsibly to reduce GHGs. Since that time, in December 2011, Canada has withdrawn from the Kyoto Accord.

In 2010, the Keystone XL Pipeline was not a contentious issue between Canada and the United States; three years later, there were few bigger issues than this between the two countries. We are now mired in arguments about GHGs as well as job creation.

In February 2011, Harper and Obama returned to the challenges concerning the border.[9] They say timing is everything in politics: the proposal that was front and centre in the first draft of the platform after the 2004 election, finally came front and centre again in the form of the Beyond the Border initiative with the United States. Canadians were willing to work in concert with a president they liked to effect virtually the same initiative that would have been rejected if it had been pursued when George W. Bush was president. So, in addition to working through the various components of the Clean Energy Dialogue, the president and the prime minister agreed to have both countries work together to resolve border issues, including the Windsor–Detroit corridor. The best catalyst for job recovery and growth was an open, yet secure border. This initiative established the Regulatory Cooperation Council to align regulations to ease the flow of goods across the border. Regulatory co-operation and harmonization has been especially successful in the automobile assembling industry.

Both the 2010 and 2011 budgets were designed in such a way that if the government was defeated because of either one, the Conservatives could use that budget as the centerpiece of the election campaign. Regardless of positive happenings for Canada internationally or with the US, it became obvious that the government would not survive through the spring of 2011, and most thought the budget would trigger an election. The 2010 budget provided the second year of stimulus spending. It also contained the much-needed commitment to return to balance and the path to get there. It projected that by 2014–15, the deficit would be reduced to $1.8 billion. None of the parties was comfortable enough with its polling results to force an election, so the government got the opportunity to present what essentially became a pre-election budget in 2011. As public policy professor Janice MacKinnon explained, the overarching message was that Canada was doing well fiscally and economically relative to other industrial countries.[10] The 2011 budget boasted of Canada's strength relative to other major economies and projected that the deficit would be eliminated by 2015–16 at the latest. As usual, connected with the promise for budgetary balance, there were targeted tax and spending measures designed for groups that might be enticed to vote Conservative. Employment insurance benefits were extended, with a credit of $1,000 per person for hirings in small businesses. Funds were provided to universities for energy and medical research, furthering the innovation agenda. Low-income seniors and caregivers were also the beneficiaries of provisions in the budget.

Even before they saw the budget, both the Bloc and the Liberals announced that they would vote against it. As Ignatieff would say, and had said in the early fall of 2009: "Mr Harper, your time is up!" The only possible support could come from the NDP, and there were measures specifically placed in the budget to garner NDP support. However, the issue that Layton most cared about – an increase in the Canada Pension Plan payments – was not included since this would need the support of two-thirds of the provinces having 50 per cent of the population of Canada. I saw Layton twice during the period 15–20 December 2010, and on both occasions, he was quite critical of the government's lack of movement on CPP; he indicated that for him this was a deal-breaker. We will never know for sure how much Layton's precarious health issues contributed to his lack of support for the budget: did he suspect this might be his last campaign, or last chance at a campaign?

The perfect storm for the opposition, which culminated in the vote of non-confidence in the government on 25 March 2011, actually began to take form early in the second mandate. When the government prorogued Parliament in December 2008, the coalition, so close to seizing power, fell apart. The opposition, especially the Liberals who lost yet another leader, took a battering. Then there was the government's refusal to share pertinent documents associated with the allegations of torture of Taliban prisoners in Afghan prisons. And yet another prorogation. Then the refusal in October 2010 to disclose to the House Finance Committee the costs associated with the proposed purchase of F-35 fighter jets, the prison build, and the implementation of the government's tough-on-crime legislation. But it was the change to the memo from the Canadian International Development

Agency (CIDA) to Minister for International Co-operation Oda – the addition of the word *NOT* – and the contradictions in the minister's story as to how the word got into the funding document that gave the opposition the courage to begin the process to bring down the government. Speaker Milliken found a prima facie case of violation of members' privileges as they may have been misled. This matter was referred to the House Standing Committee on Procedure and House Affairs. The committee was already charged with the contempt referral concerning the government's failure to produce all documents that had been requested from it or to offer a satisfactory explanation for withholding them in relation to the costs of corporate tax cuts, crime legislation, and F-35 jet procurement. On 21 March, the committee delivered its report finding the government in contempt of Parliament. Based on this report, the vote of non-confidence was carried by the opposition four days later.[11]

The actions that led to the finding of contempt and the non-confidence vote are not ones that the government should be proud of. Most governments would go out of their way to avoid such findings of censure. But this government was looking for an excuse for an election in order to finally attain a majority – and if the opposition was going to oblige in this matter, so much the better.

The stage was set for a 2011 election – with results that no one would have predicted at the outset. The Conservatives were ready for this campaign. All of the so-called scandals were, to the Conservatives – and as the results showed, also to Canadians, just so much opposition blustering. The Conservatives had their issue, their ballot question, and their leader, all focused on the economy and who was the best leader in uncertain economic times. And the "ask" from the Conservatives to the electorate was for a "strong, stable, national majority." The Liberals had their anti-democratic ballot question, based on what they perceived to be scandals, as well as other ballot questions based on their platform. The NDP had a ballot question on the same topic as the Conservatives, but with a different approach to the economy: to address the needs of low-, moderate-, and middle-income Canadians. Layton's appeal was to the economic issues of "ordinary Canadians," as exhibited by his concentration on CPP. Duceppe, of course, didn't know it in the beginning, but he was to spend the entire writ period searching for the right ballot question, which as the results indicate, he never found. This was not 2008 when the government through its announcements was going to throw another lifeline to the Bloc so it could continue to exist to defend and assert the rights of Quebecers.

The Conservative campaign was quite simple: The economy and jobs are the issues. We have guided Canada through the worldwide economic recession so that Canada has the best economic record in the industrialized world. If we are not given a majority, the opposition will combine to form a government and throw the Canadian economy into chaos. This was the recurring theme in the first weeks of the campaign. The fact that Harper had colluded with Layton and Duceppe in 2004 to possibly form a similar type of coalition was quite irrelevant.

With the economy as the number one issue and only the Conservatives and NDP addressing it, the fate of the Liberals was almost decided from the beginning. As stated earlier, the Conservatives had made all the parliamentary manoeuvring, claims of contempt, breaches of privilege, and want of confidence seem like so much partisan theatrics. This characterization was fatal to the Liberal and Bloc hopes. With the election focused on the economy, there were no real issues for Duceppe to address. He was not going to form a government, so he would not be controlling the financial levers. His major complaint with the federal government was its failure to compensate Quebec for harmonizing its provincial sales tax with the federal GST. While the Conservatives refused to budge on this before the campaign, the commitment to pay was placed in the Conservative platform released prior to the debates.

The English and French debates were quite key to the result in this election. The format returned to leaders standing at podiums (with no Elizabeth May). Harper was able to defend his government's record and, as a result of positioning on the stage in the English debate, was able to set himself apart from the other leaders, who were seen as just squabbling amongst themselves, fighting for second and third place. My only role in debate preparation occurred prior to the call of the election. I met with the PMO staff who were going to be directly involved in debate prep to give them some advice on what needed to be done and how to do it.

Layton came into the debates with a narrative and a plan to supplant Ignatieff as the leader of the opposition. No longer was Jack seeking a coalition or a working relationship with other parties. This was Jack taking the fight to Ignatieff, and the latter was not at all prepared for this. Layton raising the issue of Ignatieff's absences from the House of Commons and his missed votes was, in my opinion, a low blow. I do not believe many leaders would have gone there. Everyone knows that leaders have responsibilities beyond sitting in the House, especially when they are trying to become better known across the country. While it could be considered a low blow, it was effective – mainly because Ignatieff had no response. He could have deflected the point, and actually pushed back on Layton, by talking about the national duties of the leader of the opposition or about how effectiveness is measured in ideas to benefit Canadians, not days spent in the House of Commons. This attack on Ignatieff benefitted Layton in unexpected areas, which no doubt accounted for the NDP's final showing. Duceppe tried to engage Layton on the NDP's Quebec platform, and this gave Layton the opportunity to put on his best "le bon Jack" performance, seeming like the happy warrior he was. Layton outlined his Quebec platform: except for the lack of a separation plank, it was pretty much the same as the Bloc. It was an option that Quebecers were inclined, for the first time, to consider. As well, Layton's platform, which emphasized left-leaning social positions, was made for a Quebec audience.

With the Conservative platform already out there – basically a regurgitation of the 2011 budget – the issue coming out of the debates was the real possibility of an NDP surge. Ignatieff had given voters nothing in the debates to vote for since he emphasized everything he was against. In debate preparation, a great amount of time is usually spent on moving, during an answer, from the attack on one's opponent's program or what they have done wrong to the positive message of what you would do. In the aftermath of the debates, Canadians had little or no idea what the Liberals stood for, except perhaps some vague education support called a "learning passport." Even my youngest daughter, Emily, a student at the University of Toronto, did not believe the Liberal promise of $1,000 per student per year. If the program is viewed with skepticism by those it is supposed to help, then it has no hope with the wider population.

In Quebec, Duceppe had gone once too often to the same voter well, with the same promises in the same bucket. As explained earlier, the Bloc was in for the fight of its life in 2008, until the Conservatives gave it two issues and therefore a reason to exist. The Conservatives in 2011 were bypassing Quebec, not campaigning for Quebec, with the only promise directed at Quebec being the payment of the HST monies.

That earlier discussion with Harper came back to haunt the Conservative campaign: perhaps the "time for a change" mantra would catch on. But the agent would be Layton, not Ignatieff.

It is incredibly hard to change direction or focus in a campaign. First, there has to be a decision that change is necessary. It is hard to achieve a coherent discussion on such an issue when the various parts of the campaign are spread out across the country. One of the very few successful changes – and it was in tactics, not message – occurred in the 1988 free-trade election. After the debates, the outcome was in jeopardy, so Mulroney changed his campaign style back to the one he was most comfortable with: meeting and greeting and speaking to any group that would listen to him. He was not going to spend the second half of the campaign in a bubble. This was also the campaign where stakeholders who had remained apart from the campaign became very much involved in driving a positive free-trade message. Having made the decision to change direction, focus, or tactics, the second step is deciding what to change to, and the third is implementing the change, typically while the leader is moving from location to location in the campaign bubble. In addition, the change in direction may entail a change in messaging and perhaps even a change as to where the leader's tour will go. Doing all of this on the fly, when there is limited time left in a campaign, can prove very difficult, and sometimes impossible.

The Conservative campaign was able to make the strategic shift from focusing on the Grits to focusing on Layton and the NDP as primary opponents. Speeches were prepared and new television ads developed and approved. Conservatives went back to the original theme of coalition, this time led by Jack Layton, and warnings about the lack of NDP economic credentials, reminding voters in Ontario of the failed experiment with the Bob Rae NDP government.

As Geoff Norquay stated in an article written after the election, there were two winners and two losers in the 2011 election.[12] Both Harper and Layton accomplished what they set out to do. Harper, with a majority, could now govern without the constant threat of an election. Arguably, Jack did better than he ever imagined as the NDP, at least for a time, has replaced the Liberals as Official Opposition. The two losers were the Liberals and the Bloc as they lost both seats and leaders in this election. Ignatieff and the Liberals completely mis-read the Canadian electorate: they believed their own narrative of scandal, corruption, and loss of democracy without checking to see if anyone else felt that way. Ignatieff's performance in the debates, when challenged by Layton, and in the party leader interviews conducted by CBC's Peter Mansbridge (as he does with all leaders during a feder-al election), when convoluted rhetoric mired his efforts to put the question of coalition to bed, ended up increasing the spectre of a coalition. And finally, he was unable to make the transition from attacking his opponents to promoting his own platform. Duceppe just ran out of causes and out of steam when compared with the alter-native: Layton and his pro-Quebec platform, which he was able to promote in the debates, and the fact that with Jack, there was no threat of a referendum. It was no contest once Quebecers realized there was a pro-Quebec, socialist alternative to the Bloc. Quebecers were not going to pump up the Conservative representation as that putative love affair ended in 2008. As Lawrence Cannon said to me in my office when we were dealing with the aftermath of the 2008 elec-tion: at least we are not sitting here wondering what went wrong – we know what we did; our task now is to fix it and ensure that it never happens again. The fix never occurred, and Cannon was one of the casualties of the orange crush led by Layton. Quebecers were not going to support the Liberals either: the Gomery hangover was still present, and the Liberal Party's message and its messenger did not res-onate in Quebec.

The two winning parties in 2011 put together quite different com-binations of voters to achieve their results. The NDP's change of status from fourth party to Official Opposition could have been accom-plished by only appealing to Quebec. But, in addition, they bled off Liberal support in Atlantic Canada, Ontario, and British Columbia. In the latter areas, at least the NDP was building on some existing sup-port; the Quebec result was entirely new. Is this an aberration or a complete paradigm shift for the NDP in the Quebec political scene? Midway between the 2011 election and the next one in 2015, the jury is still out on this matter. It is difficult to say whether a Mulcair-led NDP will be able to duplicate the 2011 Layton results. The other added variable is the spring 2013 election of Justin Trudeau to the leadership of the Liberal Party. In 2015 Harper will face two parties led by new leaders.

The Conservative majority victory, unlike the 2006 election results and what could have been in 2008, did not run through Quebec. Professor and former Harper chief of staff Tom Flanagan points out that the new coalition of Conservative supporters is composed of western populists, traditional Tories in Atlantic Canada and Ontario, and "ethnic voters who share Conservative economic and social values" in Ontario and British Columbia.[13]

Voters who filled the rooms to support the merger of the Alliance and PC parties in December 2003 were predominantly white. At that time, the Liberals were thought to hold the key to the ethnic vote in Canada. As the new Conservative Party got its feet under it and the Liberal Party moved further to the left, it became clear to Harper that the economic and social policy views of multicultural or ethnic Canada were more aligned with the Conservative Party than with any other party. During debate of the same-sex marriage bill in 2005, a movement to raise awareness of the policies of the Conservative Party in the ethnic media grew to the point where Minister of Citizenship and Immigration Jason Kenney was given free rein to move among these communities extolling the values and policies of the Party. As Flanagan says, multicultural voters are middle-aged or older, married with children, imbued with family values, respectful of religion, distressed about the impact of crime, oriented toward the private sector, and concerned about high taxes and the general business climate in Canada. Once attracted to vote in support of Conservative candidates, because it is values-based support, it is difficult to see this support being fickle and falling by the wayside except if the Conservatives give it good reason to leave.

With this new foundation of support, the Conservatives formed a majority government in May 2011. The questions at that point were: what would Stephen Harper do with it, how would it change Canada, and how long would it last?

Majority Third Mandate:
The Harper Doctrines

As the dust settled and the sun rose on 3 May 2011, it was obvious to most that the general election just concluded played perfectly into the Conservative ballot question and delivered Canadians a "strong, stable, national Conservative majority government." By mid-campaign, the issues that had triggered the election, and that were held so dear by the Liberal Party, were forgotten by all but the Liberal leadership. The Conservative platform that promised job creation, support for families, deficit elimination by 2014, safe streets, and a strong military won out over what Harper termed a "reckless coalition" that at the beginning of the campaign was led by Ignatieff and post-debates by Layton. For the Conservatives. it was like the 2008 campaign without the unforced errors. The theme was the same – who do you trust to run Canada's economy in a time of worldwide economic turmoil – but without the arts-funding-withdrawal and young-offenders-in-prison moments to scuttle the movement to majority. Unlike 2008, there was no plan for the road to majority to go through Quebec. The coalition established by Mulroney and other successful Conservative leaders was no longer there or available for support. It had been replaced by an Ontario-western populist axis. The coalition that looked so promising and so permanent post-2006 election was more fragile than originally thought. Quebecers left the Conservatives since they believed the Party did not understand them and had abandoned them with the arts cuts and get-tough-on-young-offenders policies. The repetition of disappointing results in Quebec, despite the platform commitment to compensate Quebec for sales tax harmonization, demonstrated how complete the schism actually was.

The 2012 Budget. Jim Flaherty (left) and Stephen Harper presented the budget that set out the basis for the Harper Doctrine of Federalism. (Courtesy of Fred Chartrand/The Canadian Press. Reprinted by permission)

However, the overall majority result demonstrated to those who had been involved for years that all the work done to merge the two legacy parties in 2003, the policy development, and the four general elections, each with an increasingly positive result to the point of securing a majority, was all worthwhile. A new party had emerged under Harper's leadership, different from both legacy parties, yet in many ways the same. And Canadians were willing, finally, to allow this new, but at the same time not-quite-so-new, group to govern for a period of time without threat of an election, without fear of being defeated when making tough, sometimes unpopular but necessary decisions. A sufficient number of Canadians had become comfortable with the strong leadership demonstrated by Harper and the Conservative Party on the economy at home and in foreign affairs. These Canadians had experienced targeted, focused government and found they liked it. The grand interventionist Liberal programs of universal, accessible daycare, promised many times but never delivered, or personal income tax cuts, promised but never showing up in larger paycheques, were gone. The Conservatives and the Canadian people had slowly moved toward each other to settle on a new positioning of the Canadian "centre," somewhat to the right of where Martin and Chrétien had left it. The challenge for Conservatives was to maintain this political centre in its new position, build on it, and reinforce the combination of voters that brought the Party to majority.

As explained in the previous chapter, this victory did not come from maintaining the Mulroney voter base. As Tom Flanagan has pointed out, Harper had a positive view of the Mulroney electoral support: at the Ezra Levant–David Frum 1996 Winds of Change[1] conference, he told participants that the only way back to government was to reconstitute the Mulroney winning combination of populists in western Canada and rural Ontario (Reformers); traditional Tories in Ontario and Atlantic Canada (PCs); and francophone nationalists. Both Diefenbaker and Mulroney had successfully put this group together – Mulroney twice – so it was natural to think it could be done again. For a while, post-2006, it looked like it might happen, but as I have noted numerous times, that was not to be. The Conservatives hope that this new electoral combination, founded on solid ethnic or multicultural support in Ontario and British Columbia, will not be as fragile as the 2006 coalition that broke apart in 2008 and could not be reinvigorated for 2011. The populists in western Canada and in Ontario as well as the traditional Tories in Ontario and Atlantic Canada should maintain their support, as long as Harper and the Conservatives remain true to their philosophy of not moving toward implementation of elements of a social conservative agenda. These supporters like the fiscal conservative agenda of lower taxes and relying on business to drive the economy, but recognize that the needs of Canadians at the lower end of the economic scale must be recognized and addressed. The new arrivals in the combination of voters are mainly the ethnic voters from urban and suburban Ontario and British Columbia. This group is arguably the most conservatively inclined, both fiscally and socially, of those who form the combination. Jason Kenney has actively courted the support of this group; his work began to pay dividends in 2008 and reaped great results in 2011. The nurturing of this part of the group will have to be done with great sensitivity.

In pursuing this group, the Conservatives were helped by the fact that the Liberal Party, once this group's natural home, had fallen on hard times. Looking to move up from its lowest level ever in popular support, the party is developing a new policy platform. The Liberals have elected a young dynamic leader in Justin Trudeau, who may be able to reinvigorate the Liberal appeal to these new Canadians.

Could this group be poached by the NDP led by Tom Mulcair? For this to happen, it would require a colossal blunder by the Conservatives, coupled with a movement of the NDP toward the economic centre as, first and foremost, this ethnic group is composed of owners of small- and medium-sized businesses, not normally core supporters of the NDP.

If either the Liberals under Trudeau or the NDP with Mulcair are able to attract a significant number of this electoral group in the next election, a Conservative majority may be in doubt.

Will the British Columbia part of the electoral combination hold? This is particularly crucial to the future success of the Conservatives, especially with the addition of new seats in British Columbia. The issue with the British Columbia group would be whether environmental policies pursued by the NDP trump the Conservatives' economic agenda. This is the challenge faced by Conservatives as the next general election approaches. The Conservatives will have to stress the economic advantage of energy pipelines and their importance, not only to the general economy of Canada but especially for British Columbia. The NDP's environmental message is powerful, but economically unrealistic for the future since it means ignoring the growing energy markets of Asia, and particularly China.

One concern could emerge for the Conservatives should the economy not improve, and because of that, make them unable to balance the budget by 2015. If one of these two opposition parties gets its economic policies together, they could challenge the Conservatives on their strength, the economy. If this happens, cracks could show in the 2011 combination of voters.

As noted, at this point, the Quebec soft nationalists no longer form a part of the electoral group supporting the government. Going forward, this is not a positive sign for the Conservative Party. It is obviously possible to win one majority with only minimal representation from Quebec (five seats), but trying to govern and grow in the future with only a handful of members from Canada's second-largest province makes little or no sense. As the government looks forward to 2015 and beyond, it must come to grips with its lack of appeal in Quebec. It is time to revisit open federalism and begin the Quebec dialogue again. As said earlier, I believe part of the failure of the 2008 campaign was in not reaching out to those federalists in Quebec who knew it best, Brian Mulroney and Jean Charest. The same can be said about the 2011 campaign, even though it was not designed to go through Quebec – but then, it wasn't a campaign designed to lose seats there either. The NDP orange crush was to knock out the Bloc, not Conservative candidates such as Lawrence Cannon.

As between 2004 and 2006, this will take time and attention, and Harper has to rededicate himself to this task; if he does, based on the experience of 2006, he could be successful. While it is always helpful to have senior spokespersons or ministers responsible for Quebec, only the prime minister can recommit his party and his government to Quebec. Harper is the same man today as he was in 2006 when he engineered the passage of the Nation Resolution through the House of Commons. The commitments made in the 2006 platform, even the one dealing with fiscal imbalance, have been kept. And recently the sales tax money has been paid to Quebec, as promised in the 2011 platform. There is a solid base of promises made–promises kept from which the prime minister can work; hopefully he will take up the task. Coming into the next election, he would not want the failure to attain significant support in Quebec to cause his supporters in other provinces, especially Ontario, to reconsider their choices.

To make matters more complex in Quebec, both the NDP and the Liberals now draw their leaders from that province. The change in political landscape since 2011 makes it more challenging for Harper. Also, the sponsorship scandal, which hobbled the Grits from 2006 onwards, has faded from memory to be replaced by Conservative scandals. At this point, it is unclear as to whether the NDP will be able to maintain its seats in Quebec or whether they will move into the Liberal column. Surely Harper does not want to be sidelined as a spectator while these two parties divide up the seventy-eight Quebec seats in 2015.

The 4 September 2012 Quebec provincial election gave the Parti Québécois a weak minority government, with the Liberals as Official Opposition and the new party, Coalition Avenir Québec, in third place. This will present challenges and opportunities for Harper as well as Mulcair and Trudeau. The prime minister must be careful not to provide Premier Pauline Marois with the "straw man" to beat up and knock down and launch her minority into a majority. Harper, because of his views on the powers of federal and provincial governments, may actually become a willing partner should Marois want to regain control over matters that rightly belong to the province. Her victory also gives Harper a renewed opportunity to engage with Quebecers and go back to the open federalism of 2005–06. However, there is no doubt that the PQ victory presents challenges this federal government has not previously faced.

The PQ win also gives the prime minister the opportunity to place the NDP's Sherbrooke Declaration front and centre in the mind of the public. The NDP, on a separation referendum vote of 50 per cent plus one, would begin the breakup of the country. Harper's view of the application of the rule of law and strong commitment to the Clarity Act and the Constitution would be placed in sharp contrast to the NDP's more lenient program. National unity will now be an issue. Since he began to govern with a majority, it could be argued that Harper has done relatively well addressing what some would say are the three keys to establishing a dynasty: the economy, protecting the welfare state, and national unity.[2] Canada's economy is one of the strongest, if not the strongest in the G20. It has held solid through the economic downturn and recession that began in the early fall of 2008. By maintaining a strong economy, the government has not diminished Canada's social safety net. If anything, it has been improved in many aspects. Employment Insurance is now geared more toward getting people back to work, rather than simply being another source of income, similar to social assistance. Health care funding, always a litmus test of a government's social commitment, has held steady, with increases promised in the 2011 platform and the block health care funding announced by Minister Flaherty at the end of 2011. There is never enough money for health care, but the system is not being strangled by the federal government. That leaves national unity. From the time the Conservatives assumed office in 2006 until the PQ win in September 2012, there has been relative peace on the national unity front. Because of the slim minority held by the PQ, it is unlikely there will be any immediate overt move toward a referendum on separation. However, one cannot discount the fanning of separatist embers by the new Quebec government.

National unity is now squarely a challenge for Harper as it never was previously, and he approaches it from a decided point of weakness: he has few Quebec MPs, and the mistakes of the 2008 campaign led Quebecers to believe that Conservatives just don't understand Quebec. However, he has the ability to address the issues that Premier Marois will raise, as her victory gives him the opportunity to engage with Quebecers in a positive way. As a national leader with a separatist government in Quebec, he can no longer ignore the province and is bound to address separation issues should they arise. He can revisit "open federalism" from the 2006 campaign and determine how it can be expanded and made relevant in 2015. How he handles this new challenge between now and the next federal election will demonstrate whether there is truly a new dynasty in Ottawa.

As Harper looked forward to exercising the new majority mandate and the implementation of what I have termed "Harper Federalism," he had a solid foundation upon which to build. Even though Canada had been through an economic downturn, it fared pretty well, based on its sound banking and financial system. It has solid economic fundamentals, an educated and talented workforce, and natural resources in abundance. Inflation has been kept under control as one of the main parts of the mandate of the Bank of Canada. It has the second-lowest corporate tax rate in the G8. All of this has contributed to Canada's strong dollar, which makes Canada attractive to foreign investors. While the dollar has weakened somewhat in the latter part of 2013, it is still relatively strong, and its value in the low ninety cents US area may indeed increase demand for Canadian goods.

Actions in the future are usually rooted in the experience of the past, and the past for Stephen Harper has a very doctrinaire or "strict constructionist" view of the Constitution and its division of powers. This view emerged, when he was an MP between 1993–96, in his criticism of Prime Minister Chrétien's handling of the Quebec Referendum in 1995, which resulted in his subsequent support for Chrétien's Clarity Act. Harper characterized the Calgary Declaration as appeasement of those who wished to break up the country. His best-known statement of the federal–provincial separation of powers came in what is termed the Firewall Letter to Premier Klein of Alberta, published in the *National Post* on 24 January 2001.[3]

It set out what was called the Alberta Agenda:

• Withdraw from the Canada Pension Plan to create an Alberta Pension Plan offering the same benefits at lower cost while giving Alberta control over the investment fund

- Collect its own provincial revenue from personal income tax, as done for corporate tax
- Let the RCMP contract expire in 2012 and create an Alberta Provincial Police Force
- Set its own provincial health policies, and if Ottawa objects, fight it in the courts; if Alberta loses, pay the penalties
- Force Senate reform back onto the national agenda by using section 88 of the Supreme Court of Canada decision in the Quebec Secession Reference Case

In his acceptance speech when he won the leadership of the Alliance Party, Harper made it clear that his view of Canadian federalism followed a strict interpretation of sections 91 and 92 of the Constitution Act, 1867 and that Quebec grievances leading to a determination of separation as the only solution could be addressed by allowing for provincial autonomy in areas of provincial jurisdiction.

The seminal act that outlined the Harper Doctrine of Canadian Federalism came in the first year of majority government with the presentation of the 2012 budget. As Kevin Lynch pointed out, it came in the global context of the financial crisis, which he characterized as a hangover that never ends no matter how many fiscal Aspirins are consumed. In that global context,[4] Canada was faring quite well, with the budget focusing in the out years on the fact that fiscal balance and economic growth go hand in hand. The budget was used to deliver three messages. First, western Canada resources and diversification of markets for their export are an economic priority. Canada cannot be a world energy superpower with only one major customer for its energy product. Second, retirement at age sixty-five is no longer acceptable. This was as much about enhancing and enlarging the workforce as it was about saving or redistributing money. And third, there is no hidden social conservative agenda that some thought would come with a majority Conservative government, other than a careful alignment of federal and provincial responsibilities. This last part is continually under threat as some backbench MPs through private members' bills and motions attempt to bring forward various aspects of the abortion issue for debate.

Minister Flaherty's announcement of block funding to the provinces for health care was a perfect example of how Harper views the division of powers.[5] Under the Harper Doctrine, health care is solely a provincial implementation responsibility to which the federal government contributes financial resources. The Canada Health Act, so often held up as the foundation of our system is, for the most part, irrelevant. By the federal government backing away, except for the cash contribution, the hope is that the provinces will begin to innovate and experiment with different forms of care and delivery mechanisms.

Under Harper Federalism, the role of the federal government is to protect Canada's borders, keep the streets safe for law-abiding citizens, and keep taxes low, with government only taking from taxpayers what it needs to operate efficiently and effectively and pay down the debt. With regard to the economy, the government is to act as a catalyst, opening economic doors for industry, but industry has to walk through them. It is the job of government in the Harper Doctrine to keep corporate taxes low and negotiate trade agreements to give the private sector access to markets to sell their goods and earn income. This is the reason for Harper's insistence on expanding trade relations beyond the United States.

The 2012 budget[6] dealt with matters within federal jurisdiction in an economic context. Innovation, employment insurance, immigration, and old age security eligibility – all within federal jurisdiction – were addressed. The importance of energy and major energy infrastructure projects that would greatly benefit the economy were made the centrepiece of environmental regulatory reform. Concerns related to those most vulnerable in society, the First Nations, were addressed, but with tools designed to improve their economic conditions. This first majority budget demonstrated the move away from the use of the spending power and the move toward provincial and federal governments acting within their own spheres of influence. There would be no more universal, accessible daycare plans that sound great but produce little; no new federal–provincial joint programs within provincial jurisdiction without first obtaining provincial consent. The federal government is responsible for macroeconomic policy, an economy based on energy, natural resources, innovation, and international trade. The emphasis on trade in natural resources would be broadened to encourage secondary manufacturing. Just because it may be difficult to accomplish, does not mean it should not be encouraged.

However, within a year, in the 2013 budget, the federal government had moved off of this position in relation to job training. It introduced the concept of the Canada Job Grant program, which is definitely a federal–provincial joint job-training program, with industry involved as well. It is now some months since the announcement of this program, and it is unclear as to whether the provinces will buy into it. It is still difficult to determine why the Harper government moved in this direction. The main criticism of the provincial training programs was that they were not focussed on the needs of employers. Well, then, fix that problem. There is no need to take funding for training away from the provinces and set up a parallel program. It just seems like back-of-the-envelop policy-making so the federal government can say it has addressed the unemployment problem with its own jobs program – except it isn't its own program.

The Harper economic doctrine has expansion of Canada's trade relations beyond the United States as one of its cornerstones. Canada must move off the security blanket of the United States as its principal market. Canada must diversify its markets and that has led the government to set priorities for consummating trade negotiations with the European Union (EU), Japan, and perhaps South Korea. For too long, China has been ignored, but that's changing, even though negotiations will be lengthy and difficult. Canada's involvement in the Trans-Pacific Partnership is important if only because the United States is involved, and it is our largest trading partner. Beyond natural resources, Canada should be looking at trade arrangements that feature Canada's strength in financial services, banking, and insurance services as well as aerospace and IT.[7] Emerging and developing countries could do a lot worse than import Canada's best practices in financial regulations as they relate to banking and insurance. They would benefit from the input of Canada's major banks and insurance companies and the government agencies that regulate them. Canada's economic success has demonstrated the value of a strict regulatory regime for financial institutions, and of a well-run, independent central bank focused on inflation control and interest rates.

This trade agenda has been difficult to implement. Negotiations with the EU took much longer than anticipated, but in October 2013 an agreement was signed, to be put in place during the next year. It might have arrived sooner had Harper decided to involve himself earlier in the negotiations and decision-making. As has been pointed out many times in the analysis of the FTA negotiations with the United States, the agreement never would have been finalized had it not been for Prime Minister Mulroney's direct intervention with President Reagan. Hopefully this agreement with the EU will be followed by the finalization of the Trans-Pacific Partnership Agreement. Should this occur, Harper will have gone a long way toward implementing the trade part of his economic doctrine.

Implementation of the recommendations of the Jenkins panel report on innovation[8] began with the 2012 budget, but must continue if Canada is to compete in the world through means other than the development and sale of its natural resources. It has been said many times that Canada excels at research, but falls short in the commercialization of that research. Linkages between the research being done in universities and the needs of the private sector are crucial. The private sector must become the leader in this area, working with government funders and Canadian educational institutions. The 2007 budget proposed measures to attract the brightest and the best students to Canada and to keep them here. It is vital that this continue. Only through the exchange of knowledge will Canada be able to compete in the marketplace of ideas that lead to innovation and innovative solutions. These cutting-edge ideas are desperately needed in the development of our natural resources and in the reduction of GHGs and pollutants produced by that development.

In order to ensure that nothing stands in the way of innovation, the government should continue to rationalize its regulatory regime. Budget 2012 provided a good start in relation to environmental regulation and the redefinition of navigable waters. Both of these changes should have a positive effect on major infrastructure projects. The government must ensure that its regulatory approach does not impede innovation but, rather, supports it.

The development of a human capital component is at the foundation of Canada's economic progress and prosperity. Through targeted immigration, the government can address shortfalls in Canada's workforce. However, more than economic immigration is needed.

One of the issues plaguing the government is job training and job creation. It is common now to say that Canada has jobs that go wanting and a workforce that is not trained for the jobs that are available. The Temporary Foreign Worker Program provided a partial stop-gap solution, but the result was workers being imported to fill jobs that could and should be filled by Canadians. This need for training led to the announcement in the 2013 budget of the Canada Job Grant program, which would involve a partnership among industry, the provinces, and the federal government. This program is to replace the provincial labour market agreements that expire in March 2014. As stated above in relation to federal–provincial jurisdiction, this was initially a poorly thought-out solution, which with a number of changes may be effective.

Based on its view of federalism, this federal government will be reluctant to look at the effectiveness of Canada's post-secondary institutions, but such a review is long overdue. Billions of government and private-sector dollars are invested in Canadian colleges and universities, yet Canada has no capability to measure what these dollars are producing and whether these expenditures are even effective. Accountability is supposed to be the hallmark of the Harper government, yet from an economic point of view, it does not know whether the investment in post-secondary education is producing the results that will make Canada a leader in innovation, and through that innovation address the country's low rate of productivity. From solely a value-for-money-invested perspective, the federal government should conduct such a review. One of the main features of Canada's recent immigration policy is to attract and keep the brightest and the best students from around the globe. In citing Canada's advantages, it would be helpful if the government actually knew how effective its post-secondary education system was. If Canada is to be a world leader in innovation, it must have more Ph.D. students and more post-doctoral students working in research in universities. Canada has to address this deficiency, and it could start by a thorough study of the effectiveness of all forms of post-secondary education.

It seems counterintuitive, given that one of the legacy parties to the Conservative Party is the Reform/Alliance Party, but Harper has invested a fair amount of political capital in the challenges experienced by Canada's Aboriginal peoples. The Statement of Apology for the residential schools and the Crown–First Nations Gathering form the base of this part of the Harper Doctrine. This group sits, for the most part, on the periphery of the mainstream of Canada's educational initiatives and its economy. The challenges are well known. They have been studied literally to death and any further studies should not take place unless they are focused on solutions and have not been addressed in either the report of the Royal Commission on Aboriginal Peoples[9] or any subsequent studies by Parliament or think-tanks.

It is time for action, and this government has at least a couple of years ahead of it to make a significant difference in the lives of Aboriginal peoples. Treaty implementation, settlement of land claims, self-government agreements, and an overhaul of the education system on reserves are priorities; addressing these four areas will begin to unlock the economic potential of First Nations, but Aboriginal peoples must be part of the search for solutions, and the solutions must be sought in a timely fashion. The present process encourages and rewards delay.

The development of Canada's wealth in minerals and other natural resources should provide Aboriginal peoples with the kind of economic lifeline that has been needed for so long. For most, their major economic lifeline has been the federal government. While the government has a fiduciary duty to continue its overall role, opportunities in natural resources development are limitless and can be achieved while protecting and enhancing the environment. If there is a need for capacity-building for First Nations to help them deal with the development options related to natural resources, an appropriate role for government would be to help find sources of independent advice to meet that need. Prior notification and informed consent through a consultative approach are not only necessary and needed by Aboriginal peoples but also required by law. Only through co-operation and consultation will the maximum results be achieved. Without it, we all lose; with it, we all win.

The government should review the Indian Act[10] to address those parts of it that are anachronistic. Because of the varied capacities of the over 600 bands in Canada, there may always need to be some form of Indian Act; however, that should not preclude undertaking the review. Perhaps in this matter, the government can take advice from First Nations on what should be done and what can be done to the Indian Act. If the federal government and the provinces can agree to cost sharing and equalization payments to support have-not provinces, surely this type of ingenuity could be used to develop economic, social, and land ownership programs and funding for First Nation bands that would remove the yoke of the Indian Act.

The government along with the First Nations should pose together the hard question regarding the continued need for a federal Department of Aboriginal and Northern Affairs. Is there a better way to address the challenges and opportunities of the First Nations than through a large bureaucracy in Ottawa with tentacles across the country? Fundamental questions need to be asked and answered. What services need to be delivered by Ottawa? What are the capacities of individual First Nations to accept responsibility and accountability for their own affairs? These are the questions that the federal government needs to work through with the First Nations to arrive at and implement a series of jointly agreed-upon recommendations. One approach could be dividing the bands into groups having powers that the group decides it will exercise, with various levels of economic transfers and accountability.

There is also a Harper Doctrine in play in foreign affairs, which for our purposes includes international trade. Early on, as we were putting together the first draft of the new platform, post–2004 election, Harper made it clear that there would be changes with regard to Canada's conduct of foreign affairs or diplomacy and Canada's armed forces. When the Conservative Party became the government, foreign affairs would be more focused and results driven. He would say that Canada does not sit alone on the northern half of the North American continent, in splendid isolation from the rest of the world. Canada has interests abroad, Canada has allies, and Canada will act to protect these interests and work with her allies. We are part of the world, and the world, as a result of the ever-constant threat of terrorist attacks, is increasingly a more dangerous place. The foreign affairs part of the Harper Doctrine has been effectively implemented by ministers, and now, by John Baird, who has acted as the prime minister's trouble shooter in a number of portfolios. As Minister Baird has indicated, Canada will continue to belong to multilateral and multinational organizations, but it will no longer "go along to get along." Canada can no longer be counted on to agree with everyone else's agenda.[11]

Having said that, it is clear that Canada's role in the world is guided by a number of principles that, taken together, become what could be described as the Harper Doctrine of Foreign Affairs. The bedrock principle is support for Israel. While Canada does not blindly support every move Israel makes, Canada will act to ensure the survival of the Israeli democracy in the Middle East. A subset of the policy of support for Israel is the government's concern about the future intentions of Iran. Harper has made it clear – many times – that, in his opinion, Iran is the scariest, most dangerous country on earth, and its possible, or probable, ongoing move to nuclear weaponization needs to be monitored closely and carefully. Iran is even scarier than North Korea.

In addition, there is Harper's commitment to the robust advancement of Arctic sovereignty. From the time of his first trip north in the summer of 2006, he has been fascinated with its people, its wide expanses, harsh climate and environment, beauty, and economic potential for the future. All of this comes together to form the basis of the government's Northern Strategy. The plans for northern ships and a new ice-breaker, as well as a number of other components of the Northern Strategy,[12] have been slower in coming than Harper would have liked. However, the commitment is no less strong, and perhaps even more imperative. The 2010 Arctic foreign policy statement reinforces the commitment to this region and the importance of mapping this area to support Canada's claim to sovereignty. Canada's chairing of the Arctic Council in 2013 came at a convenient time in the evolution of this policy. It will give Canada the opportunity to demonstrate to other Arctic nations its resolve to claim and exercise sovereignty over this area as a basic tenet of its foreign policy.

The revitalization and rebuilding of Canada's military, as promised in the 2006 platform, is inextricably tied to the Canada First Defence Strategy[13] announced in May 2008 and Canada's foreign policy. This was a comprehensive analysis of the needs of Canada's armed forces as well as a detailed itemization of the expectations placed on the military for the future. It has three roles: defence of Canada and security; North America defence in conjunction with the United States and perimeter security; and overseas protection of Canada's interests and support of our allies. There are six core missions: conduct domestic and continental operations, support major international events held in Canada, respond to a major terrorist attack, aid the civil power in time of crisis or natural disaster, lead and/or conduct a major international operation for an extended period, and deploy forces anywhere in the world in response to crises for shorter periods. To fulfill this mandate, personnel, equipment, training, and infrastructure have to be put in place.

It is an understatement to say that the kit envisaged in this strategy has been more difficult to deliver than originally anticipated. Some parts, such as the Globemaster transport aircraft, have been delivered and put into useful service. However, it is frustrating for everyone involved when it seemingly takes forever to acquire helicopters, jet fighters, armed vehicles, and the like. Inexperience in managing large procurement projects has resulted in unacceptable delays caused by either this inexperience or the failure of contracting parties to deliver promised goods on time. Because of Canada's harsh climate, especially in the North and off the Atlantic coast, procurement specifications are such that buying off-the-shelf is not possible, since the purchase would be missing some crucial elements that would put lives in danger. A lot of thought and work went into the Canada First Defence

Strategy, and years will be lost in the procurement pipeline if it is determined that the original requirements have to be rewritten. The procurement process seems to be fraught with difficulty and has become quite politicized, when there is no need for this to occur. Without the government relinquishing control of the process, would it be possible to have either the opposition leaders or their defence critics as part of the process? They could be ad hoc members of the new military procurement body run out of Public Works. Seven-plus years into governing and now into a majority mandate, Harper would have liked the process to be much further along than it is. Given the participation of Canada's military in both Afghanistan and Libya, where it has acquitted itself well, and the discussions the prime minister and I had when the defence strategy was being developed, he would have liked to have seen the equipment promised in the January 2006 platform in place and operational now. It is to be hoped that procurement, to the extent it can be focused and streamlined, will begin to produce results under the new process implemented in 2012.

Aid to troubled and devastated parts of the world has been revisited under Harper as an integral part of how he sees Canada's role beyond its borders. Canada is no longer involved in a scattergun approach with no core theme or purpose, other than just helping out. Aid is focused in this hemisphere, particularly the Americas. Canada's commitment to Haiti after the 2010 earthquake was enormous and tested some of the recent acquisitions of the military, especially the Globemaster transport aircraft. Harper has been criticized for pulling aid away from the world's poorest continent, Africa. While this may have been the case initially, the 2010 G8 and G20 commitment to maternal and child health led by Canada has resulted in a return of aid to Africa. This is substantiated by the report "Keeping Promises, Measuring Results."[14] Similar to all other activities undertaken by this government, the watchword is supposed to be accountability, with aid that is focused, purposeful, and results oriented.

Under the Harper government, Canada has had a less than positive relationship with the United Nations. Much has been written about the fact that Canada did not achieve a seat on the Security Council, withdrawing its bid in October 2010 when, after two rounds of voting, it was clear that the seat was going elsewhere. The real question is why we tried at all, since we believed initially that it was not coming our way. When the prime minister first learned of the opportunity, he felt mounting a campaign to win the seat was not worth the effort. I'm not sure what changed his mind, but it seemed a half-hearted attempt at best. Given the results, he should have stuck with his initial instincts on this matter. During this same time, the Security Council, because of its composition and its voting and veto structure, has been unable to deal with significant crises, and has only laterally be able to confront Syria over the use of chemical weapons. Given the important role that Canada played in the founding of the United Nations, there might be an opportunity for Canada and like-minded nations to play a substantive role in reshaping the United Nations to increase its effectiveness. This would require a significant commitment of international political capital. It would also take political will to undertake such a task, but in the end, a more effective United Nations, or other such body, would be worth the effort. For example, an alternative might be to use the G8 or G20 to address various international crises. A good beginning in this regard occurred at the 2013 G8 meeting, with the situation in Syria. Having Russia at this meeting with fellow-G8 nations made negotiation of this difficult issue possible, without Russia's UN Security Council veto hanging over everyone's heads.

The negotiation and signing of international trade treaties is both an economic and foreign affairs function. For Harper, such trade agreements are crucial to growing Canada's economy. He sees trade as also linked to investment – investment abroad by Canadians and in Canada by others. Canada's vast geographic size combined with its small population creates a real need for foreign investment. While there has been some divergence from that position along the way – for example, with potash and the proposed sale of MacDonald, Dettwiler and Associates Ltd. satellite operations – Harper would argue that Canada has been open for business. The government would contend that the threshold for review of a transaction by Industry Canada under the Investment Canada Act has been raised. But the confusion around the decisions of the government concerning the China National Offshore Oil Corporation purchase of Nexen and the Petronas takeover has had a chilling effect, at least in the short term, over investments and certainly takeovers in the oil sands. But the need for investment continues, and the government is going to have to clarify where that investment can go and how much intrusion from foreign states or corporations is acceptable. At present, it seems that investment is going elsewhere.

The importance of trade diversification cannot be overstated. Canada has been and always will be a trading nation. However, since the Canada–US Free Trade Agreement came into force in 1989, followed by the North American Free Trade Agreement in 1994, trade has focused south and virtually nowhere else. Canada cannot be so reliant on trade with the United States, given that country's uneven economy. It must and is exploring and working on other options. Those include looking to the Far East with negotiations with Japan, Thailand, and Indonesia. In addition, after neglecting the fastest growing economy in the world, Canada has begun trade negotiations with China. Canada is also now participating in the Trans-Pacific Partnership. It was Harper's hope that a free-trade agreement with the European Union would have been concluded by the end of 2012. However, better late than never: the initial text of the EU Trade Agreement was signed by the prime minister in October 2013. Canada should also be looking further south, beyond the United States, to Mexico and Brazil. These negotiations may mean the end of some of Canada's protectionist measures. Supply management, which predominates the dairy and poultry industries in Quebec and Ontario, may be on the chopping block. The quotas held by these farmers would have to be either phased out or bought out by the federal government, or perhaps some innovative tax measures could be found to compensate these farmers since they will be losing their acquired rights.

The inability of the government to land a major trade agreement until October 2013 calls into question the efficacy of the international trade agenda. It is important to this part of the government's economic agenda that trade initiatives beyond the EU agreement be landed sooner rather than later. Next in line would be the Trans-Pacific Partnership agreement and then an agreement with Japan; despite its recent economic downturn and the punishing effects of the 2011 tsunami, Japan still has the world's third largest economy.

From the time of Sir John A. Macdonald, Canada's most important economic and political relationship has been with the United States, extended, on a personal level, between the prime minister and the president. Prime ministers ignore this relationship at their peril. Early on, Harper adopted former prime minister Mulroney's view that we can disagree without being disagreeable. Canada's influence in the world is sometimes measured, at least to a certain extent, by its influence in Washington, DC.

Harper had an excellent working relationship with President Bush and, through it, was able to settle the long-simmering softwood lumber dispute. It, of course, helped that Canada was an ally in Afghanistan. Canada was able to work with the Americans when, on short notice, they wanted to close the border to anyone not possessing a passport. Stock Day, then minister of public security, was able to negotiate a postponement of this being applicable to Canadians to a more reasonable implementation date. President Bush's public persona was so different from dealing with him in private. He has a great sense of humour and was quite knowledgeable about the players and security issues around the world. He had the usual preoccupation with world affairs that seems to dominate the thoughts of all United States presidents. Harper found it odd that, for all the mayhem the United States was causing – especially in Iraq, which was Bush's war – Bush really seemed to believe he was acting in God's interests as he saw them. Everything he did was driven by his deep religious faith and beliefs. The main problem for Harper in managing the relationship with Bush was to keep its closeness under wraps: Bush was not loved in Canada.

At the beginning of Obama's term in office, Harper had quite the opposite problem in dealing with the president. If anything, Obama may have been more popular in Canada than he was in the United States, and perhaps more popular than Harper. Ottawa was the chosen destination for President Obama's first foreign trip and that signalled the importance that Obama placed on this relationship. As stated above, these two men have a lot in common, and at the beginning of their relationship, Obama was looking to Harper for advice on the world's economic situation and for a frank assessment of the strengths and weaknesses of other world leaders. He also wanted to set up an agenda of matters that the two leaders could address in a positive fashion over the next few years. Since that time, their relationship has matured; they met many times at international meetings and the prime minister has visited the president in Washington. There are also a fair number of back-and-forth meetings between Obama's cabinet secretaries and our federal Cabinet ministers on matters of mutual interest. As well, both Michael Wilson and now Gary Doer have had very productive runs as Canadian ambassadors to Washington.

Lifting off from the G20 meeting held in Pittsburg and the next one held in Toronto and chaired by Harper, there has been specific co-operation on economic matters, especially on thinning the border between Canada and the United States. In addition to co-operation on international financial issues and the Clean Energy Dialogue that came out of their first meeting, Obama and Harper initiated the Beyond the Border initiative. It could be the next big idea between the two countries, the last one being the Free Trade Agreement concluded in 1988.[15] From Canada's perspective, the future relationship with the United States lies in a thinner border with trade trumping security concerns, or at least having equal weight in future deliberations. Progress on the Windsor–Detroit corridor, while initially slow, will now result in a new bridge across the world's busiest border crossing. As part of the border initiative, there is a commitment to work toward co-operation on harmonization of regulations. The Regulatory Cooperation Council has as its mandate the harmonization of regulations between the two countries. Harmonization makes sense when products are made in one country and sold in the other or in both countries, or go back and forth across the border as they are made or assembled, with workers in each country adding value. Motor vehicles are an obvious example, but this would also apply to electrical appliances, computers, and other similar products. Harmonization of regulatory regimes should result in savings for consumers and may reinvigorate the declining manufacturing base in both countries. Derek Burney, Canada's former ambassador to the United States, believes in the importance of this border initiative and has suggested that a body be established to supervise the implementation of the recommendations coming out of the negotiations. A bilateral border commission designed along the lines of the International Joint Commission could be quite effective in the next few years as recommendations flow from the Beyond the Border initiative. However, if no specific body is charged with implementation, there is always the possibility that the recommendations will be caught up in the everyday business of the two countries where only pressing and urgent matters receive attention, and simply sit on the shelf. This is the reality that Burney is trying to avoid.

One area that has become very contentious is the proposed Keystone XL Pipeline to deliver bitumen from the oil sands to refineries in the southern United States. The energy trading relationship between Canada and the United States is crucial to Canada's economy for at least the next ten years. As Canada seeks to diversify markets for its energy by expanding into the Far East, especially China, there will still be a need to access the US market. The challenges here are not only environmental but also economic as the United States begins to reduce its dependency on imported energy while more and more of its domestic oil and natural gas plays are brought on stream.

The ongoing discussions on border security, perimeter security, trade, energy, climate change, and economic issues will be crucial to ensuring a positive ongoing relationship between Canada and the United States during the next decade – and that relationship is an important part of the Harper Doctrine of Foreign Affairs. But at this point, midway through Harper's majority term, the relationship with the United States, especially as it relates to Keystone, has become exceedingly problematic.

What the Left Can Learn from the Right

The electoral divide on the right of the political spectrum began before the 1993 federal election, but was most apparent in the electoral results: much of western Canada abandoned the Progressive Conservative Party and moved its conservative support to the Reform Party. East of the Ontario–Manitoba border, voters had either forsaken conservatism altogether or split their support between the two parties on the right. The rise of Reform in the West had been coming for some time. Its strength was a surprise to the PC Party, but it shouldn't have been.

The period from 1993–97 on the right could be described as one where the PCs and Reform fought each other as vehemently as they fought the governing Liberals. On the PC side, the view was that with internal restructuring, new policies, and an attractive hard-working leader – which Jean Charest was – a comeback to respectability was one election away; forming the government would take two elections. On the Reform side, they were trying to solve the riddle of how to gain support east of Manitoba. Once that solution was found, could government be far away?

The Clark return in 1998 and the results of the 2000 election signalled a new strategy of absorption or reverse takeover. The more the Alliance MPs rebelled against Stockwell Day as leader and broke away, the more welcoming was the PC Party of new friends from the other faction on the right. The split on the right might have ended had Day won back the leadership he gave up to settle the internal divisions in the Alliance Party. Had the Clark plan worked, with Day re-elected as Alliance leader, the PC Party would have continued to welcome disaffected Alliance MPs until the right was virtually united or whole again.

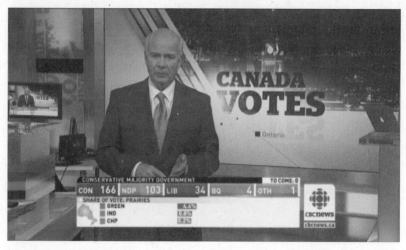

The Majority. What will be the election results for the left in 2015? (Courtesy of CBC)

It could be argued that one of the lasting gifts of the Clark leadership to the conservative movement was creating a space where PC and Alliance MPs could work together and with PC senators on issues of public policy, almost as if they were back in the pre-1988 era. The PC–DRC caucus coalition worked well; it just did not have the institutional glue to withstand Harper as the new Alliance leader.

The co-operation, then merger or reunification of the Reform-now-Alliance with the PC Party was in many ways a product of the co-operation that Clark had started and encouraged. It was not going to work with Harper–Clark, but it was going to work with Harper–MacKay. The 2003 merger of the two parties on the right is a testimony to the two leaders, Harper and MacKay, putting party and country before personal ambition. They decided not to go through the uncertainty of what might happen: Would the Martin juggernaut explode across the country, giving the Liberals the largest majority in Canadian history? Would the Alliance base in western Canada hold in the face of Martin's efforts? How would the MacKay-led PC Party fare in the various regions of Canada? Working from a base in Atlantic Canada, would the PC Party gain traction in Ontario and Quebec? They decided not to wait until after the 2004 election before commencing merger discussions. One could argue that it would have been easy for Harper and MacKay to wait: for Harper to see if the PC Party would be completely finished; for MacKay, as the new leader, to deservedly take at least one shot at a general election. But they both took a larger view of their roles and their parties' roles in the service of Canadians.

With merger, the hard work, which led to government in 2006, was just beginning. Bringing together two cultures, two policy platforms, and MPs with history in the legacy parties was quite a task. Working through challenges together, and building trust and confidence in each other and in the leadership cemented the new relationship. Bridging the gaps in the 2004 election platform with policies developed internally by caucus groups, established by the leader on topics selected by the leader, led directly to the 2006 success.

We know the effect that merger on the right had on Canada's political scene. And we can speculate what would have happened without a merger. Yes, the right may have united at some point after the 2004 election, but it would have been a substantially weakened right, possibly living in opposition through at least one if not two more elections.

What is there for the left-of-centre parties in Canadian politics to take away, learn, apply, or adopt from this period? Are there any similarities to the situation faced by the parties on the right? If so, are they significant enough to effect the same result as was achieved through the creation of the Conservative Party?

In both the NDP and Liberal leadership races, there was one candidate in each contest who advocated merger. Nathan Cullen espoused the idea throughout his NDP leadership campaign. The "new normal" of the NDP as Official Opposition was a phenomenon of the 2011 election; it had never happened before. What will happen in 2015? Was it an aberration that resulted from a weak Liberal campaign coupled with a strong NDP campaign with a likeable leader? What will be the result in elections going forward? Is it worth taking the chance, or better to maintain the status quo and find out? The answer is that it is too soon to talk of some formal merger or co-operation agreement that would integrate the NDP and Liberal Party caucuses. It took the right three general elections and one pivotal by-election to reach the merger conclusion.

The Liberals have re-energized under a new leader, Justin Trudeau. Part of his overwhelming victory was based on no merger with the NDP, no electoral co-operation. Joyce Murray, who ran a creditable campaign, was an advocate of co-operation and merger, so the idea was canvassed during the Liberal leadership. While it had some support, it was discarded.

The NDP and the Liberal Party do not come from the same place. Their origins and histories are different. The Liberal Party traces its beginnings to the nineteenth century and boasts Laurier as its first great leader. It formed the government of Canada for much of the twentieth century. To paraphrase Laurier, if the twentieth century did not quite belong to Canada, it certainly belonged to Laurier's Liberal Party. The NDP has its roots in a western Canada farmers' movement that morphed into a party representing labour more than its agrarian founders. While it has formed provincial governments and has had great leaders both federally and provincially, it has only recently begun challenging to take the federal levers of power for its own. These are two different party cultures, two different backgrounds. Merger would not be the coming back together of what once was. Neither is a piece broken away from the other.

So if not merger, then could the co-operation fostered under Joe Clark's leadership of the PC Party be a model for these two parties to follow? Clark's ultimate goal was to subsume the disaffected Alliance MPs under his leadership. As a second choice, he was willing to lead a coalition that worked together in Parliament, under his leadership, and co-operated in elections, so that the right-of-centre parties would not run candidates against each other. In constituencies cross the country where members of the coalition were running, voters would have only one right-of-centre candidate. It is such a great theory, but it is very difficult to implement. How does one decide which party's candidate runs in which riding? Party financing under the Canada Elections Act militates against this type of agreement. There is also nothing preventing independent candidates from running.

Again, any movement in this direction by the NDP and the Liberals is at least another election away. Even if the parties do contemplate such co-operation at some future point, they will find that on the left, there is no neat geographical dividing line as there was in the Alliance–PC days. Even then, there was no agreement on electoral co-operation. On the left, both the NDP and the Liberals are competitive with the Conservatives and each other in virtually every part of the country except Alberta, where there is still a Conservative hegemony. Electoral co-operation prior to merger is difficult, if not impossible, because of electoral financing laws, perception of needing a candidate in every riding to demonstrate that the party is still national in scope, and the practical reality of choosing which ridings to target for each party.

Furthermore, it is even doubtful that co-operation in legislative areas could occur. Question period and committees of the House of Commons would be the place to start. Such co-operation would have at its foundation a united front with the Conservative Party as the common enemy.

However, in order to co-operate, even in a limited way, there have to be some shared values. Both parties believe in a strong active role for the federal government in both economic and social areas. They both are strong proponents of the Charter of Rights and Freedoms and the use of the federal spending power, especially in the establishment of nationwide social programs. Due to economic realities, there may be few, if any, opportunities for such spending programs, but both parties support federal intervention in this way.

There are differences between the two parties on economic issues and on national unity as it relates specifically to Quebec. When in government, the Liberal Party believed in government support for industry, in the ultimate goal of competition, and in an economy based on a strong independent private sector. It is unclear what role the private sector plays in the NDP policy book. The next few years will probably tell us more about NDP economic policies as they are further refined. The NDP could learn a lot from the Liberal approach to the private sector and industry, since Liberals have demonstrated that a party on the left can work with the private sector in a co-operative fashion. The NDP has learned the importance of this linkage in some of the provincial governments it has formed. Time will tell whether this will carry over to the federal NDP.

On the issue of national unity, both parties are federalist in nature, but they take quite different approaches to the issue of possible Quebec secession. In fact, one of the questions raised on numerous occasions by the federal Liberals in the 2012 Quebec provincial election was which Quebec provincial party the NDP supported. The answer was really a non-answer: the NDP leader, Tom Mulcair, kept referring to the Quebec election as a local matter. Similarly, when the Canadian flag is not on display in the Quebec National Assembly, it is, for him, a local matter. In fairness, he has stressed his contribution in support of the "No" campaign in the 1995 Quebec referendum and that he is a committed federalist. The Liberals, as authors of the Clarity Act, have set out a rigorous path for the breakup of the country, or more specifically, the separation of Quebec. The NDP has a different and more lenient view, as set out in their Sherbrooke Declaration.

Fifty per cent plus one vote is enough for the NDP to start the move-ment toward breakup. This divergence was not a front-and-centre issue until the election of a PQ government in Quebec on 4 Septem-ber 2012. A PQ government, even with a slim majority, could test the commitment to Canada and to Quebec nationalism of many of the NDP MPs from Quebec. Given the significant size of its Quebec caucus, Mulcair will have to watch his caucus carefully to ensure that latent sovereigntist tendencies do not emerge.

So, if no merger is on the horizon, and perhaps only limited leg-islative co-operation, is there anything else the left can learn from the right and what it endured in the wilderness years from 1993–2006? The period from the 2004 election until the drop of the writ for the 2006 election is probably the most relevant for each party to study as far as electoral preparation is concerned. The NDP has a new leader and is trying to define itself as the Official Opposition or the govern-ment-in-waiting. The Liberals also have a new leader and are in grave need of a new policy playbook. As government for most of the last century, the Liberals only needed to renew their policy approach peri-odically. As a centrist or centrist-left government, rarely in opposition, the party possessed a centre-left, pragmatic policy agenda that was capable of being implemented. However, its last main policy push came from the work of Chaviva Hošek and Paul Martin, which resulted in the 1993 Liberal Red Book. There has been little policy introspection since then, and none, except for the ill-fated Dion Greenshift, since Martin assumed the leadership in 2003.

Both the NDP and the Liberals have time on their side since there likely won't be another federal election until the fall of 2015. There is time to focus, and time to do the hard policy work necessary to devel-op a platform before the next election. The Conservatives, after the 2004 election, used caucus as the prime source of policy development. It was a large, diverse, experienced caucus, especially when the Senate caucus was added to the mix. This group was put to work almost immediately on the various policy weaknesses that came through in the 2004 election. The whole exercise was directed by Stephen Harper and resourced by the party research branch and MPs' and Senators' staff. For Harper, bilingualism, childcare, industrial subsidies, regional development agencies, arts and culture, Quebec federalism, immigra-tion, agriculture, defence and foreign affairs, tax policy, and criminal justice were all tackled by either caucus committees or a single caucus member who had particular knowledge in that subject area.

Caucus members who were put in charge of a particular area were to consult widely with stakeholders and with their caucus colleagues. Some held hearings or meetings with interested groups across the country. Others met with representatives of industry groups or the entities that would be most affected by the new policies. The results of this process – the recommendations – were then considered for inclusion in the platform either in their totality or selectively. All caucus members saw at least some of their work reflected in the platform.

The other significant effort that contributed to the effectiveness of the 2006 platform and to the campaign itself was the targeted polling data assembled in the fall of 2005. The polling results were used not only to identify who supported the Conservative Party but also to help identify policies and programs that would specifically appeal to Conservative supporters or those within the Conservative catchment area. There is no substitute for honest self-analysis to determine where support is and where it might come from in the future. Effective analysis can be built upon and utilized to direct policy formulation.

The parties on the left have not yet exhausted each other through a general election or two or three (as did the PC, Reform, Alliance, and Conservative parties), nor has a cataclysmic event come along (as did the Perth–Middlesex by-election for the right). Without either as a compelling reason to consider closer ties, perhaps the most the left can learn from the right are the baby steps of legislative co-operation and the basic building blocks of hard work needed to identify core support, construct policies to appeal to those supporters, and broaden that support.

An Uncertain Path Forward
for the Conservatives

A look back at the past twenty years and fourteen "days" of events and decisions, people and personalities, actions and inactions that, I believe, piloted the federal conservative movement from opposition to government must, naturally, prompt a look forward. What do the past and present suggest about Day Fifteen, about the future of the Harper government and the Conservative Party?

Going back to my story about the man spinning plates on the top of poles as a metaphor for governing, it seems that attaining a Conservative majority has not brought the focus to policy development and its implementation, and to governing that one might have hoped would happen. Whether through neglect or a combination of events, plates began toppling off poles. It is hard to say definitively when this started – and perhaps there was no particular date – but at some point after March 2012, the cumulative effect was that the government seemed to no longer be in control of the policy agenda, or even worse, seemed to have no agenda at all. Maybe it is something that just happens after seven years of governing when at least half of those years are spent battling through a worldwide recession.

Given the recession, Harper tied the reputation of his government to sound economic management and an ability to grow the economy. This was his theme in both the 2008 and 2011 elections and may very well be again in 2015. The 2012 budget made it clear that economic recovery would be tied to energy development, immigration to help grow the economy, and innovation. The economic recovery has been harder to come by than the government anticipated. It had hoped that elimination of the deficit created by the 2009 stimulus budget would have been well on its way, and in fact, had promised elimination by 2014 in the 2011 election campaign. As we now know, this hasn't hap-

The Future. Where will the road lead for the Conservative Party? (Courtesy of iStockphoto LP)

pened; however, achieving balance looks quite doable for the 2015 budget. In spite of this positive fiscal situation, Canada is experiencing a job crisis, with higher unemployment at this point than envisaged by the government in its first majority mandate. In an attempt to boost employment, the Temporary Foreign Worker Program has been changed so that it is used to bring in talent from offshore only after a thorough search within Canada.

While trying to stay away from another stimulus package, the government has dedicated funds toward building infrastructure in the hope that this would help the unemployment situation. It has also attempted to deal with the problem of too many jobs remaining vacant because the skills of the unemployed don't match the skills that are needed. With the Labour Market Agreements between the federal and provincial/territorial governments expiring in March 2014, the federal government has announced that it will pursue something it calls the Canada Job Grant Program. This was announced in the 2013 budget and has all the earmarks of a policy put together quickly, without consultation or agreement from the provinces. It keeps money in the federal treasury while the federal government takes the lead on these tripartite agreements that involve contributions from industry and the provinces/territories toward job skills training for individuals. The problem, besides lack of provincial/territorial buy-in or even if it does eventually gain their approval, is that it will not immediately take people off the unemployment rolls.

Low inflation plus a low interest rate policy from the Bank of Canada has kept Canadians protected from the worst ravages of the recession. However, growth is not stellar and the unemployment rate remains stubbornly around 7 per cent.

None of this augers well for a government that prides itself on economic acumen. It leaves the government open to attacks from the opposition and to the possibility that the electorate may just decide to take a leap of faith and give the other guys a chance. Alternatively, if the economy picks up and a significant surplus is achieved, voters may decide they don't need the austerity of the Conservatives anymore and opt for change.

Continuing with the economy, it became obvious early on in the recession that Canada's manufacturing sector was faltering. To address this, the government created a development agency for Southern Ontario as well as one for the North, but even so, manufacturing declined. However, Canada's natural resource industries, and specifically energy development, not only moved in to fill the void but also enabled Canada to fare as well or better than any other G7 country throughout this period. The 2012 budget rationalized environmental regulations to help pave the way for energy development and its transportation infrastructure. Unfortunately, this plan for economic reliance on energy has run into the practical problem of lack of market access. Pipelines that were to bring Alberta's bitumen to world markets through access to west coast ports are now embroiled in environmental controversy, and in the case of the Keystone XL Pipeline, subject to approval by the United States. A new proposal from Trans-Canada Corporation to bring bitumen from the oil sands east to refineries in Quebec and St John, New Brunswick, is in its infancy and won't be operational for years, even if it does get all the necessary approvals and support from the Province of Quebec. It will be interesting to see if the application by Kinder Morgan to twin its Trans Mountain Pipeline from the oil sands to Vancouver is subject to the same level of objections. The lack of pipeline capacity has meant that Canada is not diversifying its markets and selling oil offshore at higher world prices. This has led to revenue losses both in Alberta and Ottawa.

The reliance on energy to grow the economy has run into such difficulty – to the point where one wonders whether the government actually understands its own energy economy. Keystone approval is in the hands of the United States, with caveats requiring reduction of GHGs coming from the oil sands, and President Obama has started a debate about the number of short- and long-term jobs created by the pipeline. The proposed Enbridge Northern Gateway Project received conditional approval from the Joint Review Panel in December 2013. This decision now goes before Cabinet, with all the political considerations that will accompany that discussion, including exercising the government's duty to consult with Canada's Aboriginal peoples. In the meantime, existing pipelines, which are at capacity, are being supplemented by rail transport of crude oil.

Inextricably connected with the energy economy are the government's environmental initiatives. As the recession deepened, any plans for an overarching policy on GHG reduction were scrapped for a sectoral approach federally, to be supplemented by provincial initiatives. The goal set, pursuant to the Copenhagen Accord of 2009, was 17 per cent reduction in GHGs over 2005 levels to be attained by 2020. While this was the objective, the word from Harper was that nothing was to happen environmentally that would impede economic recovery.

For this government, moving on the environment has always been viewed as playing defence. Regardless of what it did, it would never get credit from environmental groups or the population at large, so a minimalist approach was adopted. Proceed if necessary, but do no harm to the economy.

As set out above, there seems to be a lack of understanding on the part of the federal government and perhaps some parts of the energy industry – which may be deliberate – that the social licence that allows energy development to proceed is rooted in environmental action. This strategy is fine until it begins to impede energy development, as it has with both the Keystone and Gateway pipeline proposals. The economic result hurts: without the distribution links, Canada's energy does not reach lucrative international markets. Compounding this problem is the fact that relief will not be forthcoming for years. Economic recovery based on energy would seem to be some ways off.

Another part of the government's plan for economic recovery came in the form of its trade agenda. If the last big idea in Canada on this front was the Canada–US Free Trade Agreement, then the hoped-for next big idea was to be a series of free trade agreements reached by the Harper government. Sounds great, but implementation of this agenda has been more difficult than ever envisaged. Premier Charest was quite keen on a free trade agreement with the European Union, and discussions started rather casually in 2007–08. Led by the Harper government, they then moved into full-scale negotiations dealing with virtually every aspect of the economy. While the negotiations took much longer than anticipated, the deal was initialled in mid-October 2013, with the final text to follow. When implemented, this agreement should provide a much-needed boost for job creation and the economy. As negotiations slowed with the EU, the government went back to work on possible agreements with South Korea, Japan, India, China, or Thailand. All have received entreaties from the Harper government. In addition, the government sought and won inclusion in the negotiations of the Trans-Pacific Partnership. This is especially important for Canada since the United States is a leading member; being involved in any major trade agreement that also includes Canada's major trading partner is a further benefit. The United States would like to see these negotiations wrap up before the end of 2013 or soon thereafter.

The problem here, as with the energy agenda, is that even if trade negotiations on the Trans-Pacific Partnership and with, perhaps, one or two other countries are successful, the fruits of these labours will not materialize for quite some time. And the big prizes of China and India are still years away from any trade arrangement.

Another area that has been troubling for this government in 2012–13 relates to the First Nations. The First Nations agenda got off to a promising beginning in the government's first term with the apology for residential schools and in its second term when Aboriginal leaders were involved in decisions dealing with spending on infrastructure for Aboriginal communities arising out of the 2009 stimulus budget. Since that time, few advances have been made on the Aboriginal agenda. Hopes were raised with the first-ever Crown–First Nations Gathering held at the beginning of 2012 and attended by chiefs from across the country, the governor general, the prime minister, and a number of government ministers and officials. This meeting set out an agenda, but it was not realized through 2012. A working group on First Nations education was unable to reach agreement, and frustrations with living conditions and economic matters led to a confrontation with government at the end of 2012 and the beginning of 2013.

A meeting in January 2013 with Prime Minister Harper, Cabinet ministers, and Assembly of First Nations National Chief Shawn

Atleo as well as some regional chiefs dealt with a number of items that were then to be handed off to a high-level working group. This group included the Clerk of the Privy Council, the prime minister's chief of staff, and other officials as well as representatives from the Assembly of First Nations. It began to address issues such as treaty implementation, land claims, and self-governing agreements as well as the major economic issue of Aboriginal involvement in the development and transportation of energy in Canada. However, little has been accomplished. National Chief Atleo has spoken at length about free, informed consent on behalf of First Nations and partnering with industry and governments in resource development. This would lead to economic self-reliance. Education is also a must for Aboriginal youth: more are incarcerated yearly than graduate from high school. At this point, negotiations are ongoing between the government and First Nations leadership on a new First Nations Education Act. Atleo has stated that any education act must respect language and culture as well as be jointly administered by the government and First Nations. Whatever system is agreed upon must be fully funded so that it may have the desired effect on First Nations education.

What started with great promise has stalled with little, if any, improvement in the lives of Canada's Aboriginal population. This is a matter that will not go away and has the distinct possibility of exploding into open confrontation with the government at any time. Unfortunately, that confrontation will probably come with the First Nations delaying or stopping energy projects either through the courts, alleging lack of prior consultation, or through civil disobedience.

Lack of progress on the Aboriginal agenda, however, has not caused the government nearly the same amount of grief as the lack of progress on Senate reform – and the actions of certain Senators appointed by the Prime Minister. It was so easy in opposition to criticize the Senate and put forward solutions. It has been impossible for the Harper government to implement the most basic of Senate reforms, such as term limits and provision for provincial Senate elections. The first foray into Senate reform, which had the prime minister appear before a Special Senate Committee to discuss the provisions of the government's Senate reform bill, through to the Senate reference case before the Supreme Court of Canada, attempts at reform have been either mishandled by the government or stymied by the opposition.

Senate reform has become more complicated due to the actions of certain senators regarding claims for living expenses or various other expense claims. This has pointed some in the general direction of abolition, which is the last question set out in the Reference Case that the government has referred to the Supreme Court, seeking guidance on the methods by which reform could be accomplished.

The Senate expense issue has also caused political problems for Harper. His chief of staff, Nigel Wright, in an attempt to resolve an expense situation, used his own funds to pay off the debt owed by Senator Duffy to the Crown for improperly claimed living expenses. Harper has denied knowledge of this payment and, a few days after he learned of it, disassociated himself from Wright in much the same fashion as he did with Mulroney in the Schreiber affair. Whether or not one believes Harper in this matter, it has harmed his credibility and his reputation for integrity and as an effective manager of the country's business.

This has been one of those unforced errors that plagues governments of all political stripes. Effective issues management would have seen all of the facts gathered – no matter how bad they were – and only then, and one time only, would the government have explained its position in terms that would not change. This did not happen. And this matter has grown into one that has occasioned a number of external audits, the suspension of three senators appointed by Harper, and the involvement of the RCMP. It also seems to be a case of, just when you believe you know all the facts and issues, more are uncovered. The Senate expense mess has hurt the government's credibility.

The government has also been affected by complaints from backbench members that they are tired of having their independence continually under threat or challenge by the chief government whip and the Prime Minister's Office. Some argue that this is the result of an aging government with backbenchers, who believe they will never be promoted, exercising a form of independence since they no longer live in fear of the whip or the prime minister. It is my belief that the strict message discipline of the first and second minorities would seem to be no longer necessary, so MPs should be able to show some independence and begin to advance their own pet projects. When dealing with this, any initiative that touches on the subject of abortion has to be distinguished from all other subjects: Harper has been adamant from the beginning that he will not countenance any moves that will affect Canada's abortion laws.

The reality is that the government is now in a position where it can allow some degree of independence of thought; the whips need not be on backbenchers all the time. There is nothing to be gained by the government disciplining members over matters of little consequence or engineering changes in House committee membership in order to punish or embarrass a backbench member who is pursuing a private member's bill or motion that does not threaten or negate the government's agenda. The issue here is actually one of respect.

Early on, Harper made it clear that there was no hierarchy of MPs – they were all equal. In order to emphasize this fact, he did not follow the lead of other prime ministers and did not appoint a deputy prime minister. The message of equality from the first mandate would seem to have been lost not only among MPs but also among staff. In the middle of 2013, my former colleague Keith Beardsley coined the phrase that the government was being run by "boys in short pants." The moniker stuck because, to a certain extent, it was true.

As the title to this chapter suggests, the path forward for the Harper government is uncertain. Two unknowns are the economy – which takes in jobs, energy development including pipelines, and trade initiatives – and the political fallout from the Senate expense scandal. The Cabinet shuffle of mid-2013 was an attempt to put a new face on certain aspects of Harper's government, promote those whom the prime minister felt deserving, and perhaps put in place a regime more accommodating to the occasional outburst of backbench independence. The policy part for all that is new appeared in the Speech from the Throne delivered in mid-October 2013. The rest of the mandate will focus the new Cabinet team on the policies set out in this Speech as well as policies contained in the budgets of 2012 and 2013.

Moving into the last year and a half of this mandate, the Harper government cannot ignore the problems and challenges it faces. They are as much due to the style of this government as what the government has done, attempted to do, or neglected to do. The communications position of less is best may have been appropriate for the first term in office, but in a majority situation, the "us against them" mentality is not necessary. In conflicts with the parliamentary budget officer and in other contentious issues, most notably the Senate expense matter, it is the lack of fulsome disclosure more than the issue itself that has hurt the government. Continuous stonewalling and half measures in communications have led the government into a situation where, in its time of need, it has many critics but few supporters to come to its defence. In the early years, the government was dedicated to accountability, hard work, and preparation, serving Canadians who worked hard, played by the rules, and paid their taxes. To address the problems facing the current government, it is time to revisit the attitude and work ethic that came together to produce those early governments.

Whether a fourth-mandate-in-a-row win returns a majority or minority government will depend on which of two voting combinations holds together for Harper. Will it be the 2006 or the 2011 group of voters? Much depends on Conservative fortunes in Quebec and in British Columbia. Can Harper revive the Party's fortunes in Quebec when facing two opposition leaders from Quebec? Will the new Canadian and ethnic vote in British Columbia, which propelled the Conservatives to a majority in 2011, still be supportive? And there's always the possibility that "time for a change" could be a compelling opposition slogan after nine years of Conservative government.

Despite governing through trying economic times, Harper and the Conservatives – save for the usual blips immediately after new leaders of opposition parties are selected – have led the polls from day one. This situation began to change with the election of Justin Trudeau as Liberal leader and has continued throughout the Senate expense issue. If the shift persists during 2014, this will be new experience for Conservative MPs. Governing from a position where they are behind in the polls will certainly present challenges for Harper and his team. Harper's leadership has not been subject to question, even when he thought it might be after the 2008 election. It was also not challenged after the Economic Fall Update debacle in 2008 and the constitutional crisis that resulted.

A rededication to the ethics and principles that brought about a Conservative government in 2006, 2008, and 2011 is no guarantee of success in 2015, but it is essential if there is to be any hope of success. Should the next election focus on the economy, as have the past two, then with a few breaks, all might turn around. A settled trade deal, a pipeline approved and being constructed, and continued economic recovery supported by resurgence in the United States and in the European Union – these could put Harper and the Conservative Party on a winning path for Day Fifteen and beyond.

Acknowledgments

Only those who have attempted a project like this know how many people are involved behind the scenes, adding value, so that there will be a final product. This effort began with Jamie Watt's encouragement to commit to paper my experiences from over thirty years of involvement in Canadian politics. His suggestion was appealing: the issue was what parts to write about, and how to write about them in a way that would serve readers who have a passing interest in politics as well as readers who want to know how politics and government actually work. There are plenty of books on the theory of government and politics, but few written by those who have actually been there.

The idea of framing key years of my association with the conservative movement around fourteen "days" came from Liam Scott of Toronto, a skilled and innovative thinker and communicator. This construct for the period of 1993 to 2013 provided the project with boundaries and a certain amount of rigour.

On my behalf, L. Ian Macdonald submitted the proposal for this book plus a couple of others to Philip Cercone, executive director of McGill-Queen's University Press. Philip called and told me that we should go with the fourteen-days proposal first, with the others to follow. The team at MQUP has been a constant source of advice, strength, and support. In particular, Ryan Van Huijstee, managing editor; Jacqueline Mason, editor; and my copy editor, Eleanor Gasparik, have added value with every comment, and their continuous patience dealing with a first-time author was both needed and greatly appreciated.

Nothing of value is accomplished without the support of close friends and family. My children have suffered through every part of this project and given their unqualified support. Gwenda Wright and others typed parts of the manuscript – and showed me how to use a laptop. My long-time friend Gord Baker provided not only his advice but also an office to work in. Former prime minister Brian Mulroney; former senator Michael Meighen; Mike Coates, chair of Hill + Knowlton Strategies; and Reverend Dr Brent Hawkes have been a source of support and counsel. There are a number of others who provided ideas and critical commentary: you know who you are.

It is unfortunate that senators Finlay MacDonald and John Lynch-Staunton, who contributed so much to keeping the PC Party lights on and to nurturing the Conservative Party in its early days, are no longer with us to see how their efforts formed a part of these fourteen days.

As always, any errors of fact or judgment are mine and mine alone.

Notes

DAY ONE

1 André Pratte, *Charest: His Life and Politics* (Toronto: Stoddart, 1998), 230.
2 The special joint committee reviewing Canada's foreign policy reported on 15 November 1994; the joint committee reviewing Canada's defence policy reported on 21 October 1994.
3 Peter Pigett, "Playing the Waiting Game," www.helicoptersmagazine.com. Accessed on 22 November 2013.
4 The Special Senate Committee on The Pearson Airport Agreements received its Order of Reference from the Senate on 14 May 1995.
5 The Report of the Special Senate Committee on The Pearson Airport Agreements, 6 November 1995.
6 Bill C-22, An Act Respecting Certain Agreements Concerning the Redevelopment and Operation of Terminals 1 and 2 at Lester B. Pearson International Airport, introduced in 1994, in clauses 9 and 10 eliminated the right to compensation for cancellation of the contracts.
7 Pratte, 234.
8 Ibid., 239.
9 Bill C-20, The Clarity Act, was introduced in December 1999 and passed into law on 29 June 2000.
10 Bill C-341, Quebec Contingency Act (referendum conditions), was introduced in 1996 by Stephen J. Harper, MP.
11 Hugh Segal, *The Long Road Back: The Conservative Journey, 1993–2006* (Toronto: Harper Collins, 2006), 100 and 107.
12 Report of the Auditor General, 25 November 2003. The references are to the auditor general's conclusions on the sponsorship matter contained in chapters 2, 3, and 4 of her report.

13 Winds of Change conference in Calgary, May 1996; convened by David
   Frum and Ezra Levant and chaired by Stockwell Day, then Alberta
   provincial treasurer.

DAY TWO

1 Tom Flanagan, *Harper's Team: Behind the Scenes in the Conservative Rise
   to Power* (Montreal & Kingston: McGill-Queen's University Press, 2007),
   16.
2 Ibid., 20.
3 One of the main features of the MPs training college was to instill in the
   new MPs that even though the PC Party was not the Official Opposition,
   there were still many devices at their disposal to raise both local and
   national issues. Raising local issues in the House of Commons and then
   reporting on them in their MP's Householder ensures that the connection between the MP in Ottawa and constituents remains strong.
4 Pratte, 271.
5 Ibid., 275–94. Charest's own autobiography does not deal with this period in any significant depth.
6 The Honourable Robert de Cotret was one of the smartest and fundamentally decent people to ever become involved in federal politics. He
   held a number of portfolios in the Mulroney government; when he left
   Cabinet in 1993, he set to work as the lead on the restructuring-of-
   government project with Hugh Segal and others. He had always been a
   great supporter of Clark and enjoyed every minute of the opportunity
   to help his friend become leader once again.
7 Roy Norton has held a number of federal government positions; at the
   time of writing, he is Canada's consul general in Detroit.
8 Elsie Wayne, who was the deputy leader, strongly disagreed with Clark's
   position on this bill. The PC senators, however, supported Clark's position. Although passed by the Senate, the bill was the subject of intense
   questioning by PC senators.
9 Speech by the Right Honourable Joe Clark to the Quebec City Policy
   Convention 1999.

DAY THREE

1 Neither Preston Manning in 1999 nor Joe Clark in 1983, having
   resigned the leadership of their respective parties and thus initiating a

leadership race, were successful in succeeding themselves; Manning lost to Stockwell Day, and Clark to Brian Mulroney.

2 William Johnson, *Stephen Harper and the Future of Canada* (Toronto: McClelland and Stewart, 2005; 2nd ed., 2006), 289.

3 Ibid., 289–90.

4 Flanagan, *Harper's Team*, 30; Johnson, 289–90.

5 This issue arose in the latter part of the 1990s and involved Prime Minister Chrétien and his former partners and a hotel-golf course in his home riding of Shawinigan. The PM was accused of putting undue pressure on the Business Development Bank of Canada to help his former partners with financing and possible profiting from Chretien's position as prime minister. Clark pursued this issue with great vigour, but to no avail.

DAY FOUR

1 Bob Plamondon, *Full Circle: Death and Resurrection in Canadian Conservative Politics* (Toronto: Key Porter Books, 2006), 224.

2 Paul Wells, *Right Side Up: The Fall of Paul Martin and the Rise of Stephen Harper's New Conservatism* (Toronto: McClelland and Stewart, 2006), 50.

3 The issue of lack of membership in the PC Party was raised on numerous occasions; however, in the end, if the DRC members had taken out memberships in the PC Party, it would probably not have changed their reaction and the result when Stephen Harper called them home.

4 Plamondon, 226.

5 Bernard Lord was the premier of New Brunswick at the time of his speech. Unfortunately, he had just fought a provincial election where his substantial majority was reduced to a one-seat majority. He would have been an attractive candidate for the leadership – and one never knows, he may yet be a candidate for leadership of the Conservative Party when the position eventually becomes vacant.

DAY FIVE

1 These policies are taken directly from the MacKay leadership platform and were enunciated repeatedly by MacKay throughout the campaign.

2 Bob Plamondon, *Blue Thunder: The Truth About Conservatives from Macdonald to Harper* (Toronto: Key Porter Books, 2009), 402.

3 Plamondon, *Full Circle*, 262–3.

4 Segal, 136–7.

5 Word for word, this is the arrangement that MacKay and Orchard entered into.

6 MacKay wanted to ensure that, regardless of the outcome of talks with the Alliance, there would be a solid policy base for the PC Party should merger fail, or for the new party should merger succeed.

DAY SIX

1 One cannot overestimate the importance of this by-election result in the movement toward unification of the Alliance and PC parties.

2 Plamondon, *Blue Thunder* and *Full Circle*.

3 Segal, *The Long Road Back*.

4 Plamondon, *Full Circle*, 325.

5 The late Senator John Lynch-Staunton's contribution to keeping the lights on in the PC Party was enormous. It began with his election as leader of the opposition in 1993 by his fellow senators and continued until his retirement from the Senate. His measured opposition to the Liberal government and his work on the Pearson Airport hearings began the return of credibility to what was left of the PC Party. He also had confidence in the merger process and its leadership, as well as in those who eventually succeeded him in the leadership of the new Conservative Party. All of this work, with its positive conclusions, could not have been accomplished without his unflagging participation and support.

6 This letter and the sample policy pieces represent the beginning of a process that ended with the 2005 policy convention in Montreal, when the Conservative Party of Canada formally endorsed and adopted its new policy book. The work set out here, as well as other areas of agreement, were submitted to a rigorous caucus policy review led by Peter MacKay, which ultimately informed the 2004 platform.

7 Flanagan, *Harper's Team*, 126–36.

DAY SEVEN

1 Demanding Better: Conservative Party Platform 2004.

2 Flanagan, *Harper's Team*, 137–94.

3 Plamondon, *Full Circle*, 360–70.

4 Mike Coates, CEO of Hill + Knowlton Strategies, a public affairs consultancy, worked in a number of areas in the 2004, 2006, and 2008 cam-

paigns, and was largely responsible for ensuring Harper's success in the leaders' debates. He was also the Conservative representative in negotiations with the TV networks debate consortium. He brought to all of these tasks his great knowledge of the political process and the importance of intense preparation.

5 The Randy White interview on its own did not scuttle the 2004 campaign, but it fed into a narrative – that this new party was anti-gay, anti-Charter, and anti-courts – that Harper had spent the whole campaign trying to kill. White's interview coming at the end of the campaign, when there was no time to respond, gave the Liberals the ammunition they needed to bolster their fortunes going into the last weekend before election day.

6 Geoff Norquay, now a principal with Earnscliffe Strategy Group in Ottawa, combines the very best of policy knowledge and communication skills. It is rare to find both these skills, with the attendant background knowledge, in the same person. We were fortunate to have his expertise for the time he spent in Harper's OLO.

7 This was Harper's first attempt to go into Quebec to begin to enunciate the basis of a platform with policies directly affecting Quebec. In those days, it was difficult to rally a crowd or any attention at all. Harper also received a lot of advice that venturing into Quebec was a waste of time and money, but he persisted and, in 2006, succeeded.

8 The first substantive chapter of Demanding Better II was entitled "Commitment to a Single Economic Space for Canada and the United States," which detailed a continental approach to security that would facilitate Canada's trading relationship with the United States.

9 The Civil Marriage Act was introduced into the House of Commons on 1 February 2005 by the Martin government and received Royal Assent on 21 July 21 2005. It legalized same-sex marriage by providing a gender-neutral definition of marriage.

10 Commission of Inquiry into the Sponsorship Program and Advertising Activities led by Mr Justice John Gomery released its First Report on 1 November 2005, but the testimony given before the Commission was made public on a regular basis.

11 Flanagan, *Harper's Team*, 216.

DAY EIGHT

1 This was surely one of the lower points in Canadian politics in the last few years as the Liberals tried desperately to avoid defeat. We were never

quite sure how complicit some of our MPs were in this venture. Gurmant Grewal, MP, audiotaped some of the discussions he had with Liberal operatives. It was hard to determine who was playing whom as we attempted to decipher the tapes. Suffice it to say that Gurmont did not run in the 2006 election, but his wife, Nina, continues to represent a constituency in British Columbia.

2 Wells, 157.

3 John Howard was the 25th prime minister of Australia, serving from 11 March 1996 until 3 December 2007. His term in office was marked by unprecedented economic growth.

4 Johnson, 438.

5 As set out in the chapter 7, the first report of the Gomery Commission with its conclusions led Harper to determine that there was enough evidence in the public domain to support his view that the Liberals had lost the moral authority to govern.

6 The Vancouver debates were the first opportunity for the debate prep team to reinforce with Harper that his approach was to be that of a "prime minister in waiting," maintaining a calm, reassuring, positive style.

7 This speech and the follow-up renewed interest in Quebec in the Conservative campaign marked the beginning of the turnaround of the Conservative fortunes in Quebec, putting together the winning Conservative coalition for the first time since the days of Brian Mulroney.

8 L. Ian MacDonald, "How Harper Forced a Conservative Spring," *Policy Options*, March 2006, 27; see also, L. Ian MacDonald, *Politics, People, & Potpourri* (Montreal & Kingston: McGill-Queen's University Press, 2009), 62–3.

9 Ibid.

10 From a speech on a larger military presence in the Arctic given by Stephen Harper, Winnipeg, Manitoba, 22 December 2005.

11 Flanagan, *Harper's Team*, 247.

12 Ibid.

13 *R. v. Labaye*, decision of the Supreme Court of Canada, 23 December 2005.

14 Flanagan, *Harper's Team*, 256.

15 Ibid., 258.

DAY TEN

1 The Federal Accountability Act, Bill C-2, was introduced into the House of Commons on 11 April 2006 and received Royal Assent on 12 December 2006.

2 The first budget of the Harper government, entitled "Focusing on Priorities: Turning a New Leaf," was presented in the House of Commons on
   2 May 2006.

3 The best discussion of these three papers and how they relate to each
   other can be found in Charles M. Beach, Michael Smart, and Thomas A.
   Wilson, eds., *The 2006 Federal Budget: Rethinking Fiscal Priorities* (Montreal & Kingston: McGill-Queen's University Press, 2007).

4 Debates, House of Commons, 11 June 2008.

5 The motion was tabled in the House of Commons on 22 November
   2006 and approved on 27 November 2006.

6 Ibid.

7 The decision to change the taxable status of income trusts was kept even
   tighter than decisions about what would go into the annual budget,
   perhaps learning from the debacle that faced the Liberals in 2005 when
   they tackled this matter.

8 The emergency legislation to order the reopening of the Chalk River
   nuclear power plant was introduced into the House of Commons on 11
   December 2007 and received Royal Assent on 12 December 2007.

9 Tom Zytaruk, *Like a Rock: The Chuck Cadman Story* (Madeira Park, BC:
   Harbour Publishers, 2008).

10 Report of the Oliphant Commission of Inquiry, 31 May 2010.

DAY ELEVEN

1 Report of the Independent Panel on Canada's Future Role in
   Afghanistan, January 2008, 5.

2 Ibid., 37.

3 Charles M. Beach, Michael Smart, and Thomas A. Wilson, eds., *The 2006
   Federal Budget: Rethinking Our Priorities* (Montreal & Kingston: McGill-
   Queen's University Press, 2007).

4 Media release of the Government of Nova Scotia, 13 July 2008.

5 Canada's Clean Air and Climate Change Act, Bill C-30, tabled in the
   House of Commons on 19 October 2006. The government never proceeded with this legislation since it would have been subjected to unrea-
   sonable amendments proposed by the opposition.

6 Minister Prentice did his very best to move this along but continually
   met with arguments raised by Minister of Finance Flaherty that the proposed arrangements created a financial risk to the government, albeit a
   risk thirty years out. Prentice thought this argument to be unreason-
   able, but it carried the day.

7 The Greenshift was presented in June 2008 by Liberal leader Stéphane Dion and proposed an ecotax on carbon and reductions in personal and corporate taxes.

DAY TWELVE

1 Conducting a strategic review of government expenditures is a tricky venture at the best of times, but even more so when in a minority situation. The purpose was to have all departments comply with the proposals for expenditure reduction contained in the 2006 platform.
2 Conservative Party Platform, "True North Strong and Free: Stephen Harper's Plan for Canadians," 7 October 2008.
3 Michael Valpy, "The 'Crisis': A Narrative," in Peter H. Russell and Lorne Sossin, eds., *Parliamentary Democracy in Crisis* (Toronto: University of Toronto Press, 2009), 16.
4 Budget 2009, Canada's Economic Action Plan, 27 January 2009.

DAY THIRTEEN

1 Christopher Dornan, "From Contempt of Parliament to Majority Mandate," in Jon H. Pammett and Christopher Dornan, eds., *The Canadian General Election of 2011* (Toronto: Dundurn, 2011), 9.
2 "Economic Impacts of the Petroleum Industry in Canada," Canadian Energy Research Institute, July 2009.
3 Alan Arcand, Michael Burt, and Todd A. Crawford, "Fuel for Thought: Economic Effect of Oil Sands Investment for Canada's Regions." Study by the Conference Board of Canada, October 2012.
4 Budget 2010, Leading the Way in Jobs and Growth, 4 March 2010.
5 Military Police Complaints Commission, "Commission's Final Report: Concerning a Complaint by Amnesty International Canada and the British Columbia Civil Liberties Association, June 2008," 27 June 2012.
6 Richard Colvin evidence before the Special Committee on the Canadian Mission in Afghanistan, 18 November 2008.
7 Lawrence Martin, *Harperland: The Politics of Control* (Toronto: Penguin Canada, 2011), 197.
8 Environment Canada regulations on coal-fired electricity plants will come into force on 1 July 2015.
9 The "Beyond the Border Action Plan," which was a result of these negotiations, was announced on 7 December 2011.

10 Janice MacKinnon, "Balancing the Fiscal Plan with a Campaign Blueprint," *Policy Options*, April 2011, 18.

11 The vote in the House of Commons was 156–145 in favour, holding the government in contempt of Parliament.

12 Geoff Norquay, "The 'Ballot Question' in the 2011 Election: Two Wins, Two Losses," *Policy Options*, June–July 2011, 50.

13 Tom Flanagan, "The Emerging Conservative Coalition," *Policy Options*, June–July 2011, 104–8.

DAY FOURTEEN

1 Flanagan, *Harper's Team*, 16.

2 Lawrence LeDuc and Jon H. Pammet, "The Evolution of the Harper Dynasty," in Jon H. Pammet and Christopher Dornan, eds., *The Federal General Election, 2011* (Toronto: Dundurn, 2011), 307.

3 Stephen Harper, Tom Flanagan, Ted Morton, Rainer Knopff, Andrew Crooks, and Ken Boessenkool, Open Letter to Ralph Klein, *National Post*, 24 January 2001.

4 Kevin Lynch, "Fiscal Austerity and Economic Renewal," *Policy Options*, May 2012, 13.

5 On 19 December 2011, Finance Minister Flaherty announced that the Canada Health Transfer (CHT) would continue to grow at 6 per cent annually until 2016–17, and starting in 2017–18, the CHT would then grow in line with a three-year average of nominal GDP growth (with a minimum increase of 3 per cent per year guaranteed).

6 Budget 2012, Jobs, Growth and Long-Term Prosperity, 28 March 2012.

7 Derek Burney, "Getting Smarter in a Changing Global Economy," *Policy Options*, April 2012, 20.

8 Expert Panel on Research and Development final report, "Innovation Canada: A Call to Action," 17 October 2011.

9 "Report of the Royal Commission on Aboriginal Peoples," November 1996.

10 An Act Respecting Indians, originally enacted in 1876, has been amended from time to time to broaden the definition of Indian or to protect rights, but it is a relic of a former age and needs to be dealt with, but in consultation with those whom it directly affects.

11 L. Ian Macdonald, "A Conversation with the Minister of Foreign Affairs," *Policy Options*, April 2012, 10.

12 Canada's Northern Strategy, 17 August 2012.

13 Canada First Defence Strategy, 12 May 2008.
14 World Health Organization, "Keeping Promises, Measuring Results," 19 May 2011.
15 Derek Burney, "Boldly Bilateral – Thinking Big Again," *Policy Options*, March 2011, 50–2.

Index